Transnational Protest and Global Activism

People, Passions, and Power

Social Movements, Interest Organizations, and the Political Process
John C. Green, Series Editor

After the Boom: The Politics of Generation X edited by Stephen C. Craig and Stephen Earl Bennett

American Labor Unions in the Electoral Arena by Herbert B. Asher, Eric S. Heberlig, Randall B. Ripley, and Karen Snyder

Citizen Democracy: Political Activists in a Cynical Age by Stephen E. Frantzich

Cyberpolitics: Citizen Activism in the Age of the Internet by Kevin A. Hill and John E. Hughes

Democracy's Moment: Reforming the American Political System for the 21st Century edited by Ron Hayduk and Kevin Mattson

Gaia's Wager: Environmental Movements and the Challenge of Sustainability by Gary C. Bryner

Multiparty Politics in America edited by Paul S. Herrnson and John C. Green

Rage on the Right: The American Militia Movement from Ruby Ridge to Homeland Security by Lane Crothers

Rethinking Social Movements: Structure, Meaning, and Emotion edited by Jeff Goodwin and James M. Jasper

Social Movements and American Political Institutions edited by Anne N. Costain and Andrew S. McFarland

The Social Movement Society: Contentious Politics for a New Century edited by David S. Meyer and Sidney Tarrow

The State of the Parties: The Changing Role of Contemporary American Parties, 3rd ed., edited by John C. Green and Daniel M. Shea

The State of the Parties, 4th ed., edited by John C. Green and Rick D. Farmer

Teamsters and Turtles? U.S. Progressive Political Movements in the 21st Century edited by John C. Berg

Transnational Protest and Global Activism edited by Donatella della Porta and Sidney Tarrow

Waves of Protest: Social Movements since the Sixties edited by Jo Freeman and Victoria Johnson

Forthcoming

The Art and Craft of Lobbying: Political Engagement in American Politics by Ronald G. Shaiko

Chimes of Freedom: Student Protest and the American University by Christine Kelly

Coalitions across Borders: Transnational Protest and the Neo-Liberal Order edited by Joe Bandy and Jackie Smith

The Gay and Lesbian Rights Movement: Changing Policies! Changing Minds? by Steven H. Haeberle

Ralph Nader, the Greens, and the Crisis of American Politics by John C. Berg

The U.S. Women's Movement in Global Perspective edited by Lee Ann Banaszak

Transnational Protest and Global Activism

Edited by
Donatella della Porta and Sidney Tarrow

ROWMAN & LITTLEFIELD PUBLISHERS, INC.
Lanham • Boulder • New York • Toronto • Oxford

ROWMAN & LITTLEFIELD PUBLISHERS, INC.

Published in the United States of America
by Rowman & Littlefield Publishers, Inc.
A wholly owned subsidary of The Rowman & Littlefield Publishing Group, Inc.
4501 Forbes Boulevard, Suite 200, Lanham, MD 20706
www.rowmanlittlefield.com

P.O. Box 317, Oxford OX2 9RU, UK

British Library Cataloguing in Publication Information Available

Library of Congress Cataloging-in-Publication Data

Transnational protest and global activism / edited by Donatella della
Porta and Sidney Tarrow.
    p.   cm.— (People, passions, and power)
  Includes bibliographical references and index.
  ISBN 0-7425-3586-X (cloth : alk. paper)—ISBN 0-7425-3587-8 (pbk. :
alk. paper)
    1. Social movements—International cooperation.   2. Protest
movements—International cooperation.   3. Social action—International
cooperation.   I. Della Porta, Donatella, 1956–   II. Tarrow, Sidney G.
III. Series.
HM881.T75   2005
303.48′4—dc22   2004003834

Printed in the United States of America

♾ ™ The paper used in this publication meets the minimum requirements of
American National Standard for Information Sciences—Permanence of Paper for
Printed Library Materials, ANSI/NISO Z39.48-1992.

*To Alberto
who is missed
as friend, colleague,
and teacher*

Contents

Figures

Tables

Preface

This volume builds on a rich tradition of research that goes back over fifteen years. In 1986, a group of sociologists and political scientists met at the Free University in Amsterdam to launch what turned out to be a fruitful development in the general area of social movements and contentious politics. The group had the goal of bringing together European and American specialists on social movements, labor conflicts, and contentious politics, and, more generally, trying to bridge what seemed at the time like a wide gap in approaches between the European "new social movement" approach and the American "resource mobilization/political process" approach. The collective volume that came out of that conference did indeed stimulate cooperation and dialogue among political scientists—for whom social movements had often been marginal to politics—and sociologists—for whom collective action was a central category of analysis—and led to a series of collaborations between American and European scholars.

Not only did the Amsterdam meeting produce a widely read book, *From Structure to Action: Comparing Social Movement Participation* (1988); under the leadership of Bert Klandermans, it launched a series of volumes under the general rubric *International Social Movement Research* and laid the foundation for a continuing transatlantic dialogue among Europeans and Americans, sociologists and political scientists working in the social movement field. Successive meetings—in Washington in 1992 (McAdam, McCarthy and Zald, 1996), in Lausanne in 1998 (della Porta, Kriesi, and Rucht, 1999), and in Scotland in 2000 (Diani and McAdam, 2003)— extended the range of collaboration to the next generations of social movement specialists from both disciplines and on both continents.

As a result of these efforts, there is now a truly international and interdisciplinary core of specialists in social movements and contentious politics, ranging from the original group of participants at the Amsterdam conference, to a second generation of now-established younger scholars, and to a third generation just coming into their own. Many of these younger scholars are going beyond the initial consensus that emerged from the Amsterdam conference and expanding their interest into new areas of contention and conflict resolution. This is all to the good, and in doing so, they are forced to engage in dialogue with areas outside of social movement scholarship in the strict sense: urban policy and politics, democracy and democratization, organizational sociology, international relations, party politics, and public interest groups.

Members of the older and younger generations met again in the summer of 2003 at the Rockefeller Foundation Study and Conference Center in Bellagio, on Lake Como, where the idea of this book emerged. Our goal in Bellagio was to advance cross-national transatlantic and interdisciplinary collaboration during a period in which a new cycle of protest was emerging. After the dramatic challenge of the World Trade Organization (WTO) meeting in Seattle, this new wave of contention has become more and more visible, more and more insistent, and of wider and wider scope. Compared to the relative "normalization" of protest over the previous two decades, it produces new challenges to scholars, to movement activists, and to their opponents. As we explain in the introduction to this volume, transnationalization is the most important of these challenges. But it is by no means the only one: new forms of electronic communication, the rise of network and affinity group forms of organization, and challenges to corporate governance are additional features of this new cycle of protest. These were the issues that we debated in Bellagio and that we bring to a wider audience in this book.

The Villa Serbelloni provided an invaluable setting for our meeting, allowing for four days of both intense debate and informal discussions. The decision to bring together an "old" network of social movement scholars—many of them with previous experiences of collaboration—with younger scholars from both Europe and the United States proved especially fruitful. Mutual trust allowed for constructive disagreement, but also for the development of what appears to be an emerging consensus on the nature and the importance of this new wave of activism and mobilization.

While some research in the recent past has focused on transnational campaigns and, more recently, on the rise of a "global justice" movement, this volume aims instead at linking local and global conflicts by looking at the way in which global issues are transforming local and national activism, as well as at the interaction between local, national, and supranational movement organizations. Although all of our authors share an interest in the empirics of recent contention, they also share a theoretical and methodological interest in the adaptation of the concepts and hypotheses developed in the social movement literature to what appears to be a new cycle of protest at the global level.

We are grateful to the Rockefeller Foundation (and, in particular, to Signora Gianna Celli, managing director; Ms. Susan E. Garfield, New York manager at the Bellagio Study and Conference Center; as well as the residents at the Villa Serbelloni in July 2003) for their generous and kind hospitality, as well as to the Ford Foundation and the GRACE (Gruppo di ricerca sull'azione collettiva in Europa) at the University of Florence for logistical support. For the many challenges and opportunities of the debate they animated, we are indebted to all the participants. We particularly wish to thank Massimiliano Andretta, Simone Baglioni, Manuela Caiani, Maria Fabbri, and Lorenzo Mosca at the University of Florence; Michelle Beyeler and Hanspeter Kriesi, Institut für Politikwissenschaft, Universität Zürich; Bert Klandermans, Faculteit der Social-Culturele Wetenschappen, Free University Amsterdam; Ruud Koopmans and Dieter Rucht, Wissenschaftszentrum Berlin für Sozialforschung, Berlin; and David S. Meyer, Department of Sociology, University of California, Irvine for their contributions to our discussions at Bellagio. Our contributors showed such a strong commitment to our collective enterprise that the revised manuscript was able to be sent to press a mere six months after our final collaborations. The merit for this record timing is shared by Sarah Tarrow, who edited the texts and tables with care and efficiency, and by Jennifer Knerr, Renée Legatt, and Jehanne Schweitzer of Rowman & Littlefield for the prompt and efficient production of this book.

Transnational Processes and Social Activism: An Introduction

DONATELLA DELLA PORTA AND SIDNEY TARROW

Modern social movements developed with the creation of the nation-state, and the nation-state has for many years been the main target for protest. Although social movements have often pushed for a conception of "direct" democracy, the institutions and actors of representative democracy have long structured movements' political opportunities and constraints within the boundaries of institutional politics. In fact, for most of the history of the modern national state, political parties were the main actors in democratic representation, linking the formation of collective identities with representative institutions. But at the turn of the millennium, nation-states face a host of new challenges:

- From without, there is the contemporary challenge of terrorism and the rejection of pluralistic and secular government on the part of broad sectors of the world's population;
- from within, there is both widespread disaffection from conventional forms of politics and disillusionment with the active state;
- linking these internal and external challenges are the uncertainties of new forms of internationalization and globalization that connect citizens to a global market but reduce their control over their own fates.

Although the power of the nation-state has by no means disappeared, since the 1960s, social, cultural, and geopolitical changes have begun to transform social movements' institutional and cultural environments. In particular, there has been a shift in the locus of political power—a shift symbolized by the growing use of concepts like "multilevel governance," "the world polity," and "global civil society," which point to the following internal and external developments. *Internally*, there has been a continuing shift in power from parliaments to the executive, and, within the executive, to the bureaucracy and to quasi-independent agencies. Power has moved from mass-parties to parties that have been variously defined as "catchall," "professional-electoral," or "cartel" parties (for a review, see della Porta, 2001), and therefore from party activists to the "new party professionals." *Externally*, there has been a shift in the locus of institutional power from the national to both the supranational and the regional levels, with the increasing power of international institutions, especially economic ones (World Bank, International Monetary Fund [IMF], World Trade Organization [WTO]), and some regional ones (in Europe, the European Union [EU]; in the Western hemisphere, the North American Free Trade Agreement [NAFTA]).

Meanwhile, informal networks have spread across borders (such as international agreements on standards; nongovernmental organization [NGO] coalitions in the areas of human rights, the environment, and peace; and, in a darker vein, drug and human trafficking networks). Many see a shift in the axis of power from politics to the market, with neoliberal economic policies increasing the power of multinational corporations and reducing the capacity of traditional state structures to control them. Taken together, these changes have led to the development of a system of "complex internationalism," which provides both threats and opportunities to ordinary people, to organized nonstate actors, and to weaker states, as we shall argue in our conclusions.

How are social movements reacting to these power shifts in terms of their organizational structures, their collective action frames and identities, and their repertoires of action? At first, scholars assumed that international movements would be similar to those that had developed within the nation-state. More recently, a growing stream of research on social movements has identified three important processes of transnationalization: diffusion, domestication, and externalization. By *diffusion*, we mean the spread of movement ideas, practices, and frames from one country to another; by *domestication*, we mean the playing out on domestic territory of conflicts that have their origin externally; and by *externalization*, we mean the challenge to supranational institutions to intervene in domestic problems or conflicts.

These processes are all important and appear to be widespread. However, the recent evolution of movements focusing on "global justice," peace and war, or both, suggests some additional processes. The most important of these, and the one that emerges most clearly from the chapters in this book, is what we call "transnational collective action"—that is, *coordinated international campaigns on the part of networks of activists against international actors, other states, or international institutions.* In the first section of this introduction, we will rapidly survey findings on the three better-known processes of diffusion, domestication, and externalization. In the second section, we will try to specify how the process of transnational collective action has developed in recent years. In the third section, we will suggest some hypotheses about its forms and dynamics. In the fourth section, we will summarize the contributions to the volume.

DIFFUSION, DOMESTICATION, AND EXTERNALIZATION

Three broad processes link transnational politics today to the traditions of social movement studies in the past and lay the groundwork for the major changes that we see occurring in the contemporary world.

Diffusion

Diffusion is the most familiar and the oldest form of transnational contention. It need not involve connections across borders, but only that challengers in one country or region adopt or adapt the organizational forms, collective action frames, or targets of those in other countries or regions. Thus, the "shantytown" protests that were used to demand American universities' divestiture from South Africa were a domestic example of diffusion (Soule, 1999), while the spread of the "sit-in" from the American civil rights movement to Western Europe was a transnational one (Tarrow, 1989). Research on protest in Belgium, France, and Germany has also indicated the existence of important cross-national diffusion effects (Reising, 1999:333).

A variant on diffusion is what Tarrow and McAdam, in chapter 6, call "brokerage," through which groups or individuals deliberately connect actors from different sites of contention. This process was evident as early as the spread of the antislavery movement from England to the European continent in the late eighteenth century (Drescher, 1987) and, in more recent history, in the transfer of the American student movement's themes and practices to West Germany, through students who had studied in the United States in the 1960s (McAdam and Rucht, 1993). In their contribution, Tarrow and McAdam identify the brokerage elements that built the Zapatista solidarity network around the world after the Chiapas rebellion of 1994.

One of the factors that characterizes the new international system is the greater ease with which particular practices or frames can be transferred from one country to another through cheap international travel, the knowledge of common languages, and access to the Internet (Bennett, 2003, and chapter 9 in this volume). But underlying these advantages lies a disadvantage. Every new form of communication both heightens ties between those who already know one another, and raises the walls of exclusion for those lacking access to the new medium of communication (Tilly, 2004). Not only that: although it is undoubtedly easier and faster for information about protest to be communicated across national lines today than it was fifty years ago, the Internet also creates the risk of diffuseness, as those with Internet skills learn to mount their own websites and set themselves up as movement entrepreneurs. In general, research indicates that sustained diffusion processes both require and help to produce transnational networks and identities, to which we will turn in the next section.

Internalization

By internalization, we mean the playing out on domestic territory of conflicts that have their origin externally. Previous research on protest events, collected mainly from newspaper sources from Western Europe, stressed the small number of protests that target international institutions directly. A good part of this research focused on the EU. Using Reuters World News Service and the Reuters Textline, Doug Imig and Sidney Tarrow (2001; also see 1999) found a limited (but growing) number of such protests. Similarly, in Germany, Dieter Rucht (2002a) observed a low (and declining) proportion of protests aimed at the international level (with the high point coming in 1960–1964) or at EU institutions. Meanwhile, Marco Giugni and Florence Passy (2002) noted how rarely protests on migrant rights targeted the EU, notwithstanding the increasing Europeanization of legal competences regarding border control. Even environmental action was rarely turned on Brussels: protests with EU targets ranged from 0.8 percent in Italy to 4.6 percent in Germany in the last decade, with no discernible increasing trend (Rootes, 2002). Similarly, few protest events have addressed international organizations other than the EU.

Protest events analysis, however, indicated that protest often addressed national governments regarding decisions that originated or were implemented at a supranational level. In their analysis of protest in Europe, Doug Imig and Sidney Tarrow (2001) found that most EU related events (406 out of 490) were in fact cases of domestication—that is, conflict about EU decisions, but mounted at the national level. And processes of domestication in fact characterized many mobilizations of European farmers (Bush and Simi, 2001). Outside of Europe, as well, many important mobilizations against international institutions followed a similar dynamic. The anti-IMF "austerity protests" of the 1980s took a largely domesticated form (Walton, 2001). Recent Argentine protests were similarly triggered by the pressure of international financial institutions but directed against domestic institutions (Auyero, 2003).

The low level of protest targeting the supranational level might be explained by the political opportunities available to collective actors at other territorial levels of government. In addition, the undeniable "democratic deficit" of international institutions—lacking both electoral responsiveness and accountability in the public sphere (Eder, 2000)—plays an important role. Such mobilizations might in fact be seen as proof of the continued dominance of the nation-state. However, a more careful look shows the emergence, in the course of these campaigns, of innovations both in the organizational structure and in the frames of the protest (della Porta, 2003a), as we will see below.

Externalization

A third area in which researchers have observed the emergence of clear transnational trends is in studies focusing on movement organizations that become active supranationally. Within this approach, scholars of international relations have analyzed informational and lobbying campaigns in which national and international NGOs attempt to stimulate international alliances with nationally weak social movements (Keck and Sikkink, 1998; see also chapter 7 in this volume). These researchers stress that organized interests and social movements look to international institutions for the mobilization of resources that can be used at the national level. A variant is the construction of transnational coalitions of international NGOs, which reach into these institutions to find allies on behalf of the claims of weak domestic actors in countries of the South (Fox and Brown, 1998).

The strategy of externalization (Chabanet, 2002) has often characterized the mobilization of national groups targeting the EU in attempts to put pressure on their own governments for material or symbolic resources. For instance, British environmental organizations paid increasing attention to the EU (even playing a leading role vis-à-vis other environmental groups) when political opportunities at home were poor (Rootes, 2002; see also Rootes in this volume). To give another example, with their Eurostrike in 1997, Spanish, French, and Belgian Renault workers protested at the EU level against the closing of the Renault factory of Vilvorde in Belgium (Lefébure and Lagneau, 2002).

Some international institutions have indeed emerged as arenas for the articulation of collective claims (Smith, Chatfield, and Pagnucco, 1997). On the rights of indigenous populations or women, the United Nations seems able to produce international norms that, though weaker than national regulation, can be used to strengthen and legitimize these groups' claims (see Soysal, 1994). In Western Europe, the European Parliament has worked as a main channel of access for various organizations, especially in areas like the environment, in which parliamentary committees are active. Feminists, environmentalists, and unions have also been able to obtain favorable decisions from the European Court of Justice, especially with the increasing competence of the EU with respect to environmental and social policies (Dehousse, 1998; Balme and Chabanet, 2002).

In their dealings with international institutions, some movement organizations receive material and symbolic resources, such as the financing of particular projects, or recognition of their legitimacy. On their side, international institutions benefit from low-cost work from voluntary associations; from the information they can provide; from access to local populations; and, of course, from legitimization (for instance, Mazey and Richardson, 1997:10). For the institutionally weak European Parliament, alliances with NGOs provide resources for legitimization vis-à-vis the more powerful European Commission and the European Council. Similarly for the United Nations, NGOs active on human rights help a weak bureaucracy to acquire specialized, and, in general, reliable knowledge, while development NGOs offer high-quality, low-cost human resources (for a summary, see della Porta and Kriesi, 1999).

Externalization processes have, however, some limits. First of all, "boomerangs" and "insider/outsider coalitions" are more likely to emerge when "(1) channels between domestic groups and their governments are blocked or hampered or where such channels are ineffective for resolving a conflict, setting into motion a 'boomerang' pattern . . . (2) advocates believe that networking will further their missions and campaigns, and actively promote networks; and (3) conferences and other forms of international contact create arenas for forming and strengthening networks" (Keck and Sikkink, 1998:12). Moreover, they are potentially more effective for movements focusing on internationally established norms (such as human rights) than for those struggling against internationally hegemonic discourse (such as the liberalization of markets for goods and services).

To summarize: these three forms of transnational relations represent an important part of what some scholars have been calling "global social movements" and what others, more modestly, call "transnational politics." They are extremely important, and may be increasing in scope and scale, but they do not represent the most dramatic change we see in the world of contentious politics. This is what we call "transnational collective action," to which we turn in the following section.

TRANSNATIONAL COLLECTIVE ACTION

Transnational collective action is the term we use to indicate coordinated international campaigns on the part of networks of activists against international actors, other states, or international institutions. Both in Western Europe, where it takes a more institutionalized form, and outside Europe, where more vigorous forms have developed in recent years, we see it developing out of the more traditional forms that we have outlined above. We can vividly illustrate this development of new forms from old with the example of anthropologist Hilary Cunningham, who has studied activism on the U.S./Mexican border for over ten years. She began in the early 1990s by studying the "border crossing" of a group of activists linked to the U.S. Sanctuary movement, who offered safe havens to Central American refugees. She compares this experience to more recent activism to reduce the negative effects of the NAFTA agreement (2001:372–79). Between these two episodes, both occurring on the same border and involving the same populations, Cunningham observed a shift from a state-centric movement to a transnational coalition (379–83). In fact, as the movement developed, the role of the state was transformed for its activists. This transformation developed out of environmental, cognitive, and relational changes. We can use these categories to examine the forces behind the development of transnational collective action.

Environmental Change

Since the late 1980s, three kinds of changes in the international environment have helped to produce a transnationalization of collective action. First, the collapse of the Soviet bloc encouraged the development of forms of nonstate action that had previously been blocked by Cold War divisions. This produced a wave of Western governmental support for NGO activity in both East-Central Europe and the former Soviet Union (Mendelson and Glenn, 2002), as well as the development of homegrown nonstate groups that might otherwise have been branded as "procommunist" in the days of the Cold War. At the same time, the explosion of secessionist movements, border wars, and warlordism that followed the breakup of the Soviet bloc fed an increase of humanitarian aid movements around the world.

 Second, the development of electronic communications and the spread of inexpensive international travel have made it easier for formerly isolated movement actors to communicate and collaborate with one another across borders. Related to this, there has been a massive increase in migration flows across borders, which has stimulated both benign forms of immigrant activism (Guarnizo, Portes, and Landolt, 2003) and the more transgressive forms of diasporic nationalism that have exacerbated ethnic and linguistic conflicts (Anderson, 1998).

Finally, the importance of the international environment has been highlighted by the growing power of transnational corporations and international institutions, treaties regulating the international economy, and international events like the global summits of the World Bank, the Group of Eight, and especially the World Trade Organization. These are of course framed by activists as threats, which they indeed are for broad sectors of the world's population; but it is the internationalization of the global environment that produces opportunities for activists from both North and South to engage in concerted collective action. Together, these changes combine into what we call "complex internationalism," and will describe at greater length in our conclusions.

While some analysts appear to think that globalization is sufficient to produce global social movements, changes in the global environment are not sufficient to produce a transnationalization of collective action. Cognitive change within and relational changes between actors must be the active forces for such a fundamental change. The former can best be seen in the changing perspective of nonstate actors active on the international scene, while the latter can be observed in the formation of sustained networks of transnational activists.

Cognitive Change

Since social movements are "reflective" actors, their international experiences have been critically analyzed. Tactics and frames that appear to succeed in more than one venue have been institutionalized—for example, in the spread of the practice of demonstrating on the occasion of the periodic meetings of the great international institutions, first within Western Europe in the 1990s and then globally, against the World Bank, the IMF, and the WTO. The formation of the "World Social Forum," created to highlight the distortions of the annual Davos World Economic Forum, eventually produced regional social fora such as the European one that took place in Florence in 2002. Moreover, the tactical adaptation of governmental and police strategies to movement challenges at a transnational level demanded the common elaboration of plans for collective action on the part of activists.

With respect to domestication, although still mainly addressing national governments, many groups of protesters have learned from people like themselves in other countries. This was the case, for instance, for Italian farmers, during the struggle against the implementation of EU quotas on milk production (della Porta, 2003a). Similarly, the local movements of the unemployed have learned to pay greater attention to their transnational connections (Chabanet, 2002; Baglioni, 2003). Though it was "domestic," the wave of attacks on McDonald's in France gave rise to a spontaneous wave of similar attacks in other countries and to the popularity of the theme of the "Americanization" of mass culture and commerce.

As for externalization, the "vertical" experience of individual national movements operating internationally has placed many actors in contact with others like themselves and thus encouraged them to develop a more globalized framing of their messages and their domestic appeals. We can see this in the indigenous peoples' movements throughout Latin America, which have adopted many of the same cognitive frames in countries with little else in common (Yashar, 2005).

Relational Changes

The most striking developments of the last decade have operated through the relational mechanisms that are bringing together national actors in transnational coalitions. The existence of international institutions as common "vertical" targets has helped to produce the "horizontal" formation of transnational coalitions through the networks of activists that form around them. For example, at the European level, networks of organizations of regionalist movements (Hooghe, 2002), women's organizations (Mazey, 2002), and labor unions (Martin and Ross, 2001) gained some success in the EU. In the same way, indigenous people and human rights organizations have coordinated their efforts and gained access to the United Nations (for a summary, see della Porta and Kriesi, 1999). In parallel, although more slowly, women's concerns and ecological issues advanced in the United Nations, as well as in the World Bank. National women's organizations that participated in the UN NGO conferences for women, especially in Beijing in 1995, encountered others like themselves and forged long-lasting transnational coalitions. The same is true of the "counter-summits" organized around the economic summits at Davos and elsewhere. According to a survey of NGOs, a major perceived advantage of the counter-summit is the consolidation of transnational and trans-thematic linkages between transnational movement organizations (Pianta, 2001).

Relations between movements and governments are a major source of change. Social movements do not act in a vacuum, and, in fact, the strongest influences on their behavior and tactics are the behavior and tactics of the governments they challenge. The last decade has shown that governments also imitate one another, therefore leading to increasing similarities in the contexts in which movement campaigns and protests take place.

Increasing interaction facilitates the growth of common identity, and therefore reduces national particularism. One of the major changes in the last half decade has been the adoption of new and more violent tactics on the part of the forces of order against international protesters. This came to a head in Genoa in 2001, but it has been evident since the 1999 protests in Seattle that police forces are following similar strategies in protecting international institutions and conferences.

In summary, reflecting on the successes, but also on the failures of transnational collective action, as well as the experience of working together on temporary campaigns, has led to the creation of transnational organizational structures and the framing of transnational identities. Certainly, social movements have retained their national character, remaining tied to the types of political opportunities present in individual states; but they have also increasingly interacted transnationally. As has been noted, if social movements are to work with success in supranational arenas, they must develop a base of cross-national resources and global strategies that will be significantly different from those deployed in national arenas (Smith, Pagnucco, and Romeril, 1994:126). These arenas offer activists of different world regions the opportunity to meet, form organizational networks, coordinate activity, and construct global frames and programs (Passy, 1999; Smith, 1999).

EMERGING FORMS AND DYNAMICS OF
TRANSNATIONAL CONTENTION

All four forms of transnationalization described above facilitate the spread of movements targeting international institutions, practices, and relationships, producing a growing concern with global issues. In the last few years, research has begun to develop on the ways in which transnational collective action is organized and on how transnational conflict and alliance structures are formed. Knowledge has increased, for example, regarding the lobbying efforts of international NGOs or networks of NGOs, working patiently within the ambit of international institutions (O'Brien et al., 2000); on the construction of international treaties and agreements with the active participation of transnational actors (Klotz, 1996; Price, 1997; 1998); on the service or information-based politics of foreign NGOs or networks within individual societies that are not their own (Keck and Sikkink, 1998); on the framing of domestic protest activities against "globalization" without significant foreign participation (such as the 1995 Chiapas rebellion against the Mexican government, framed against the handy symbol of NAFTA [Olesen 2003]); on the actions of local movement actors active on global issues, such as local social fora

(Andretta et al., 2002 and 2003); and on transnationally organized contentious claims-making against international economic actors, institutions, and states (Andretta et al.; also della Porta, 2003b).

Building on this knowledge, but adding new elements of research, the chapters collected in this volume pose one or more of the following questions:

- What are the organizational forms that have developed to connect very loose networks of activists ("movements of movements," as they have been called)? What is the role of the Internet ("the net of the networks")?

- How do repertoires of protest adapt to address institutions with low democratic accountability and transparency? To what extent are movements able to build new public spheres, or arenas, for critical political debates?

- Are movement identities undergoing changes in their content and structure as the result of transnational exposure and activism? Is there a return to "materialistic" concerns? Is tolerance for internal differences growing? Is the opposition to neoliberal globalization an emerging master-frame?

- What are the main resources (knowledge, capacity for disruption, legitimacy, links to institutional actors, etc.) that movements mobilize in order to address the political claims in a complex system of governance? Where do social movements find their "social capital"?

- How do national (or even local) political opportunities influence the strategies of social movements that are active on global issues? Are the political parties of the Left still perceived as potential allies? And what are the differences between movements' adaptation to multilevel governance at the center and at the periphery?

Looking at the effects of the development of conflicts over global issues at the domestic level, as well as at the transnational dynamics of contention, the contributions to this volume begin to provide responses to these questions.

With respect to organizational structure, they clearly indicate that recent forms of transnational contention are far from exclusively organized around transnational social movement organizations. Instead, they are rooted at the local and national level, turning simultaneously to various governmental levels. In particular, transnational mobilizations create linkages between different social and political actors: not only do domestic and international populations of movement organizations interact (see Johnson and McCarthy in this volume), but coalitions involving local groups are formed through local social fora and changes in the framing of domestic political conflicts. New technologies reduce the costs of participating in transnational networks, even for small local groups, helping in the development of global protest campaigns.

Also at the local level, "global social justice" has become a masterframe of new mobilizations, including those addressing the environment and the conditions and rights of women and workers, native people, peasants, and children (see Diani in this volume). This in turn produces loosely coupled transnational networks that organize around particular campaigns or series of campaigns, using a variety of forms of protests, adopting and adapting repertoires of protest from the traditions of different movements. Specific concerns with women's rights, labor issues, the defense of the environment, and opposition to war survive, but are bridged together in the opposition against "neoliberal globalization." In order to keep different groups together, "tolerant," inclusive identities develop, stressing differences as a positive quality of the movement.

As for the repertoire of action, after years of using more moderate tactics, a new propensity for "taking people to the street" has developed, in particular, with the development of forms of civil disobedience. Yet, protest is also combined with educational campaigns, comic presentations, and attention to the mass media, stressing not only the power in numbers but also the importance of the presentation and diffusion of the message (on the importance of media work for ATTAC, see Felix Kolb's contribution to this volume). Whether a qualitatively new repertoire of contention has developed around transnational contention remains to be seen, but what is clear is that new targets, new frames, and new combinations of constituencies have produced major innovations in the existing repertoire. As we will see in this volume, this evolution modifies trends that have been observed in contentious politics at the domestic level in many countries:

- If social movement organizations appeared increasingly institutionalized and bureaucratic during the 1980s and 1990s, new types of loose organizational structures have emerged around the issue of global justice, with a capacity to penetrate the public sphere, bringing new issues into the public sphere;
- if movement strategies appeared increasingly moderate and contained, direct action and civil disobedience have combined with them, increasing the disruptiveness of protest;
- if social movement discourses appeared to privilege specialization, they have recently shown a taste for more general issues.

What do social movement scholars have to teach in response to these changes? Explanations for these new developments can be found in the resources and opportunities available to movements—as the social movement literature suggests. But these changes can only be captured if we shift from a static to a more dynamic definition of resources and opportunities: for example, from resources and opportunities as "they are," to resources and opportunities as they are perceived and constructed by the activists; from specific collective action frames to the process of framing entire episodes, the actors, and the issues within them; and from studying individual forms of collective action to the process of innovation and interaction between challengers and their opponents (della Porta, 1995:9–14; della Porta and Diani, 1999:223–24; McAdam, Tarrow, and Tilly, 2001: ch. 2).

In terms of the mobilization of resources, two emerging challenges for movements can be mentioned. First, the fragmentation in the social structure has increased social heterogeneity, in particular with a decline of the social groups (the working class, but also the "new middle class") that had provided the social bases for many previous movements. Second, an increasingly individualized culture has been read as reducing the bases for solidarity values in the society, therefore increasing a tendency to free-riderism and diminishing the propensity for collective action.

However, our findings suggest that transnational mobilization is facilitated by the adaptation of movement strategies to the changing environment (including a shift in the type of resources available to challengers). In particular, the flexible networks that have been encouraged by a looser and less crystallized social structure make it possible to connect heterogeneous social bases with movement organizations inherited from previous waves of protest. At the same time, a redefinition of political involvement that emphasizes diversity and subjectivity (see chapter 8 in this volume) taps into cultural changes—which some have called "postmodern"—that build on the thesis that "the personal is political." In this way, "apolitical" personal lifestyle changes that are becoming common to many young people across the globe have become an intangible but rich source of movement mobilization.

Similarly, if we look at political opportunities, both the supranational and the national levels appear to be quite closed in traditional terms. On the one hand, even the most developed among the international institutions lack the basic features of democratic responsiveness and accountability—granting at best informal and limited access to movement organizations or, more generally, to citizens. On the other hand, the traditional allies of social movements, the left-wing parties, have been far from supportive of recent protests, both in their content and forms. But here again, recent mobilizations have attempted to redefine the concept of politics, putting an emphasis on the role of "politics from below," and expressing a strong distrust of representative institutions. Addressing public opinion directly, the activists seem to attempt (with some success) to create public spaces that are autonomous from the political parties, but also from the commercial logic of the mass media. That is, faced with few institutional opportunities, the activists aim at redefining politics.

THIS VOLUME

The chapters collected in this volume address these theoretical issues on the basis of empirical studies of contemporary social movements and their interactions with opponents, authorities, and international institutions. Global protest campaigns, counter-summits, cross-sectoral alliances among movements and NGOs, the refraction of transnational protest activity into the domestic arena: these are some promising research subjects that can help to better specify and operationalize the dynamics sketched above.

This volume builds on a rich tradition of scholarly collaboration that goes back over fifteen years to a meeting of social movement scholars at the Free University of Amsterdam in 1986. At that time, distinct research traditions divided social movement scholarship among Europeans and Americans, sociologists and political scientists, advocates of "new social movement theory" and of resource mobilization (Klandermans and Tarrow, 1988). The Amsterdam meeting set out to bridge those gaps. It not only succeeded in producing a much-read volume (Klandermans et al., 1988), but it gave rise to an international book series, *International Social Movement Research*, and created a loosely linked international network of social movement scholars who met every few years, renewed and broadened their composition, and helped set the agenda for social movement research for years to come (Klandermans et al., 1988; McAdam et al., 1996; della Porta, Kriesi, and Rucht, 1999; Diani and McAdam, 2003). This volume is dedicated to the memory of our friend and colleague, Alberto Melucci, who was part of the first "Amsterdam" generation, and whose work has influenced many of us.

While some research focused in the past on transnational campaigns and, more recently, on the rise of a global justice movement, this volume aims at linking local and global conflicts by looking at the way in which global issues are transforming local and national movements, as well as at the interaction between local, national, and supranational movement organizations. Using recent cases of transnational contention—from the European Social Forum in Florence to the Argentinean human rights movement and British environmentalists, from movement networks in Bristol and Glasgow to the Zapatistas—the chapters presented in the volume adapt the concepts and hypotheses developed in the social move-

PLAN:

ment literature to what appears to be a new cycle of protest developing around the globe, after the "low ebb" of mobilization in the last decade.

Part I of the book contains two chapters devoted to the analysis of the effects of the emergence of a "global vision" of conflict at the local and national level. We will show how global justice issues affect local and national movement organizations, first by helping to structure local movement networks and then by widening the issue scope of national organizations. Next, we analyze how activists in transnational protest campaigns engage in collective action at the local level, developing a multilevel challenge to traditional politics. Finally, we show how transnational movement organizations adapt to national opportunities, helping to diffuse concern over global injustice at home.

In particular, in chapter 2, Christopher Rootes discusses the degree and forms of transnationalization in the environmental movement. Using rich databases on the British case, the chapter assesses a limited transnationalization in terms of protest action as well as organizational structures. In-depth analysis of some movement organizations points, however, to the changing character of the British environmental movement as it wrestles with the challenges presented by its need to act locally while at the same time increasingly recognizing the growing importance of transnational economic and political institutions.

In chapter 3, Mario Diani addresses the general question of whether and to what extent transnational issues, such as North–South inequalities, third world debt, or globalization processes, affect local politics and the structure of local civil society in West European countries. On the basis of evidence coming from structured interviews conducted with 124 organizations in Glasgow and 134 organizations in Bristol, the author stresses the influence of global issues on the network structure of the groups, suggesting that interest in transnational issues does indeed shape the structure of civil society networks.

In part II, we turn to the processes through which domestic contention diffuses to other countries and to the international level. In chapter 4, Erik Johnson and John McCarthy look at the interactions between national and transnational social movement organizations. Comparing the coevolution of the populations of transnational environmental movement organizations with the national populations of environmental movement organizations in the United States (based on various issues of the *Yearbook of International Organizations*, and the *Encyclopedia of Associations, National Organizations of the U.S.*), with particular attention to the timing of the founding of movement organizations, the chapter discusses the "top-down" versus "bottom-up" hypotheses, stressing the role of state-level movement organizations in stimulating the rise of transnational ones.

In chapter 5, Felix Kolb focuses on the role of social movement organizations in shaping the European debate on global issues. On the basis of research on the successful anti-neoliberal group, ATTAC (combining a content analysis of newspaper coverage with archival sources), the chapter shows how transnational protest, mass media, and organizational strategy interacted in the making of the German branch of this important transnational movement organization.

In chapter 6, Sidney Tarrow and Doug McAdam address the mechanisms and processes through which transnational contention is organized, and in particular on "scale shift," which signifies a shifting trajectory of contention from small to larger arenas (or, in contrast, from larger to smaller ones). The authors specify this process through four main mechanisms and two alternative paths ("brokerage" and "diffusion") and speculate about the properties and implications of each for the durability of trajectories of mobilization. Each of these paths is illustrated with well-known cases of scale shift, ranging from the American civil rights movement to the Zapatista network and the nuclear freeze movement.

Part III turns to various patterns of the internationalization of contentious politics. In chapter 7, Kathryn Sikkink addresses the question of how the interaction of national and international political opportunity structures influences the strategies of social movements that are active on global issues. On the basis of a series of case studies, especially in Latin America, the chapter discusses how activists, aware of the possibilities created by this dynamic interaction, choose strategies attuned to opportunities at both the international and domestic levels. Using the basic idea of closed and open structures at the domestic and international level as an analytical starting point, it suggests four different characteristic patterns of activism, linking them with different policy issues (such as human rights, trade, and money).

Donatella della Porta, in chapter 8, discusses the conception of democracy and politics in the movement for "globalization from below." Using data from a survey with 2,800 activists of different nationalities who took part in the European Social Forum in Florence, and focus groups of activists in Florence, it discusses the movement's responses to challenges related to various aspects of transnationalization, looking at some characteristics of "global activists," such as their involvement in complex political and social networks and their range of previous experiences of political participation. Finally, the chapter addresses the activists' definition of politics, looking both at their criticisms of representative democracy and their image of a democracy "in movement."

Lance Bennett, in chapter 9, contrasts "traditional" and "new" patterns of transnational activism. Looking at the movement organized loosely around "global justice" issues, the author suggests that it challenges earlier accounts of transnational activism cast largely in terms of NGO-centered, single-issue policy networks that run centrally organized campaigns based on brokered coalitions, aimed mainly at policy reforms. The new transnational movement is instead described as composed of loose activist networks adopting self-organizing communication technologies and advocating multiple issues, multiple goals, and inclusive identities. The implications of the emerging organizational model for political effectiveness and democracy-building are discussed.

The conclusion addresses three main issues. First, we look at how the international environment intersects with globalization to produce a system that we call "complex internationalism," in which states, international institutions, and nonstate actors regularly interact around issues of global importance. Second, we turn to the progress that has been made in scholars' understanding of transnational contention since the first studies of the phenomenon appeared in the 1990s. Finally, we turn to some of the unresolved and recently opened issues in transnational contention, such as the rise of militant political Islam and the apparent turn of the United States to a more hegemonic project that threatens much of the progress in multilateral governance made over the last few decades.

Part I

TRANSNATIONALISM
FROM THE INSIDE

2

A Limited Transnationalization?
The British Environmental Movement

CHRISTOPHER ROOTES

Although environmental issues are increasingly recognized as transnational issues that can only rarely be addressed satisfactorily within the confines of a single national state, the transnationalism of environmental movements remains problematic. Transnational protests against international or supranational institutions such as the World Trade Organization (WTO), World Bank, and European Union (EU) have often raised environmental issues, but they have not been primarily environmental protests. Although environmental movement organizations (EMOs) have often publicly sympathized with the critique of those institutions, they have not generally been prominently involved in the protests.

In any case, the proliferation of protests does not itself constitute a social movement. As Diani (1992, this volume) insists, it is the *networking* of collective action that constitutes a social movement. Transnational movements are most likely built upon the foundations of national environmental movements, so to explore the prospects for transnational movements we need to examine developments within national movements as they attempt to address the imperatives of globalization and come to terms with new opportunities for transnational action.

This chapter examines changes in the key constituents of the British environmental movement as they wrestle with the challenges presented by their need to act locally, while at the same time responding to the growing importance of transnational economic and political institutions. The most immediately compelling of such institutions are those of the EU. Both the potential for and the difficulties of transnationalization are illuminated by the experience of British EMOs in and in relation to Europe.

21

THE EUROPEANIZATION OF
ENVIRONMENTALISM?

It is often claimed that the increased numbers of nongovernmental organizations (NGOs) operating on a transnational basis is a sign of the emergence of a global civil society. Perhaps so, but political action is shaped by the opportunities offered and constraints imposed by political institutions. The international institutions that have so far been constructed are almost always just that—inter-*national*, or even simply intergovernmental; there is as yet no global polity comparable to the nation-state. The pattern of action adopted by transnational NGOs is, in consequence, an adaptation to an international political milieu dominated by intergovernmental negotiations and agreements. As Sidney Tarrow has observed, "transnational groups organize [around] international institutions, which serve as sources of group claims, as targets for their protests, and as sites that can bring parallel groups together internationally" (2001a:246–47).

But would the establishment of formal political institutions on a truly global scale remove all obstacles to the development of transnational social movements? It is instructive to consider the most plausible contender in the most favorable circumstances, the most globally conscious social movement in the most highly developed existing supranational polity: the environmental movement in the EU. However, as we shall see, despite the development and increasing powers of EU institutions, especially with regard to environmental policy, their impact upon national environmental movements has been less substantial than we might have expected. In each of the three elements essential to the identification of an environmental movement—networks, engagement in collective action, and shared concern (Rootes, 1997:326, cf. Diani, 1992)—the transnationalization of environmentalism is at best limited, even within the EU.

Networks

The most obvious sign of the transnationalization of environmentalism is the advent of new pan-European organizations. These groups formed because their founders recognized that, so long as it was ad hoc, effective cross-national collaboration between environmental campaigners was rare. They were also responding to the European Commission's (EC) increasing interest in environmental policy (Rootes, 2002, 2004). The EC's growing environmental competence not only emphasized the need for transnational organization; it also provided the opportunity. Following its first Environmental Action Programme and its desire to promote a broadly representative forum bringing together environmentalists from across Europe, the EC in 1974 provided financial assistance for the formation of the European Environmental Bureau (EEB).[1]

Other, more specialized networks also established representation in Brussels, both because they recognized the efficiency of concentrating their European lobbying activities in one place, and because they saw the EC as a more important producer of environmental policy than any EU member state. Thus Friends of the Earth (FoE) established a Brussels office in 1985, followed by Climate Action Network (CAN) in 1989, at least partly in order to prepare policy advice for the European Parliament (Rucht, 1993:81).

Both EMOs' own recognition of the value of transnational coordination and the EC's desire to disseminate environmental awareness encouraged the formation of European networks. However, because the EC remains a bureaucracy with a relatively small staff, it has sought, even more urgently than national governments, to limit the number of interlocutors with which it deals. This has encouraged closer cooperation and aggregation of interests among the various EMOs and EMO networks represented in Brussels. In order to accommodate the EC's preference for dealing with a single peak organization broadly representative of the environmental movement, a "super umbrella" network was formed. Initially comprising the EEB, FoE, Greenpeace, and the World Wide Fund for Nature (WWF), the "gang of four" has become Green-8, which now also includes CAN Europe, the European Federation for Transport and the Environment, Friends of Nature International, and BirdLife International.

Nevertheless, within the EU, the transnational networking of environmental groups is more limited than might be supposed. At first glance, British EMOs are relatively well embedded in European networks: the EEB counts more member organizations from Britain than from any other country, and British-based organizations played prominent roles in the formation of other European environmental networks. However, a 1998 survey of the European links of British EMOs found that although their heavy reliance on one another when dealing with EU matters encouraged networking among EMOs *within* the United Kingdom, it did not produce extensive collaboration with organizations in other European countries (Ward and Lowe, 1998). Although four-fifths of the thirty groups surveyed claimed membership in a European network, twenty different networks were mentioned. One in three claimed membership in the EEB, but most saw it only as a vehicle for the exchange of information.

A more extensive survey of British environmental groups undertaken as part of the Transformation of Environmental Activism (TEA) project produced similar results. Of 117 national-level EMOs surveyed in 1999–2000,[2] only thirty-two claimed even to have exchanged information with the EEB during the previous twelve months, and only ten claimed to have collaborated in a campaign with the EEB (see table 2.1). Believers in the transnationalization of environmentalism might draw comfort from the fact that the organizations most often nominated as recent interlocutors or partners were the transnationally oriented FoE, WWF, and Greenpeace. However, these references were almost certainly to the British national organizations of these EMOs, rather than their transnational operations. Indeed, the relatively small and thematically specialized Council for the Protection of Rural England (CPRE), which operates within only one of the nations of the United Kingdom, was nominated far more often than any unambiguously transnational EMO. Moreover, in response to an open-ended question asking representatives of British EMOs to name their most important collaborators, of a total of 232 nominations the

TABLE 2.1
Networks of Information and Campaigning of 117 British National EMOs (1999–2000)

Number of British EMOs reporting that they had during the previous 12 months

I. Exchanged information/expertise with named EMOs

II. Collaborated in campaigns with named EMOs

I. Exchanged information with named EMOs during previous 12 months

Organization

Frequency	EEB	CAN	FoE	WWF	Greenpeace	Other[a]	CPRE
Often	7	8	39	32	25	47	22
Sometimes	10	6	37	38	31	15	17
Rarely	15	13	15	16	19	4	23
Never	55	69	17	21	32	2	37
No answer	30	21	9	10	10	49	18

II. Collaborated in campaigns with named EMOs during previous 12 months

Organization

Frequency	EEB	CAN	FoE	WWF	Greenpeace	Other[a]	CPRE
Often	1	3	15	13	4	19	7
Sometimes	5	3	34	17	25	9	11
Rarely	4	2	8	9	13	5	13
Never	80	86	46	58	61	5	65
No answer	27	23	14	20	14	79	21

[a] Refers to the first named "other" organization; respondents could indicate up to three.

EC/EU was mentioned only twice, and not a single European EMO or network was named (Rootes and Miller, 2000).

These modest numbers are hardly a reflection of a peculiarly British lack of enthusiasm for European collaboration. Similar surveys in the six other states covered by the TEA project suggest that EMOs elsewhere in the EU were scarcely more active in European networks than their British counterparts. The proportion of EMOs reporting that they had never during the previous twelve months exchanged information with the EEB ranged from about half in Greece, Spain, and Sweden, through 60 percent in Britain and Germany, to almost 80 percent in Italy.

Transnational environmental movement networks within the EU are, then, neither very dense nor very active. Most are highly specialized, and most EMOs remain primarily oriented toward national rather than European arenas. Cross-nationally collaborative *action* tends to be confined to the larger multinational organizations such as FoE (Ward and Lowe, 1998:162). Otherwise, British EMOs appear to prefer to operate within the familiar milieu of British politics. There are good reasons for this.

Scarcity of resources is a major constraint upon collaboration among European EMOs. Because their constituencies—and, hence, their resource bases—are mostly at the national level, most EMOs focus upon maintaining or strengthening their national organizations rather than providing the substantial resources required by disproportionately expensive organization at the European level. Another obstacle is the persistence of national differences. EMOs depend for their legitimacy and resources upon their ability to command public support and, in the absence of a European public sphere, must respond to public opinion at the national level. EMOs in smaller states with less highly developed national environmental movements may look more often to the European level, but there is nothing to suggest that those in other EU states have been more successful than the British in escaping the long shadows of national institutions and patterns of action (Long, 1998:117).

Indeed, particularly in the 1980s, British EMOs appeared more active in European arenas than their German counterparts. It has been suggested that the EU is especially congenial to the British because the structure of power in the EU (weak legislature, strong executive, and preference for informal policy networks) is similar to that in Britain (Hey and Brendle, 1992, cited in Long, 1998:109). However, British EMOs' relatively ready embrace of Europe is better explained by temporary difficulties at home. It was especially under the environmentally unresponsive Thatcher governments (1979–1990) that British EMOs sought to increase their leverage by appeals to European institutions (Dalton, 1994; Ward and Lowe, 1998:156). The greater responsiveness of British governments since the early 1990s has meant that action at the European level has appeared less necessary.

A preference for action within nation-states is not, however, simply a rational response to the pattern of opportunities. Comparison of the orientations of British and German EMOs toward European arenas suggests that habits of action learned at the national level are so deeply ingrained that EMOs are disinclined to acquire the knowledge and skills necessary to operate effectively on the European stage (Roose, 2003a, 2003b). The period of greatest British enthusiasm for action at the European level was an extraordinary conjuncture in which a government peculiarly fixed upon economic development was deaf to the appeals of the environmental movement, at a time when public concern with environmental issues was increasing. The changed structure of opportunities represented by the increasing competence of EU institutions has had only a limited impact upon the behavior of British EMOs.

Collective Action

Although environmentalists have staged transnational demonstrations in Brussels or Strasbourg and at recent EC summits, the great majority of environmental protests in the EU have taken place *within* nation-states. Of all the British environmental protests reported in *The Guardian* during the ten years from 1988 to 1997, only very small numbers were European in their level of mobilization, the scope of the underlying issues, or their targets. Similar patterns emerge from the systematic study of reports of environmental protest in a leading national newspaper in each of France, Germany, Greece, Italy, Spain, and Sweden over the same period (Rootes, 2003b; Rootes, ed., 2003). There was no evidence from any of these countries of a trend toward transnationalization. In the EU, publicly visible environmental movement activity occurs almost exclusively at local, regional, or national levels, and it has mainly been focused upon local or national issues and aimed at local or national targets.

The development of the EU has created new opportunities, but EU institutions do not encourage deployment of all the strategies and tactics customarily adopted by EMOs to influence national governments. The European Parliament has until very recently been a toothless forum largely invisible to the European public, while the European Council consists of delegates of national governments whose positions have been prepared in advance and at home. As a result, where channels of communication to national governments are relatively open, it makes more sense to direct action at targets closer to home.

Moreover, even if environmental policy is now largely made at the EU level, its implementation is still national and local. A great deal of environmental movement action is focused not upon policymaking, but upon the ways in which, and the sites at which, policy is implemented. National EMOs know that their vitality depends upon maintaining involvement with local campaigns (Rootes, 2003c), and so local and national issues and arenas remain crucial to them.

Even if national governments appear increasingly to be mere agents of the EC, environmental activists tend to mobilize against those local tokens of European power rather than against the EC itself (cf. Imig and Tarrow, 2001). By comparison with the institutions of nation-states, EU institutions are remote and inaccessible. But national and local targets may be tactically appropriate as well as accessible. Even mobilizations restricted to the national—or the local—level have the power to disrupt EC-favored projects and thereby to alert the EC to the issues in contention. Moreover, to the extent that such protests put pressure on national governments, they may tip the balance within the European Council and thus determine European policy.

Shared Concerns?

Even if evidence of organization and collective action at the EU level is slight, Europeanization may nevertheless occur in the form of the development of common issues among the various national movements and mass publics. Yet previous research has revealed considerable differences in the conceptions of environmental problems among Europeans and has shown how these are reflected in the policies and actions of national EMOs (Dalton, 1994). Surveys conducted during the 1980s demonstrated that, although large majorities of people professed concern about the environment everywhere in the EU, environmental concern in southern Europe was more often expressed as "personal complaint" than in the North (Hofrichter and Reif, 1990).

The pattern of issues raised in environmental protests from 1988 to 1997 in the seven EU states covered by the TEA project confirms this pattern of variation. Pollution and the effects of environmental degradation upon human health were more frequently raised in Italy, Spain, and Greece than in northern Europe. More surprising, however, was the diversity of issues raised in the four northern European countries. In Britain and Sweden, protests were relatively evenly spread among transport, animal rights, nature conservation, pollution, and urban/industrial issues; but in France, protests concerning nature protection and, especially, animal welfare were relatively rarely reported. Most strikingly, in Germany, where animal rights protests were also rarely reported, over half of all protests involved nuclear energy, an issue rarely raised elsewhere in recent years. Not only was there no common pattern, but there was no

TABLE 2.2
Leading British National Environmental Organizations (c. 2002)

	Year Founded in UK	Members/ Donor Supporters (thousands)	Income/ Budget (million GBPs)	Staff Employed	Local Groups	Manage Property/ Reserves
RSPB	1889	1,020	58	1,300	160[a]	yes
National Trust	1895	3,000	166	4,000+		yes
Wildlife Trusts*	1912	413	*	1,517	47	yes
CPRE	1926	59	2	50	200	no
Civic Trust*	1957	330	*	*	900	
WWF	1961	320	31	260	c. 200	not UK
Friends of the Earth	1971	119	5	110	c. 220	no
Woodland Trust	1972	115	16	216		yes
Greenpeace UK	1977	224	9	100	100[b]	no

Sources: Social Trends 33 (2003); annual reports and websites of EMOs themselves.
*Umbrella groups representing autonomous local/regional groups
[a] Plus 130 youth groups
[b] Estimated in 2000; probably fewer in 2002 as a result of policy of merging existing groups.

general trend toward transnational convergence (Rootes, ed., 2003). The pattern of protest was dominated by the particular concerns of the citizens of particular nation-states.

Viewed in the aggregate, environmentalism in Europe is still more strongly shaped by national circumstances than by European institutions. Nevertheless, change occurs within those national contexts. Thus far, we have examined evidence of publicly visible action that suggests that even within the charmed circle of the EU, the transnationalization of environmentalism has been at best limited. But not all changes are so publicly visible. We might yet find evidence of transnationalization if we consider more closely the recent history of EMOs. We shall therefore focus upon the five EMOs that our surveys (Rootes and Miller, 2000) show to be the core of the network that is the British environmental movement: Friends of the Earth (FoE), Greenpeace, the World Wide Fund for Nature (WWF), the Royal Society for the Protection of Birds (RSPB), and the Council for the Protection of Rural England (CPRE).[3] Table 2.2 presents some basic information about these and other large environmental organizations.

DEVELOPMENT AND CHANGE IN THE BRITISH ENVIRONMENTAL MOVEMENT

In the course of the past three decades, British EMOs have changed considerably. Some of those changes are attributable principally to changes in the contexts within which they operate. But many—including some that have considerable implications for the transnational aspirations, links, and actions of British EMOs—are largely endogenous. We shall consider here the development of their agenda; their institutionalization, both internal and external; and the enduringly problematic relationship between national EMOs and their local members, supporters, and wider public constituencies.

Broadening Agenda

One of the most striking ways in which British EMOs have changed is in the expansion of their agenda, most conspicuously, but not exclusively, to issues of transnational significance. The older conservation organizations have embraced biodiversity and sustainable development, and, in some cases, the resulting transnational linkages, while FoE has extended its agenda to issues of social justice, both transnationally and domestically. Thus, the broadening of EMOs' agenda extends not only to other environmental issues, but also beyond what have conventionally been considered environmental issues.

A major stimulus to new thinking in established conservation organizations was the dramatic rise during the 1980s of the new campaigning EMOs—FoE and Greenpeace—and the emergence of informal networks and ad hoc campaign alliances. This was not entirely new: from the very beginnings of environmentalism in Britain, there has been a large measure of cooperation among EMOs, as well as recognition of a specialized division of labor (Lowe and Goyder, 1983). Nevertheless, interorganizational influences increased in the 1980s and 1990s due to increased networking and the formation of national and international umbrella groups. This appears to have diffused among quite different groups a new shared concern, grounded in a more systemic analysis of the sources of environmental ills. All now speak the language of sustainability and biodiversity. FoE, Greenpeace, the WWF and Earth First! all recognize, albeit in differing ways, the contributions of transnational capital and markets to ecological degradation, and the RSPB is increasingly prepared to examine the social forces that affect wildlife habitats. The emergence of smaller groups concerned with the conservation of single species has encouraged the WWF to see its role as complementary to those of other organizations. Thus the WWF has assisted other, more activist groups, donating money toward the purchase of Greenpeace's first ship, and helping to fund some anti-roads protests in the 1990s (Rawcliffe, 1998:138). Capitalizing upon the agenda-setting actions of more radical groups, the WWF has been able to present itself as the reasonable voice of positive and practical environmentalism, and has enjoyed excellent standing with governments.[4]

The exchanges among British EMOs are not only interorganizational. As the voluntary sector in Britain has developed, campaigning has emerged as a professional career; there are increasingly frequent movements of personnel, even at the most senior levels, among EMOs and between EMOs and other nonprofit organizations in fields such as civil and welfare rights. These developments tend to smooth interaction among EMOs and facilitate an effective division of labor. They also improve the linkages between the environmental movement and other actors in both public and private sectors, maximizing the possibilities for EMOs to efficiently and effectively influence the formation and implementation of public and corporate policy.

However, although conservation organizations have certainly developed in the context of communication within an enlarged and transformed environmental movement, ecology as a discipline has developed in tandem with the environmental movement; it is not simply or mainly a product of that movement. The drift from old-style conservationism reflects the development of scientific understanding of ecology at least as much as contact, collaboration, or competition with newer, more radical EMOs.

The WWF provides a good example of this shift. By the end of the 1970s, the WWF had already evolved from a small organization focused on endangered species and habitat destruction into an international EMO concerned with conservation of biodiversity generally. In 1980, the WWF expanded its agenda to embrace development issues and first introduced the term *sustainable development* (Denton, 1993). In 1986, in order to reflect the wider scope of its activities, it changed its name from World Wildlife Fund to the World Wide Fund for Nature.

As a direct result of the UN Conference on Environment and Development (UNCED) process and the 1992 Rio Earth Summit, the WWF widened its ambit to work with other NGOs to form a common agenda on development and environment. In 1993, with Action Aid, Cafod, Oxfam, Christian Aid, Save the Children and FoE, it produced a report calling for fundamental changes in foreign and domestic aid policy (Rawcliffe, 1998:217).

Always transnational in the scope of its organization and the geographical range of its activities, but nervous about alienating traditional supporters, in 1998 the WWF undertook a "corporate review" that included a survey of public and other audience perceptions. To the WWF's surprise,

> our audiences had a much better understanding that we should be covering a wide range of issues. . . . we felt that our audiences expected us to be much

closer to the conservation end of things, when in fact . . . they could see that sustainable development was a key element of that (Niall Watson, interview, July 2000).

The slogan subsequently adopted for internal purposes—"WWF takes action to protect the environment for people and nature"—"doesn't seem very radical, but the focus on environment and getting people in there as well is quite a significant step for us" (Niall Watson, interview, July 2000).

Although WWF-UK describes the conservation of species as "still the core of our business," in 2000–2001 and 2001–2002 it spent four times as much (about one-third of its total budget) on "levers for change," a portfolio including education and information for schools and businesses, an International Development Policy program in conjunction with the humanitarian NGO CARE International, and preparations for the 2002 World Summit on Sustainable Development (WWF-UK Financial Report, 2001–2002). The WWF sees its move toward increasing concern with sustainable development as a logical development from its initial objectives and its analysis of the promotion of those objectives, but its concern with the environment remains fundamental.

We'll tackle poverty issues and environmental issues at the same time . . . because environment is fundamental to poverty issues and aid issues. . . . unless the environment is at the heart of all those other organizations that are dealing with aid, and dealing with relief, and dealing with development, it's very difficult to make it sustainable (David Cowdry, interview, July 2000).

The RSPB, too, has become more transnational as a consequence of increasing knowledge and more sophisticated understanding of the implications of its relatively narrow issue focus upon birds and their habitat. Recognizing that there was little point in putting great effort into conservation projects in the United Kingdom if key habitats were being destroyed along important migratory routes elsewhere, the RSPB was instrumental in establishing BirdLife International in 1992, and supports BirdLife and its European partners by more than GBP 1 million per year. Not least through its activities in BirdLife, the RSPB has evolved from a strictly national bird protection organization into one increasingly concerned with global environmental change, and was keenly involved with the 2002 World Summit on Sustainable Development. In June 2003, in addition to opposing a mooted airport on the North Kent marshes, an important habitat for migratory wading birds, the RSPB's headline campaigns included reform of the EC's Common Agricultural Policy, the protection of marine life, support for tough new EC proposals to impose upon polluters the costs of cleanup, and the promotion of solar energy.

Since the mid-1980s, FoE has broadened its portfolio to include deforestation and mainstream political issues such as economy and health, and has become increasingly involved in campaigns to promote human rights and economic development in the global South. To some extent, this shift reflected the views of its members and supporters who, FoE's research suggested, were often members or supporters of groups such as Amnesty International or Oxfam, but not necessarily of other environmental groups such as Greenpeace (FoE national spokesman, interview, 2003). In its early days, FoE UK shared a mailing list with Amnesty International. More recently, personal contacts between FoE and aid and development charities have proliferated as the network of NGO employees has expanded and as movement from one to another has become increasingly common.

Greenpeace has, until very recently, been more disciplined in its maintenance of a focus upon a few core environmental issues, but its increasing commitment to "solutions campaigning" has brought it into closer contact with corporations and toward a more comprehensively critical understanding of the structures of power in modern societies.

The use by FoE and the WWF of the concept of sustainable development to promote a comprehensive reformist agenda is clearly a more overtly political project than the simple collection of environmental issues with which they began, and has lured even the CPRE into tentative extensions of its agenda. All these developments suggest that EMOs increasingly recognize that just as the preservation of a particular species requires a more holistic ecological perspective, so the environment as an issue domain cannot be isolated from a wider range of human concerns.

Institutionalization

The increased resources that have accompanied the growth in the numbers of members and supporters during the past three decades have enabled EMOs to professionalize their organizations and their activities. Indeed, they have necessitated it. Substantial organizations with substantial budgets require accountants, office managers, membership secretaries, and lawyers. Increasingly, they have also required professional fund-raisers and public relations and media experts. As these are organizations committed to basing their arguments on sound science, they have also needed scientifically educated experts and often research scientists. Few have gone as far as Greenpeace, which has even secured the services of seconded diplomats to conduct its negotiations, but the salaries indicated in EMOs' annual reports demonstrate that these are no longer organizations of amateurs or mere enthusiasts. Professionalization has enabled EMOs to more effectively conduct their activities; it has made them more reliable interlocutors with their counterparts in other countries as well as with other organizations, governments, and corporations at home; and it has undoubtedly contributed to the disproportionate role British EMOs have played in transnational networks.

But if EMOs' internal institutionalization has enhanced their transnational roles, the implications of their external institutionalization are more ambiguous. In response to their evident ability to command public support—and occasionally to mobilize their supporters—governments, official agencies, and sometimes corporations have sought to engage EMOs and to draw them into *domestic* policy networks.

This "external institutionalization" has clearly brought opportunities for EMOs, but it has also created dilemmas about how best to deploy their energies. Even large EMOs have limited resources, and, if real power now lies in Europe, such an embedding of EMOs in relationships at the national level might be considered a distraction. However, so long as national governments are receptive to the appeals and advice of EMOs, the character of the EU means that this is not a disadvantage. Insofar as it is the European Council rather than the Parliament or the Commission that makes the critical policy decisions, applying pressure to national governments is an appropriate and efficacious strategy and may be the best route, albeit an indirect one, to Europe.

In any case, the official networks into which EMOs have been drawn are often precisely those created to promote transnational environmental agenda, or to facilitate British participation in the formation of those agenda. To this end, successive British governments have recognized and sought to draw upon the expertise of EMOs. Thus, as early as 1990, a WWF representative was invited to join the official British delegation to UNCED. The WWF-UK integrated its activities as part of a broad-based international campaign in the two years leading up to the Earth Summit in 1992, sought to coordinate the inputs of various British NGO sectors, and was involved in the IIED/UNEP coordination process. RSPB is (along with FoE, the CPRE, and the WWF) actively involved in the UK government's roundtable on sustainable development, was the lead organization in the establishment of the government's Biodiversity Challenge Group, and has played an important role alongside government in key international environmental fora.

Nor is it only the conservation EMOs that have changed. Since the mid-1990s, FoE has broadened its contacts with government departments from Environment to Trade and Industry, Agriculture, Health, Treasury, and the Prime Minister's Office. According to FoE's director, "this reflects this broadening of the agenda away from being about dicky birds and hedgerows towards about being about jobs, health and economy." This shift is partly a response to past success on classic environmental issues within

Britain: "it's quite important to recognize when you've won. . . . on a lot of issues we are in a different mode now and . . . talking to people in different ways" (Tony Juniper, interview, March 2000).

FoE's considerable interaction with other groups, mostly informal and between specialist campaigners in particular fields, increasingly extends beyond the environmental movement to include, among others, aid and development charities, organized labor, and "the socially progressive sector." If its linkages help to set FoE's international agenda, they have also encouraged its embrace of domestic social justice issues. Following the example of FoE Scotland, FoE has recently embarked upon a community development initiative in an economically deprived and heavily polluted area of Teesside, in northeast England. Here, FoE was not mobilizing its own members; it was mobilizing people in a community where there were *no* FoE members. After conducting a factory watch and mapping pollution against poverty, FoE went in and stated, "We think that this is the problem":

> We wanted to make particular arguments to the governments about social exclusion and the environment and poverty and those links and joining them up. So we wanted a project that could start to make the political arguments about the links between pollution and poverty (FoE Senior Local Campaigns Officer, interview, 2003).

In the summer of 2003, FoE adopted a five-year action plan whose strategic aims are to integrate well-established work on sustainability and biodiversity with a concern for environmental justice at home and abroad.

Partnership?

It is not only policy*making* into which EMOs are drawn by increasing institutionalization. They are also increasingly involved in policy *implementation*. Most EMOs are now focused upon "solutions campaigning," and some have readily embraced opportunities to enter partnerships with government agencies and sometimes corporations. The RSPB is notable in this respect. It derives an increasing proportion of its income from grants, is increasingly engaged in the management of its growing number of nature reserves, and aspires to act in partnership with government agencies in the protection of the habitats that are central to its concerns. As a result, the RSPB, which had so recently appeared more willing to join with others as a campaigning EMO, now denies even that it is a lobbying organization (RSPB spokesman, interview 2003).[5]

Other EMOs, however, are more resistant to such external institutionalization. FoE is very clear about its role. Although it has sought to engage government agencies, FoE does not seek an ongoing partnership with them in implementing environmental policy. FoE "is a campaigning organization" whose job "is to raise the standards" that others are charged to implement (FoE Senior Local Campaigns Officer, 2003).

Greenpeace has been even more resistant to becoming locked into time-consuming and resource-sapping consultative relationships with government. If FoE has attempted to manage its relations with government by being selective in accepting invitations to consultation, Greenpeace has been so little inclined to accept that it is not routinely invited. In part, this reflects Greenpeace's analysis that power has shifted decisively from governments to corporations, and so it has focused its energies upon the latter. Because its agenda envisages the fundamental reinvention of business to ensure sustainability, Greenpeace has increasingly been drawn beyond simple critique to the proposal of alternatives and the demonstration of their practicability. However, despite the notable exception of its partnership with an electricity utility to establish the United Kingdom's first major offshore wind farm, Greenpeace's "constructive engagement" with industry has rarely gone so far that it could be considered a "partnership." Greenpeace, like FoE, remains primarily a campaigning organization and, even more than FoE, has aimed to deploy its limited resources where its leaders consider they might have greatest effect. Its campaigns against genetically modified organisms (GMOs) and the nuclear industry continue, and recently Greenpeace has returned to high-profile campaigning against waste incineration and against the oil company Esso. Its new director, appointed in 2001, emphasizes Greenpeace's commitment to nonviolent direct action (NVDA) and to "bearing witness." Far from becoming a "domesticated" environmental lobby group, Greenpeace has preserved its autonomy and has become a mature and impressively flexible and resourceful campaigning organization.

Larger, better-resourced organizations appear able to sustain a wider range of activities. The RSPB's devotion of its energies to partnerships at home has not been wholly at the expense of the transnational. The RSPB was one of the first British EMOs to pursue its campaigns through the EC, it played an influential role in the formulation of the European Birds Directive (1988), and most of its campaigns make explicit reference to the EC, sometimes against positions adopted by the UK government. The RSPB continues to campaign for and against EU policies, and highlights its transnational efforts through BirdLife International and with its European partners and its role in the World Summit on Sustainable Development (Annual Report, 2002).

Institutionalization does not necessarily imply de-radicalization. The RSPB widened its political (rather than simply conservationist) scope, even as it became more institutionalized and professionalized; the WWF, even more so. The CPRE has become an active, professionalized campaigning organization without losing its ready access to political elites. FoE and Greenpeace have become more professionalized and enjoy more influence upon governments and corporations than they did in the 1970s. As they have acquired assets and obligations to their employees, so their increased vulnerability to litigation has compelled caution; but it is not so much that they have abandoned protest as that the range of their other activities and their opportunities for advancing their causes by other means have grown.

The novelty of the new EMOs of the 1970s was less their ecologism or their internationalism than the style of their campaigning—their populism and, especially, their exploitation of the opportunities provided by modern mass media. They—and especially Greenpeace—blazed a trail that others have increasingly followed. As FoE and Greenpeace have become less distinctively protest organizations, the distance between them and older environmental groups such as the WWF, RSPB, and CPRE has diminished. The latter groups may generally confine their campaigning to conventional lobbying, but they have become increasingly adept in their use of mass media and more prepared to take public stands critical of governments and corporations. Ironically, Greenpeace has become more sanguine about mass media, but it has nevertheless reasserted its core identity as a campaigning organization committed to "bearing witness."

We have focused here upon the EMOs that constitute the core of the British environmental movement, but any account of recent developments in British environmentalism would be incomplete without mentioning the 1990s rise of radical "disorganizations" such as Earth First! and Reclaim the Streets. Their experience demonstrates the dilemmas of radical activists who wish to address the big issues, including global issues, but to do so without formal organization and while prioritizing direct action that is necessarily local rather than global in its bases of mobilization. Such groupings made common cause with anticapitalist and antiglobalization protesters in various protests in Britain in the late 1990s and early 2000s, but were on occasion severely discomforted by the repercussions of those protests. Not all the radical disorganizations have vanished, but, although those attracted to and active in them share commitment to the cause of global anticapitalism, they have yet to fashion forms of organization that give their campaigns any very visible continuity between intermittent protest events.

THE LOCAL, THE NATIONAL,
AND THE TRANSNATIONAL

The involvement of EMOs in national policy networks has implications for the relationships between EMOs and their local constituencies. If even their paths to the European centers of power pass through national governments, national EMOs must be certain to maintain their legitimacy in the eyes of those national governments, and the ability to demonstrate wide public support is at least an important contributor to that legitimacy. But just as their embeddedness in national policy networks makes it more important for EMOs to maintain healthy relationships with their local supporters, it also makes it more difficult to do so.

As the CPRE has found, it is one thing to engage with policy elites on the basis of mutual respect grounded in shared knowledge and expertise, but quite another to satisfy local supporters focused upon the particulars of policy implementation rather than the broad outlines of policy. This dilemma is a general one for EMOs that at national level ground their claims on the attention of policymakers in their expertise and mastery of the relevant science. These are resources only serendipitously present at local level. More usually, local members' understanding of the issues is rooted in the particulars of their local circumstances and an absolutist conception of risk that is quite different from the probabilistic calculations of science.

The need to maintain the loyalty and commitment of their members and supporters is a universal constraint upon EMOs. FoE was sharply alerted to this early in its history, when an alliance between national office staff and local groups challenged the strategy of the leadership and dominance of the board of directors. The resolution of this dispute had an enduring impact upon FoE's constitutional structure and identity. Although FoE national officers attempt to set campaign priorities based upon expert, science-based advice, they are acutely aware of the need to be responsive to members' local and often scientifically questionable concerns. FoE's campaign agenda are, consequently, products of compromise (FoE national spokesman, 2003). Both the RSPB and the WWF are formally membership organizations, and although in practice their national leaderships are able to set campaign priorities according to their own assessment of scientific advice, they too have been cautious not to lose touch with members.

Even Greenpeace, structured to ensure the autonomy of its governing elite, is not immune from the constraints of the local. Greenpeace is not a mass-membership organization, but if this gave Greenpeace an unusual degree of flexibility and autonomy, it was limited by the need to maintain income and supporters' commitment. During the 1990s, the numbers of supporting donors fluctuated according to the proportion of resources devoted to donor recruitment, and its local support groups, limited to fund-raising, suffered high rates of attrition. In 1995, in response to criticism from without and growing feeling within, Greenpeace permitted its local groups to participate in centrally directed campaigns, and in 1999 established an "active supporters" network in order to harness the energies of the many supporters who its own research showed wanted to be more involved in campaigns, but who had no wish to attend monthly meetings. "Active supporters" receive news by e-mail or newsletter, as well as suggestions about how they might assist in Greenpeace campaigns; they are offered training in NVDA, political and corporate lobbying, and communication, legal, and media skills. Seen as a locally based campaigning arm of Greenpeace UK rather than as fund-raisers or distributors of information, "active supporters" were, for example, encouraged to participate in the 1999 "True Food" campaign. Although still concerned to retain control, Greenpeace has become more open to the views of its local supporters and more adept at employing their energies.

Yet, Greenpeace has not lost its commitment to transnational concerns. Among the ten campaign issues listed on its website in June 2003 were the Iraq war, global warming, renewable energy, GMOs, toxic chemicals, oceans and whaling, nuclear issues, star wars, and the protection of ancient forests. Nor has Greenpeace abandoned multinational protests. On December 4, 2003, twenty-two British Greenpeace activists were among the forty volunteers from across Europe who invaded the site of a nuclear station in Normandy to protest the French government's decision to build another nuclear reactor rather than exploit wind power.[6]

Of the British EMOs we have considered, three have in various ways responded to the desires of their supporters to "be more involved." Greenpeace and, more tentatively, the WWF, have followed FoE down the path of engaging active supporters. Their experiences reveal some of the tensions and strategic dilemmas involved in seeking to be effective players on the national and international stages, while harnessing the commitment of their most energetic supporters. To put this in perspective, however, it should be remembered that would-be activists and participants in campaigns are, for each of these EMOs, a small minority among their supporters and potential constituencies. EMOs' commitment to respond to them is, therefore, more a matter of conscience (or anxiety), born out of a desire to use the resource their would-be activist supporters represent, than a necessity to maintain allegiances. Attending to the interests of local supporters does not, however, necessarily mean that EMOs are thereby drawn away from the transnational. As both the WWF and FoE found from their membership surveys, transnational issues were more important to their supporters than EMOs' national officers had supposed.

The difficulties the CPRE has experienced in reconciling the demands of influencing policy at national level with nurturing its local base are indicative of the dilemma a truly transnational but centrally directed EMO might face, but it is the CPRE that is least constrained by any ideological commitment to the transnational. Whatever opportunities external circumstances present, an EMO's identity is a factor in the strategic choices that must be made. The WWF escapes the dilemma to the extent that it has an unambiguously transnational identity and remit. For broad spectrum EMOs such as FoE and Greenpeace, the dilemmas are more complex. On the one hand, they need to pay sufficient attention to domestic issues to persuade local supporters of their practical relevance; on the other hand, they must satisfy other supporters' concerns with the transnational. FoE's decentralized organizational structure has enabled it to satisfy both constituencies more easily than has Greenpeace's centralized structure, albeit at the price of continuing compromises over campaign priorities.

The fact that the numbers of members and supporters of FoE and Greenpeace have leveled off since the early 1990s while older, less activist and less transnationalist EMOs (such as the National Trust, the Wildlife Trusts, the RSPB and the CPRE) and some newer, uncomplicatedly national organizations (such as the Woodland Trust) have continued to grow, is a sharp reminder that not all public concern with the environment is readily assimilated to the transnational.[7]

CONCLUSION: TRANSNATIONALIZATION AND ITS LIMITS

It was always a parody of older environmental organizations to suggest that their conservationism was some kind of blinkered failure to recognize the superior claims of political ecologism. Nevertheless, it is clear that some things have changed. When the International Union for the Conservation of Nature (IUCN) was the standard-bearer for international environmental concerns, it would have been a prodigious feat of imagination even to envisage the mobilization of a transnational environmental movement.

Of the five EMOs on which we have focused, three (FoE, Greenpeace, and the WWF) were always transnational in inspiration and aspiration. All three have in recent years become more effectively transnational, both in the conception of their agenda and their alliances. The main stimulus to this has not, however, been the changed pattern of opportunities represented by the development of the EU, but the Rio Earth Summit of 1992 and the processes initiated or consolidated there. At Rio, the vociferous protests of activists from the global South obliged Northern EMOs and NGOs to take stock, and to take more seriously the perspectives and sensitivities of the peoples of the less industrialized world.

FoE considers its international network to be a key strength that distinguishes it from other EMOs:

> when we are . . . talking about global issues . . . we can fairly say that we know what people in the South think about this, because they are part of our network and they are working on it as well. . . . I think [that] is a clear difference between us and say Greenpeace or . . . WWF. Both do the work, but to be a member of the FoE International, groups apply to join . . . we don't go into countries and set up an office and start up a group. It is still very much grassroots power (FoE national spokesman, interview, 2003).

FoE UK also plays a prominent role in FoE Europe, where the focus is more upon building up the European FoE network than lobbying European policymakers. Lately, it has been particularly active in supporting local EMOs in the countries of the former Soviet bloc (see, e.g., Fagan and Jehlicka, 2003; Fagan, 2004 on the Czech Republic).

By contrast, the CPRE has not undergone significant or sustained transnationalization of its agenda or, indeed, of its alliances and networks. The CPRE is disproportionately influential and central in domestic movement and policy networks, but has appeared to retreat from formal transnational networks. Tightly focused upon its national and local concerns, the CPRE's agenda is narrower and more geographically restricted than those of the other EMOs we have considered. Even its concern with sustainable development is articulated in local and national rather than global terms, and its organizational structure, to which the local branches are so important, makes even national coordination difficult (Lowe, Murdoch, and Norton, 2001).

Nevertheless, while director of the CPRE, Fiona Reynolds was also vice president of the EEB and a member of the EC's Consultative Forum on Sustainable Development. Although it remains a member of the EEB, the CPRE has largely forsaken regular links with other European organizations in favor of ad hoc campaign alliances with a smaller number of thematically similar national EMOs in Western Europe. Even those links appear to be pursued only because the CPRE needs allies in increasingly important EU arenas. Its recent work at the European level focused mainly on agricultural policy, but the CPRE foresaw the need for European liaison among groups concerned with "cultural landscapes" and enjoyed good relations with its counterparts in Italy, Ireland, Denmark, and Germany (Interview Conder, June 2000). The CPRE's recent history thus appears less a retreat from Europe than the clear-eyed strategy of an EMO thematically specialized upon landscape and countryside protection, which sees its potential international partners as similar bodies in other European countries, and is alert to the constraints of its limited resources.

The British environmental movement today is a more convincingly transnational *movement* than it was thirty years ago. There is an increasing sense of EMOs as part of a global movement dealing with global issues. But this is not, for EMO elites themselves, a radical departure so much as an incremental development of already existing perspectives and aspirations. The more dramatic change is the development of a substantial *non-elite* audience/constituency for such views. Of this, mass media has been both progenitor and reflector, but it is perhaps especially the expansion of higher education that has created a more confident, more knowledgeable, and more critical audience and constituency for EMOs.

Nevertheless, it is striking that so many of the efforts and resources of even the most internationalist of British EMOs are devoted to particular campaigns within Britain, targeted at British governments and corporations about essentially domestic issues. Even the WWF, among many campaigns that are clearly international, included in June 2003 a campaign to encourage the UK government to focus on the future of sustainable energy resources and adopt a Sustainable Energy Bill, setting binding targets for renewable energy and energy efficiency; it is also campaigning for higher design standards for new housing developments on the Thames Gateway. Although FoE, Greenpeace, and the WWF are all members of the OneWorld partnership—formed in 1996 to bring together more than fifteen hundred organizations from across the globe to promote sustainable development, social justice and human rights—only FoE advertises the fact on its website.[8]

There are several reasons for this effort to highlight the national even to the extent of occluding the transnational. Even internationalist EMOs need to make connections between their global programmatic concerns and practical actions potentially affecting their domestic constituencies. In part, this is simply good environmental education. But there are more pragmatic reasons as well. The resources of EMOs are limited, and limited resources dictate selectivity in campaigning. Inevitably, there will be a tendency to select those campaign issues that have greatest visibility among those who might be expected to join or support the EMO in question, and so a bias toward responsiveness to domestic concerns is built in.

However, it is not only the resources of EMOs that are disproportionately distributed domestically. So, too, are their opportunities for effective action. It is national and local arenas that are most easily understood, where action is most likely to be effective, and where the dividends on investment are most likely to be apparent to the constituencies upon which EMOs depend. Greenpeace has since the early 1990s declined, even disappeared, in a number of countries. The reasons vary, but the common thread is the perception that, in its insistence on being a transnational elite-dominated EMO, it was insensitive to the local and domestic concerns and perspectives of many who had previously supported it.

The main driver toward the transnationalization of the British environmental movement has been EMOs' broader and more sophisticated understanding of the complex and interrelated issues entailed by effective action on issues of central concern. Another is the changing pattern of opportunities as national governments have yielded sovereignty on environmental issues to transnational organizations, most notably the EU. But such changed circumstances represent a new pattern of constraints rather than simply the lure of opportunity; British EMOs *have* to address European institutions because that, on many issues, is where critical decisions are now made. But action at the transnational level generally remains secondary to their national activities because the arenas and the actors in them are less familiar and less accessible, because the costs of sustained action at the European level are daunting even for relatively well-resourced EMOs, and because the most efficacious route to Europe is still often via national governments.

There is, nevertheless, evidence of increased transnationalization in the coordination of EMOs in transnational networks of various kinds. Ad hoc campaigns are made easier and more effective by more or less regular, if not necessarily frequent, contact through rather skeletal networks.[9] Sklair (1995) may well be right: more formal transnational organization may simply be too burdensome for EMOs that are still, by comparison with governments and transnational corporations, relatively ill-resourced. Loose networks that enable coordination of campaigns without heavy investment in permanent transnational organizations may be optimal for EMOs. Nevertheless, while networks may be more or less loose, they are generally effective in proportion to their density and activity, and the evidence is that, even in the relatively favorable circumstances of British EMOs in Europe, existing transnational networks are neither very dense nor very active.

It is sobering to consider that in Britain as elsewhere, the transnational EMOs that grew so dramatically in the 1970s and 1980s remain small by comparison with established nature and wildlife protection organizations. Although the latter may be linked by international umbrella organizations to other, similar organizations in other countries, the largest remain primarily national as well as specialized in their scope and orientation. The broadening of their agenda to embrace biodiversity and sustainable development may be small compensation for the relative stagnation in the numbers of supporters of more committedly transnational EMOs.

NOTES

I am indebted to Debbie Adams, Sandy Miller, Clare Saunders, and Ben Seel for their assistance with the collection and/or analysis of much of the data discussed here. The research upon which this chapter is based was mostly funded by the EC Directorate General for Research and undertaken as part of the TEA project (contract no.: ENV4-CT97-0514), a description of which may be found at: www. kent.ac.uk/sspssr/TEA.html. I am indebted to those of my collaborators in the TEA project—Olivier Fillieule and Fabrice Ferrier, Dieter Rucht and Jochen Roose, Maria Kousis and Katerina Lenaki, Mario Diani and Francesca Forno, Donatella della Porta and Massimo Andretta, Manuel Jiménez, Andrew Jamison, and Magnus Ring—who were responsible for collecting the data for France, Germany, Greece, Italy, Spain, and Sweden. I am also grateful to Julie Barnett for permission to use material from interviews she conducted in 2003 as part of the project "Working with Special Interest Groups" contracted by the Environment Agency.

1. In 2003, the EEB described itself as "a federation of 141 environmental citizens organisations" ranging "from local and national to European and international," and listed 134 members in 26 countries, including all the EU member states, Turkey, Algeria, and most of the "accession" states accepted for early entry to the EU (www.eeb.org).

2. As the United Kingdom is a multinational state, but one in which a single nation—England—is overwhelmingly dominant, it is often difficult to distinguish the strictly English from the British/UK; I have therefore adopted an inclusive definition, treating as "national" all organizations that operate in one or more of the nations that comprise the United Kingdom. Of the 117 EMOs surveyed, 97 were British/English, and 20 operated only in Scotland, Wales, or Northern Ireland.

3. The discussion that follows draws in part upon research and interviews undertaken by Ben Seel (on FoE and Greenpeace) and by Debbie Adams (on the WWF, RSPB, and CPRE) in 2000, as well as on interviews conducted in 2003 by Julie Barnett. The most accessible history of FoE is Lamb (1996). On CPRE, see Lowe, Murdoch, and Norton (2001).

4. It is claimed that the WWF was described by Michael Meacher, UK environment minister from 1997 to 2003, as "his alternative civil service" (Stuart White, interview, July 2000).

5. Fillieule (2003) attributes the demobilization of the French environmental movement in large part to EMOs' increasing involvement as agents of the local implementation of environmental policy.

6. www.Greenpeace.org.uk (December 5, 2003).

7. van der Heijden (2002) observes a similar phenomenon in the Netherlands.

8. Third-level links for "world development" on the Greenpeace UK website do not mention OneWorld, but do include a range of aid and development NGOs (ActionAid, Amnesty International, Intermediate Technology [ITDG], Oxfam, Survival International, and the World Development Movement).

9. FoE may be part of the most convincingly global transnational network, but FoE International has a secretariat of just nine professionals and four volunteers that is little more than a node for the network of its sixty-six autonomous national member organizations (Stokke and Thommessen, 2002:296–98).

3

Cities in the World: Local Civil Society and Global Issues in Britain

MARIO DIANI

In the North as well as in the South, collective actions against neoliberal approaches, promoting a different model of globalization, have grown substantially over the last few years, suggesting a reemergence of social movements on a scale surely unparalleled since the 1960s. Available evidence illustrates the rise of globalization as a major contentious issue in public discourse (Andretta et al., 2002:10); the growth of voluntary and/ or political organizations mobilizing on transnational issues (Smith, 1997) as well as of the density of interorganizational collaborations between them (Smith, 1997; Rohrschneider and Dalton, 2002; Caniglia, 2001); the embeddedness of participants in major "no global" gatherings such as Genoa 2001 or Florence 2002 in other social movements (Andretta et al., 2002:ch. 3; della Porta and Diani, 2004b; Walgrave and Verhulst, 2003); and the consolidation of a transnational community of professional activists and campaigners (Keck and Sikkink, 1998).

While the most conspicuous displays of "no global" (or new global) activism taking place in the various counter-summits across the globe have attracted considerable attention (e.g., Smith, 2001; Andretta et al., 2002), less attention has been paid to how global issues and concerns affect the structure of civic and political life at the local level. Are the most visible transnational demonstrations/gatherings the products of largely occasional coalitions of actors that are mostly integrated in domestic networks, focusing on other types of issues and identities? Or can we instead identify some continuity between the two levels? In other words, can we find at the local level any evidence of global issues shaping grassroots political organizations' strategies and orientations? In this chapter, I address these questions by looking at citizens' organizations in two Brit-

45

ish cities, Glasgow and Bristol. In particular, I assess the extent to which globalization issues

- represent a distinctive set of policy interests for these organizations, rather than the articulation of already established interests such as those related to the environment, ethnic and minority rights, or class inequality;
- translate into a distinctive set of collective actions;
- attract organizations with a distinctive profile;
- may be associated with specific social movement dynamics, rather than being the focus of ad hoc coalitions or of organizations with little or no interest in promoting joint collective action across organizational boundaries.

Glasgow and Bristol are remarkably different in their social and political histories. In Glasgow, one must take into account the strength of the "Red Clyde" tradition of left-wing labor politics and the strong working-class presence; the role of ethnic minorities—especially Pakistanis—in the Labour political machine; and, more recently, the impact of devolution and the reshaping of center–periphery relations this has prompted. Coupled with a struggling industrial economy, and despite a fairly successful conversion of the city toward a more diversified and more service-driven economy, these traits have created a context that by theoretical standards appears particularly conducive to the persistence of collective action addressing social inequality, including action from a specific class perspective. One should also take into account the persisting impact of religious sectarianism, in particular its contribution to an explicitly confrontational political style.

Despite its city politics having also been dominated by Labour in the last decades (at least until the May 2003 local elections), the overall profile of Bristol is very different. Historically, the city has switched between Labour and Tory control, yet in a context of political moderation. Since the closure of the docks in the 1960s–1970s, working-class presence in the city has been increasingly modest. While areas of deprivation undoubtedly exist—and some are included in this study—Bristol is a very affluent city with a strong presence of professional bourgeoisie and highly qualified white-collar workers. Its main employers are high-tech firms like those in the aeronautic industry; firms in the service sector, especially the financial sector; and big public employers such as the Ministry of Defense. Unemployment rates are extremely low (around 2.5–3 percent), in stark contrast to Glasgow where social deprivation still represents a major issue. The ethnic scene is larger—with some neighborhoods approaching 20 percent minority residents—and more diversified than in

Glasgow, with a substantial presence of Indian, Pakistani, Asian, and Afro-Caribbean communities and a legacy of minority activism, which at times even took radical forms, most notably in the St. Paul's riots of 1981. Bristol has also been one of the main centers for cultural innovation, with a flourishing milieu of youth subcultures and alternative lifestyles addressing issues of health, alternative food, and body care. This has corresponded—if not necessarily overlapped—with a lively presence of environmental organizations and activism, including environmental direct action in the 1990s (Rootes, 2000).

This study focuses on organizations mobilizing on environmental, ethnic and minority, community, and social exclusion issues. These organizations provide a particularly interesting unit for the analysis of coalition building and interorganizational networking: they are distinct enough to work independently, yet have enough potential areas of convergence to render cross-sector alliances a feasible option (e.g., on issues such as North–South relations, peace, refugees, urban decay, and racism). Moreover, they can easily be articulated in terms consistent with a no/new global perspective, and linked into global agendas. Between 2001 and 2002, face-to-face interviews took place with 124 representatives of organizations in Glasgow and 134 in Bristol. These included both local branches of UK-wide organizations (in Glasgow, also Scotland-wide), and independent local groups with varying degrees of formalization and bureaucratization. All the organizations that played a citywide role were contacted;[1] as for community organizations, rather than taking a small sample from across the city, efforts were concentrated on two areas, both relatively deprived economically.[2]

ISSUES, EVENTS, AND ORGANIZATIONS

The nature of "global issues" can hardly be deduced by the contents of the specific problems on which organizations mobilize. In principle, environmental degradation, the protection of labor conditions, and the protection or expansion of migrants' rights can all be conceived of as global issues; yet they were public issues long before the term *globalization* even appeared on the scene. They may or may not represent "global issues," depending on the meaning attributed to them—that is, depending on their interpretation by social actors. Likewise, even topics most easily associated with globalization, such as sweatshop child labor or developing countries' debt, may or may not be perceived as a specific set of issues. They may as well be treated as a further specification of already existing agendas, such as traditional Left internationalism, or solidarity humanitarian campaigns by well-meaning Western charities. Before exploring the nature of the "new global movement," it is therefore appropriate to look at the structure of issues regarded as crucial by citizens' organizations (as Laumann and Knoke [1987] did in reference to policy networks), to see whether a distinctive space for "global" issues may actually be identified.

Moreover, even the presence of a distinctive set of issues need not imply that protest activities and other forms of collective action on such issues will be promoted, even less so that they will be linked into sets of activities that stand out from other episodes of collective action on cognate topics. From the point of view of protest events, social movements are best conceived of as sustained series of campaigns, where single incidents are linked into broader chains of protest activities through framing and discursive practices, but also through actors' multiple involvements in a variety of events. Analogously to what happens for issue interests, it is how such events combine that qualifies collective action. For instance, although interest in globalization issues may encourage organizations to promote actions on environmental and peace issues alike, the two may just as well be conducted independently from each other and linked to independent sets of events. Their combination into a broader, "globalization-related" protest agenda is far from granted. It is an empirical question to be explored, not a datum for the analysis.

Finally, even if distinctive, both the interest in global issues and the promotion of specific episodes of collective action are not necessarily the preserve of actors with specific profiles. They may be found among organizations and activists with very diverse orientations, resources, or political backgrounds. Although one need not expect actors associated with a specific social movement to display a very specific set of traits, analysts have often attempted to identify the defining properties of the actors engaged, if not in specific movements, at least in "movement families" (della Porta and Rucht, 1995), the most obvious example being the association between left libertarian "new social movements," high levels of formal education, and new middle-class social location (Dalton, 1996:chap.4). All else being equal, the more global issues are linked with specific actors' profiles, the more one can expect to witness a distinctive social process rather than the simple diffusion of new issues across the different sectors of a given civil society.

In this chapter, I would like to assess the impact of four different sets of organizational properties that may be correlated with interest in, and action on, mobilization issues. The first refers to *organizational traits*. Two competing hypotheses may be put forward. One posits that organizations less endowed with resources and less institutionalized will be more likely to develop an interest in less established issues like global issues. If organizations, as they develop, tend to secure control of specific issue domains and to acquire "issue ownership" (Hilgartner and Bosk, 1988; Petrocik,

1996), then the emergence of new issues such as those linked with global concerns might offer new and/or less established organizations an opportunity to secure new niches for themselves. Conversely, more established ones might be slower to adapt their agendas to accommodate new themes. An alternative hypothesis suggests that interest in global issues is most intense among organizations operating on a larger—possibly global—scale and relying on massive organizational resources. The complexity of the issues linked with globalization places greater demands on organizations: they need substantial professional expertise among their activists; the costs attached to conducting collective action on themes that well exceed the boundaries of any specific locality are substantial; and the coordination with actors interested in similar issues may be difficult. All these requirements may result in organizations with larger resources developing a distinctive interest in global issues (see e.g., Rohrschneider and Dalton, 2002). Formalization and professionalization are obviously most present among organizations promoting transnational actions on a global scene, and are often directly involved in dealings with transnational or national institutions (Keck and Sikkink, 1998). However, one could expect them to be present also at the local level, for instance through the local branches of major organizations such as the World Wide Fund for Nature (WWF), Amnesty International, or Oxfam.

Involvement in global issues may also depend on the strength of an organization's *political identity*. Organizations regarding themselves as critical political actors, or at least as actors willing to play an explicit political role, might be more likely to develop an interest in global issues than would those who think of themselves mainly as voluntary organizations, concerned with service delivery rather than political campaigning. The rationale behind this hypothesis has once again to do with the low degree of institutionalization of global issues in comparison with other issues analyzed here. As issues become institutionalized, they also tend to be broken down into sub-issues. Their controversial element is taken out, and they become "technical" problems for specialists. This is both a reflection of, and an incentive to, growing divisions of labor among organizations, leading in turn to the specialization and issue-ownership tendencies mentioned above. In contrast, newly emerged issues tend to be more multifaceted and encompassing, and boundaries between sub-issues are not well defined—there is not even a clear, shared understanding of what belongs in a certain issue domain and what does not. Their largely undefined nature leaves more room for attempts to turn them into genuine political issues, that is, issues that can be framed within a broader political project. Accordingly, such issues may be more interesting to organizations that explicitly regard themselves as political.

Specific *action repertoires* might also characterize action on global issues.

Consistent with what has been argued with reference to the organizational model, two possible relationships with global issues could be hypothesized. On the one hand, the complexity of issues at stake, and the level of involvement of domestic and transnational agencies and institutions in globalization-related problems, might suggest that organizations inclined to adopt established techniques of pressure should be particularly involved in those issues. On the other hand, one could argue that groups prepared to engage with a more varied range of repertoires of action should feel more confident regarding their chances of attracting attention to issues that are relatively less institutionalized. In particular, action on global issues might be facilitated by a group's propensity to engage in protest activity, as well as in repertoires specifically challenging corporations and other major economic actors—such as boycotts—or actively promoting alternative economic relations—such as fair-trade practices.

Finally, the stronger their interest in *related issues*, the more one could expect organizations to be more attracted to global issues, that is, issues that may be logically associated with global ones. Taking into account the characteristics of the organizations involved in this study, we should look at three different types of issues. First, global issues might be most strongly related with themes of the new social movements tradition, such as environmental or gender issues. They might also attract greater attention from organizations interested in social inequality issues such as poverty, housing, and basic education, consistent with the renewed emphasis on both inter- and intranational deprivation processes. Finally, they might be closely associated with multiculturalism and identity issues, such as those addressed by most ethnic minority and migrants' organizations.

PARTICIPATION ON GLOBAL ISSUES OR (NO/NEW) GLOBAL MOVEMENTS?

Social movements cannot be reduced to sectors of public opinion interested in certain issues, public events, or organizations sharing distinctive traits, although they are hard to conceive of in their absence. Their specificity lies at the intersection of three elements: dense networks of informal exchanges between individuals and/or organizations, shared collective identities, and conflictual interactions with opponents (Diani, 1992, 2003; Diani and Bison, 2004). Different combinations of these elements define different collective action dynamics.[3]

When collective action on global issues is mainly conducted within the boundaries of specific organizations, it is difficult to speak of no/new global movements. If organizations broadly interested in the same themes are not involved in dense collaborations, and do not share any specific identity, some of the most visible and distinctive traits of the social movement experience are missing. In such cases, *organizational processes* will prevail, as organizations focus on the strengthening of both their structures and their identities and securing control of specific issues or subsets of issues. Collaborations with other groups will be relatively rare and, most importantly, scattered across a broad range of different organizations. There will be no densely connected networks of organizations sharing similar interests, nor will strong feelings of collective identity develop between different organizations.

Other organizations will be involved in dense collaborative exchanges with groups with similar concerns, addressing specific issues. However, these linkages will not correspond to identity bonds between the organizations involved. Groups will join forces to push forward a certain agenda but will not feel linked to each other by a shared identity once the specific actions and campaigns are over. In other words, alliances and collaborations will be mostly driven by an instrumental logic. Specific events will not be linked by actors into more encompassing narratives that might assign them a broader meaning and make them part of a sustained series of collective actions. Under those circumstances, collective action will be most effectively conceptualized as a *coalitional process*.

Finally, although coalitions are clearly an important component of social movement activity, the two cannot be reduced to each other. In a *social movement process* there will be more than networks of alliances and collaborations. Of course, organizations involved in a movement dynamic will share both material and symbolic resources in order to promote more effective campaigns, and will be fairly closely linked to each other. But, most important, they will also identify each other as part of a broader collective actor, whose goals and existence cannot be constrained within the boundaries of any specific protest event or campaign. The existence of collective identity linking organizations to each other will enable them to feel part of the same collective effort even when specific actions may be over, and to develop more joint actions on that basis.

From the perspective of mobilizations on global issues, the more they were conducted by organizations with a clear division of labor between them and very little in terms of joint initiatives, the more the so-called "no/new global movement" would actually come close to a set of independent organizations, and consist mostly of organizational processes. Likewise, if alliances on global issues limited themselves to fight specific battles, with little identity and solidarity between the organizations involved, and no attempts to connect to broader frameworks, there would be little analytical gain from labeling as a "social movement" what would ultimately be little more than sets of organizations, instrumentally pooling resources in temporary, single-issue coalitions.[4] We can only talk of no/new global movements if dense interorganizational networks and shared collective identity may actually be found among organizations mobilizing on no/new global issues.

GLOBAL ISSUES IN GLASGOW AND BRISTOL

This being first and foremost a study of organizations focusing either on social exclusion and inequality, environmental problems, or ethnic and minority rights, identifying the space for global issues means looking at their space within issue agendas largely driven by other priorities. In order to explore the structure of issues in the two cities, respondents were asked whether they would "likely" or "possibly" promote initiatives on any of forty-nine issues. The list of those issues does not cover all the most important problems in contemporary British society. Rather, it identifies a set of themes, which could be central to at least some of the organizations we surveyed. However, some issues, with which none of the respondents could be automatically linked, such as "military installations," "third world debt," or "third world poverty," are also included. It is possible to group the different issues into five broader, underlying sets of concerns.[5] Four of them largely correspond with the main focus of our organizations, being associated with "social exclusion," "housing," "environment," and "ethnic and minority rights." However, the fifth set of concerns, which stands out as relatively independent from the others, does not match any of the main types of groups we included in our population. Instead, it can be broadly associated with "globalization." Interest in the broad issue with the same tag is strongly correlated with interest in third world poverty and third world debt. It is also significantly correlated, if more weakly, with attention to peace issues ("military installations"), concerns regarding manipulation of living organisms ("genetically modified food"), and interest in animal rights ("hunting" and "animal welfare").

This is, admittedly, a distinctive combination of issues that would be better tested with longer batteries of specific questions. Even as it stands, however, it is a meaningful combination. It is consistent with the integration of interest in global inequality, ecopacifist orientations, and animal rights activism that has often been found among radical grassroots activists in contemporary Britain (see e.g., Doherty, Plows, and Wall, 2001). Although the levels of interest in "global" issues are lower than those expressed in other issues—unsurprisingly so, given the way our organizations were selected—it seems possible to argue that those issues are dis-

TABLE 3.1
The Structure of Issue Interests (maximum likelihood factor analysis, Varimax rotation)

	Percentage Interested	Social Exclusion	Environment	Ethnic & Minority	Globalization	Housing
Lone Parents	39%	.776				
Children's Services	44%	.698				
Drugs	40%	.652				
Welfare Rights	47%	.639				
Unemployment Issues	49%	.615				
Poverty	57%	.596				
Health	65%	.588				
Disability	50%	.557				
HIV-related Issues	30%	.556				
Crime in Neighborhoods	35%	.553				
Homelessness	47%	.553				
Access to Higher Education	39%	.540		.358		
Community Services	61%	.534				
Quality of Basic Education	45%	.526		.368		
Minimum Wage	24%	.510				
Gender Equality	47%	.507		.322		
Women's Issues	55%	.498				
Elderly People	43%	.467				
Community Cultural Activities	48%	.429		.393		
Community Economic Growth	48%	.355				
Pollution	37%		.803			
Nature Conservation	28%		.771			
Waste	29%		.741			
Energy	33%		.699			
Environmental Education	54%		.657			
Farming, Forestry, Fishing	20%		.652			
Science and Technology	19%		.601			
Food	35%		.593			
Transport	36%		.583			
Genetically Modified Food	21%		.558		.538	
Animal Welfare	15%		.544		.538	
Tourism	17%		.408			
Building Conservation	18%		.391			
Racial Harassment	42%			.714		
Minority Citizenship Rights	35%			.607		
Minorities' Access to Public Office	24%			.597		
Multiculturalism	42%	.321		.577		
Asylum Seekers	44%			.574		

TABLE 3.1 (continued)

	Percentage Interested	Social Exclusion	Environment	Ethnic & Minority	Globalization	Housing
Minority Entrepreneurship	23%			.538		
Independent Education for Minorities	23%			.462		
Third World Debt	24%				.829	
Third World Poverty	27%				.761	
Globalization	26%		.428		.689	
Military Installations	15%		.314		.427	
Hunting	8%		.322		.346	
Tenants' Rights	35%	.466				.680
Housing Quality	38%	.509				.654
Housing Privatization	21%					.629
Housing Developments	40%					.540
Explained Variance		15%	12%	8%	7%	5%

tinctive according to citizens' organizations' perceptions of their issue priority. They should not be regarded as a mere extension of more established concerns such as those with the environment or inequality.

If global issues occupy a specific location in the agendas of citizens' organizations in the two cities, is the interest in those issues accounted for by specific organizational traits? The hypotheses, outlined in the previous section, were tested with an ordinal regression analysis (table 3.2). The basic model looks at the impact of organizational consolidation (measured as an index, summarizing different organizational traits: see appendix A for details) on attention in global issues, controlling for city. No significant differences emerge between Glasgow and Bristol here, nor in any of the models, to suggest a low impact of local political cultures and opportunities on organizations' issue priorities. Instead, organizational consolidation turns out to have a negative impact on mobilization potential (table 3.2, model 1): groups with a formal bureaucratic structure, a substantial budget, and who have been in existence for a longer time are less likely to express interest in global issues than less-established groups with a looser structure. The contribution of these factors remains consistently significant even when other variables are introduced in the models (table 3.2, models 2–4). All in all, less-established organizations seem inclined to develop stronger interests in global issues.

The explanatory capacity of the model, however, increases significantly when we bring in organizational identities. The hypothesis that global issues are more appealing to political actors is tested here by means of

TABLE 3.2
Ordinal Regression Estimates of Interest in Global Issues
(standard errors in parentheses)

Model	1	2	3	4
Glasgow	.153	.227	.195	−8.563E-03
	(.253)	(.259)	(.281)	(.329)
Organizational Consolidation				
(see appendix A for details)	−.547***	−.277*	−.332*	−.558***
	(.131)	(.145)	(.155)	(.172)
Identities				
Identity as Charity		−.469	−.493	−.343
		(.315)	(.338)	(.367)
Identity as Political		1.341***	.956**	.949**
Organization		(.300)	(.334)	(.361)
Repertoires				
(see appendix B for details)				
Protest			1.935E-03	−8.39E-04
			(.006)	(.007)
Pressure			6.880E-03	6.355E-03
			(.006)	(.006)
Consumerist			2.449E-02***	1.294E-02**
			(.005)	(.005)
Issue Interests				
Social Exclusion				−1.00E-02
				(.006)
Housing				3.957E-03
				(.005)
Ethnic & Minority				2.291E-02***
				(.006)
Environment				4.153E-02***
				(.005)
Nagelgerke R Square	.08	.18	.37	.57
-2 log likelihood	631384	607525	549424	463879

*p < .05; **p < .01; *** p < .001

two indicators: self-representation of organizations as charities and as
political groups.[6] Self-identification as political organizations, potentially
more open to pick up salient and controversial topics and to articulate
them in political projects, greatly raises the chance of being interested in
global issues. The impact of political identity remains significant, even
though its relative contribution decreases, when we introduce repertoires
in the equation (table 3.2, model 3). Here, I differentiate between three
types of repertoires, a classic *protest repertoire*, including demonstrations,
sit-ins, blockades, and other forms of direct action; a *pressure repertoire*,
including classic lobbying strategies; and what I call a *consumerist reper-*

toire, combining protest-oriented actions such as brand boycotts with more moderate styles of behavior such as adoption of fair-trade practices.[7] The propensity to adopt pressure or protest repertoires does not seem to have any relation with attention to global issues: they appear to be neither the preserve of the radical direct action sectors, nor of the lobbyists. Rather, interest in global themes seems to be higher among actors with a propensity to adopt innovative styles of action, such as product boycotts and fair-trade practices, which go beyond conventional distinctions between pressure and protest. These try to address the weak spot in contemporary corporate strategies, their exposure to consumer pressure, either directly through boycotts or indirectly through the latter's support to alternative forms of production and commercialization.

Finally, the performance of the model improves dramatically when we take into account organizations' attention to interests other than global issues. In principle, as I noted in the previous paragraph, there might be good reasons to expect a correlation between global issues and any of the other policy issues included in our dataset. In practice, global issues appear to be related to environmental issues as well as—if to a smaller extent—to ethnic and minority ones, that is, to those sets of issues that are most easily associated with the transnational dimension. No correlation is found, in contrast, between global and social inequality issues. These appear to be the preserve of organizations whose main focus may vary considerably: it can lie entirely on the specific problems of the most deprived sectors of British society (an orientation most likely to be found among institutionalized charities) or reflect an explicit attempt to connect local and global sources of discrimination (table 3.2, model 4).

PROMOTING GLOBAL ACTIONS IN LOCAL SETTINGS

How does interest in global issues translate into collective action? Similar to what we noticed in reference to issues, it is not always obvious how to tell a "global" protest event from an environmental or an ethnic one. In both cities we asked respondents to tell us about their organizations' involvement in a range of public events (sometimes, campaigns), which had taken place in recent years. More precisely, we asked about organizations' involvement in twenty-six events in Glasgow and seventeen in Bristol, broadly addressing environmental, ethnic, or inequality issues with varying degrees of radicalism. In both cities we could identify three distinctive sets of events with a similar profile,[8] although with a different relative weight (table 3.3). First, we could identify strong links between a set of actions addressing several aspects of ethnic and minority issues,

TABLE 3.3
Participation in Public Events in the Two Cities (maximum likelihood factor analysis, Varimax rotation)

	Percentage Taking Part	Ethnic & Minority	Global Inequality	Environmental Justice
Glasgow				
Chokar Family Campaign	26%	.782		.307
Imran Khan's Murder	15%	.699		
Annual Antiracist Demonstration	25%	.671		.357
Glasgow Mela	23%	.624		
Council Cultural Diversity Meeting	21%	.596		
Kick Racism Out of Football	15%	.592		
Council Police Racism Event	11%	.587		
Council Equality Policy Event	20%	.570		
Asian Youth Festival	13%	.483	.401	
Mothers Against Drugs	11%	.456		
Asylum Seekers	47%	.455		
Council Stock Transfer	16%	.331		.327
Faslane Peace Camp	18%		.916	.425
Trident Ploughshares	16%		.908	
Global Resistance Campaign	16%		.692	
May Day Parade	20%		.507	
Abolish Clause 28	18%	.306	.358	
Swimming Pool Closures	22%		.344	.321
M77 Extension	13%			.695
Mobile Phone Masts	7%			.681
M74 Extension	15%		.331	.621
Hospital Waste Incinerators	6%			.557
Gap Demonstration	9%		.437	.520
Save Our Hospitals	16%			.481
Kelvingrove Music Festival	11%	.348		.471
School Closures	11%	.381	.331	.411
Explained Variance		18%	14%	13%
Bristol				
Stop Avon Ring Road	6%			.954
Ashton Court Quarry	8%			.849
Ikea Breath Free	7%			.707
M32 Reclaim the Streets Party	5%			.548

TABLE 3.3 (continued)

	Percentage Taking Part	Ethnic & Minority	Global Inequality	Environmental Justice
Claimants' Action	3%			.538
Jubilee 2000	11%		.906	
Global Resistance	10%		.612	.323
Baby Milk	7%		.544	
Local Agenda 21	31%		.442	
Sort It Youth Festival	9%		.362	
Asylum Seekers	18%		.311	
Easton Community Festival	34%	.692		
Respect in the West Festival	31%	.651		
St. Paul's Carnival	16%	.616		
Bristol Community Festival	26%	.307		
Hartcliffe & Withyood Carnival	8%			
International Women's Day	35%			
Explained Variance		10%	13%	18%

ranging from annual multicultural festivals with a largely symbolic character to militant actions on specific instances of racial hatred or discrimination. This turned out to be the most salient set of events in Glasgow, but the least salient in Bristol. We then identified a set of actions sharing what could be called an "environmental justice" approach, linking urban ecology events, from opposition to local motorways, incinerators, or quarries, to the fight for social services in the local communities or for better working conditions. In this case the relation between the two cities reversed, with environmental justice events accounting for the highest share of variation in event attendance in Bristol, the lowest in Glasgow.

Finally, one could identify initiatives, which from different perspectives could be associated with "global inequality." In Glasgow, these events centered around peace actions such as the peace camp in Faslane or the Trident Ploughshares campaign, and antiliberal "no global" initiatives such as the Global Resistance campaign. However, they also included more traditional internationalist events such as the May Day parade and actions challenging local as well as global instances of social exclusion, such as the protests against well-known brands like Gap, or the high-profile campaign to save public swimming pools from closure. In Bristol, global inequality events included a combination of fairly institutional and more confrontational events: the debt-related Jubilee 2000 campaign, initiatives linked with Local Agenda 21, and a youth festival among the former; demonstrations to support asylum seekers, Global Resistance events, and the Baby Milk Action Campaign, targeting multinational Nestlé, among the latter.

What characteristics differentiate organizations that have taken part in at least one global inequality event over the last few years, from those who have not? There are some important differences with respect to the explanations provided for interest in global issues. The impact of organizational consolidation and repertoires disappears altogether, and that of "political organizational identity" is drastically smaller: all in all, organizational traits and know-how seem to matter very little when it comes to engaging in global actions. To the contrary, issue interests matter a lot. Part of this finding is unsurprising, namely, the expected positive correlation between interest in, and action on, global issues, and the lack of correlation between global inequality events and interest in social exclusion issues (consistent with what we found in table 3.2, even though in theory a correlation was surely conceivable).

Far more interesting, and somehow puzzling, is that the sign of the relationship between ethnic and minority issues, environmental issues, and globalization is now reversed. If interest in both sets of issues predicted interest in globalization issues, it predicts poor involvement in global actions on related topics (model 4). Of course, this might depend on an inadequate choice of the episodes included in our lists. But I do not think this is the case. Rather, this finding suggests that organizations interested in issues that they perceive as close to global issues (hence the correlation when looking at issue linkages) may struggle to translate that interest into specific collective action. It is as if strong interest in cognate issues discouraged action on themes perceived as compatible in principle, but alternative in practice, when it comes to the use of scarce mobilization resources. The negative relation between ethnic, environmental, and global issues persists even if we bring into the equation involvement in the other two types of local public events (model 5). For the latter there is, however, a positive correlation with global events, to suggest that once organizations are strongly involved in local events, they tend to be so across the board. But unless such commitment exists, mere interest in cognate topics does seem alternative to action on global issues, rather than conducive to it. It is also worth noting that, when all relevant variables are introduced, location in Bristol turns out to be positively related to active mobilization on global inequality events. This suggests an independent role for local political conditions in accounting for involvement in global events.

TABLE 3.4
Binary Logistic Estimates of Actual Participation in Global Inequality Public Events (B coefficients; standard errors in parentheses)

Model	1	2	3	4	5
Constant	−.878***	−1.011***	−1.016***	−.929*	−2.545***
	(.198)	(.282)	(.285)	(.400)	(.582)
Glasgow	.290	.259	.330	.246	−1.410**
	(.271)	(.278)	(.285)	(.313)	(.445)
Organizational Consolidation (see appendix A for details)	−.161	.019	.070	.167	.082
	(.136)	(.156)	(.161)	(.175)	(.202)
Identities					
Identity as Charity	−.229	−.192	−.236	−.131	
		(.330)	(.333)	(.348)	(.389)
Identity as Political Organization		.855**	.639	.393	.658
		(.328)	(.356)	(.388)	(.439)
Repertoires (see appendix B for details)					
Protest			.011	.013	.004
			(.007)	(.007)	(.008)
Pressure			.000	−.001	.001
			(.006)	(.006)	(.007)
Consumerist			−.003	−.006	.001
			(.005)	(.006)	(.006)
Issue Interests					
Social Exclusion				.009	.008
				(.006)	(.007)
Housing				−.003	−.003
				(.005)	(.006)
Ethnic & Minority				−.013*	−.023**
				(.007)	(.008)
Environment				−.014*	−.018*
				(.007)	(.008)
Globalization				.024***	.027***
				(.007)	(.008)
Participation in Public Events					
Ethnic & Minority Events					.893**
					(.359)
Environmental Justice Events					2.524***
					(.467)
Nagelgerke R Square	.01	.06	.08	.14	.37
-2 log likelihood	318686	309696	306407	294797	243454

* p < .05; ** p < .01; *** p < .001

GLOBAL ISSUES BETWEEN SOCIAL MOVEMENT, COALITIONAL, AND ORGANIZATIONAL LOGICS OF ACTION

Let us now refer back to the discussion of different logics of collective action, which differentiates between social movement dynamics, coalitional dynamics, and organizational dynamics. The question I want to address is whether attention to global issues characterizes organizations involved in any specific dynamic, in particular, given the relative novelty and lack of institutionalization of those issues, in social movement dynamics. An analysis of alliance networks[9] in the two cities (Diani and Bison, 2004) identified for each city three groups of organizations that occupied distinctive positions in the alliance network, being linked to other actors in a similar way—a position that network analysts would define as "structural equivalence."[10] I then checked whether organizations in each group were also internally connected to each other by identity bonds, in order to be able to differentiate between purely contingent alliances and alliances that might be embedded in stronger and deeper links. As a proxy for identity bonds I used the connections, originating from organizations' past participation in the same public events (at least three out of those listed in table 3.3), and the sharing of core activists. This enabled me to identify three different collective action processes operating in both cities.

In both Glasgow and Bristol, a number of organizations (33 percent of the total in the former, 19 percent in the latter) could be associated with *social movement processes*. They were connected through dense alliance networks and were also relatively frequently linked by shared participation in past events, or by joint activists. The relational dimension stretched beyond collaborations between organizations, which might in themselves also be purely instrumental, to suggest bonds and shared identities, which secured continuity to the network. This was not the case for another set of organizations (36 percent in Glasgow, 37 percent in Bristol), for which interorganizational networking was limited to collaboration on specific issues. *Coalitional processes* seemed to be operating there, as the gap between the density of organizational exchanges and the density of those links, measuring continuity of commitment over time and activists' personal involvement, was pronounced. Finally, both alliance links and identity links were very sparse for 31 percent of organizations in Glasgow and 44 percent in Bristol, suggesting their involvement in *organizational processes*. The main focus for those organizations seemed to be their own organizational activities; they were not involved in distinctive sets of alliances, nor were they linked by connections implying some level of collective identity with other groups. The relational dimension of social movement action was distinctly absent there.

The distribution of issue interests across organizations involved in different processes in the two cities shows no significant differences, but for one minor and one major exception (table 3.5): interest in environmental issues is significantly higher among organizations involved in social movement processes in Bristol, while—most important to us— globalization issues are the only ones to be consistently most popular among organizations involved in such processes in both cities. In both Glasgow and Bristol, organizations that either act on their own or only engage in instrumental coalition work seem less likely to invest in global issues. As findings reported in table 3.2 suggest, global issues may create more opportunities for less-established political players than others,

TABLE 3.5
Issue Interests (1–100 scales) by City and Type of
Collective Action Process

	Glasgow			
Type of Process	*Coali- tional*	*Organi- zational*	*Social Movement*	*Total*
Social Exclusion	48	57	45	50
Environment	25	25	35	28
Ethnic & Minority	32	47	44	41
Globalization	10	15	44	23***
Housing	43	52	44	47
N	45	38	41	124
	Bristol			
Social Exclusion	39	41	40	40
Environment	26	25	56	31***
Ethnic & Minority	25	26	25	25
Globalization	18	18	38	22*
Housing	30	23	19	26
N	50	59	25	134

Note: The scales measure the proportion of issues, correlated with one of the factors identified in table 3.2, in which organizations expressed interest. For example, on the average, Glaswegian organizations were interested in 23 percent of the issues correlated with global inequality, but this percentage equaled 44 percent for those involved in a social movement process, only 10 percent for those adopting a coalitional logic.
*** Difference significant at 0.001 level; * difference significant at 0.05 level.

where a division of labor between organizations has probably consolidated.

As for involvement in public events, the picture is partially different. In Glasgow, organizations involved in social movement processes stand out from organizations involved in other collective action processes not only for their participation in global inequality, but also in environmental justice events (table 3.6). There, over 70 percent of organizations of that type have taken part in at least one global inequality event (68 percent in an environmental justice event), whereas only 32 percent (16 percent for environmental justice events) have done so in Bristol, in both cases close to the city average. In Glasgow, participation in global events seems to be a powerful source of differentiation among civic organizations, whereas the same does not apply to Bristol. To understand why this is the case, as well as the reasons why Bristol seems to be a more conducive environment for action on global issues once other factors are controlled for, requires a thorough discussion of the logics guiding citizen politics in the two cities. Unfortunately, this cannot be addressed in the present chapter (for a very preliminary effort, see Purdue and Diani, 2003).

TABLE 3.6
Percentage of Organizations Involved in at Least One Global Inequality Event, by City and Type of Collective Action Process

Type of Process	Coalitional	Organizational	Social Movement	Total
Glasgow				
Global Inequality	9%	11%	71%	30%***
Ethnic & Minority	64%	50%	68%	61%
Environmental Justice	36%	26%	68%	43%***
N	45	38	41	124
Bristol				
Global Inequality	36%	39%	32%	37%
Ethnic & Minority	36%	51%	48%	45%
Environmental Justice	16%	5%	16%	11%
N	50	59	25	134

***Difference significant at 0.001 level

CONCLUSION

The analysis of two different local UK settings suggests that, far from being a mere addition to the new social movements milieu, or the mere revitalization of established agendas on social inequality, or ethnic and minority rights, mobilizations on global issues constitute the focal point of specific alliances, based on specific identity bonds within British civil society. We may attempt the following provisional conclusions regarding the role of global issues in local politics:

- Global issues are both pervasive and distinctive. Pervasive, as interest in them is equally present in two territorial areas, which are profoundly different in both social and political terms. Distinctive, as they are perceived by civil society organizations as an independent set of concerns, which are internally correlated and cannot be reduced to any of the other major issues around which mobilization attempts in the two cities develop. They do not overlap, even though they are linked to them, either with "new social movement" issues like the environment, or with ethnic and minority issues. They show no correlation at all to social exclusion issues. There is the potential for a distinctive agenda there.
- Global issues are not equally appealing to the whole spectrum of civic organizations. On the contrary, they attract disproportionate attention from organizations with a distinctive profile: low levels of formalization and consolidation; a view of themselves as political groups rather than charities; a propensity to adopt a distinctive action repertoire, emphasizing consumers' role—whether as boycotters of certain products or as promoters of fair-trade practices. Global issues are, in other words, appealing to actors structurally more prepared to experiment with new strategies of action, and to use their political orientation to secure a niche, which their uncertain formal status cannot grant them. Consistent with this picture, in both cities global issues appear particularly attractive to organizations engaged in social movement processes: in other words, involved in dense alliance networks that are also backed by relatively strong identity links.
- The picture changes substantially if we look at how interest is turned into action on specific events. None of the factors mentioned above are consistent, significant predictors of actual participation in "global inequality" actions. The latter is positively correlated to interest in global issues, and to participation on other local events on issues such as ethnicity, but negatively correlated to interest in cognate issues such as the environment and ethnic and minority rights. Most important, propensity to engage in other important local events on

ethnic and minority issues and environmental justice issues also predicts engagement in "glocal" actions. The inclination to cover such a broad agenda reflects what was recently found by analysts of direct action participants in the United Kingdom (Doherty, Plows, and Wall, 2001).

- Finally, differences between cities seem to operate in an unusual way. If we look at differences in the orientations and behavior of individual organizations, they seem to matter very little. Neither organizations' interest in global issues, nor their involvement in specific public events, is affected by their location in Glasgow or Bristol. Substantial differences can be found, in contrast, if we look at how organizations involved in specific collective action processes actually operate in the two cities. When it comes to collective action on global issues, organizations engaged in social movement processes in Glasgow differ markedly from those following different logics, whereas differences are not significant at all in Bristol. In Glasgow, where political culture still reflects drastic differences between moderatism and radicalism and inequality-based issues are still central, "global inequality" events do not seem to be an option for organizations that follow mostly coalitional or organizational logics. In Bristol, availability to act on global inequality does not shape civil society, as involvement in those actions is spread across the civic sector. These differences suggest that the embeddedness of actions conducted on global issues in specific niches of interorganizational networks is strongly mediated by the features of local civil societies and political systems.

NOTES

This chapter originates from an investigation of "Networks of civic organisations in Britain" that I conducted with Isobel Lindsay (University of Strathclyde in Glasgow) and Derrick Purdue (University of West of England, Bristol) from June 2000 to September 2003. The project was part of the *Democracy and Participation Programme*, funded by the Economic and Social Research Council (contract L215 25 2006), and directed by Paul Whiteley. I am grateful to Paul for his constant support, to Juliana Mackenzie for her assistance with data entry and data collection in Glasgow, and to Derrick Purdue's collaborators at UWE for their work on data collection in Bristol.

1. There are strong reasons to believe that all of the most central organizations in both cities were contacted: while many other organizations that were not among those interviewed were mentioned by respondents, none received more than three nominations. On the other hand, umbrella bodies like the Glasgow Council for the Voluntary Sector (GCVS) or the Scottish Council for Voluntary

Organisations (SCVO) in Glasgow, or the Voluntary Organisations Standing Conference on Urban Regeneration (VOSCUR) and the Black Development Agency (BDA) in Bristol, are excluded from the present analysis. Their role as providers of services to the voluntary and community sector, rather than as direct promoters—or opponents—of change on substantive issues, renders them very different from the other organizations contacted, when it comes to alliance building.

2. These were the Southside in Glasgow, an area with massive historical presence of the working class, including neighborhoods such as Govan, Govanhill, Gorbals, and Pollokshields, and the area including the neighborhoods of Easton, Knowles, Withywood, and Hartcliffe in Bristol, featuring a strong presence of ethnic minorities.

3. In contrast to what I have done elsewhere (Diani and Bison, 2004), in this chapter I will not consider the distinction between conflictual and consensual collective action. By the latter, I mean, with John Lofland (1989:163), a form of collective action conducted in the absence of specific social and/or political opponents. Consensual collective actors blame lack of information, skills, or education, rather than other social groups, for the grievances they address. In principle, we might have both consensual and conflictual organizational, coalitional, and movement dynamics (Diani and Bison, 2004). In practice, however, such differences had no impact at all on the analysis of collective action on global issues presented here.

4. Of course, nothing prevents a coalitional dynamic from evolving into a social movement dynamic, but it is still important to recognize the analytical difference between the two processes.

5. A maximum likelihood factor analysis generated ten rotated (Varimax solution) factors with *eigenvalue* above 1. The first five are reported in table 2.1 and represent the focus of my analysis (see Kim and Mueller [1978] for a basic introduction to factor analysis).

6. Although the two should be mutually exclusive by British law, their correlation is only -.38: significant, but far from perfect, suggesting a gap between formal criteria and subjective perceptions.

7. See appendix B for details on how these indicators of repertoires were constructed. A fourth repertoire, support to local and national candidates in elections, was not included in the models given its limited relevance.

8. A maximum likelihood factor analysis was used here too.

9. Respondents were asked to identify up to five of their most important partners in alliances. They were also invited to identify any additional important collaboration with groups belonging to any of the following categories: environmental organizations, ethnic organizations, community organizations, churches, political parties, unions and other economic interest groups, other voluntary organizations, other organizations. The resulting data on alliances should be treated not as a list of the groups with which our respondents exchanged most frequently or most intensely in objective terms, but of those they perceived as their most important allies at the time of the interview. Accordingly, the matrix of alliances, which represents the basis of our analysis, is best interpreted as an indicator of perceptions of closeness rather than objective intensity of exchange. It reflects, in

other terms, how organizations perceive their social space and identify their most relevant contacts within it.

10. In the language of network analysis, organizations are structurally equivalent when they are linked to the same actors, regardless of whether or not they are connected to each other (Diani, 2002:191–94; Wasserman and Faust, 1994:chap.9).

Part II

DIFFUSION AND SCALE SHIFT

4

The Sequencing of Transnational and National Social Movement Mobilization: The Organizational Mobilization of the Global and U.S. Environmental Movements

ERIK JOHNSON AND JOHN D. MCCARTHY

Conventional logic would suggest that movements are built from the ground up, that national movement organizational populations[1] expand as an outgrowth of the spread of local groups and, as well, that transnational movements are established as the outgrowth of national movements.[2] The first U.S. national antitoxics organizations, for example, were the outgrowth of informal networking between groups engaged in autonomous local struggles (Szasz, 1994). At the international level, Chatfield (1997) asserts, "TSMOs [transnational social movement organizations] mainly began as informal networks of people who shared common concerns, often in national associations" (28). Similarly, David Westby in his study of the Swedish anti-bomb movement argues "that many TSMs originate specifically in a national context, suggesting that many of them become transnational through a step-like process in response to political opportunity" (2002:1).

Organizationally, this implies that transnational foundings are dependent upon the expanding vitality of national populations of social movement organizations (SMOs). Empirically, however, the sequencing of aggregate national and transnational movement organizational mobilization remains very much an open question.[3] One alternative to the bottom-up thesis is that the emergence and growth of populations of transna-

71

tional SMOs may be important factors in the emergence and growth of their sister populations at the national level. In particular, David Frank and his colleagues (1999; Frank, Hironaka, and Schofer, 2000; Meyer, Frank, Hironaka, Schofer, and Tuma, 1997), strongly suggest that transnational mobilization of the environmental movement preceded mobilization of national environmental movements as well as national public policy attention to environmental issues.

The approach of these scholars emphasizes the extent to which definitions of nation-states are embedded in world society and the institutionalization of these *global* definitions of what nations should do and how. Like many other areas of state action, "blueprints of nation-state environmentalism" are developed first in world society before being diffused and acted upon by individual nations. They assert that environmental TSMOs form first and are later followed by intergovernmental treaties and organizations before nation-states finally begin to formalize environmental issues within state level agenda-setting structures. They argue that "[T]he top-down global explanation proves stronger than the bottom-up domestic alternative: The global institutionalization of the principle that nation-states bear responsibility for environmental protection drives national activities to protect the environment. This is especially true in countries with dense ties to world society" (Frank, Hironaka, and Schofer, 2000:96), such as the United States.

Several case studies of recent mobilizations buttress expectations of the importance of top-down, transnational to national organizational processes. Two transnational social movement organizations, Earth Action (Smith, 2002a) and Peoples' Global Action (Wood, 2002), for instance, have worked to facilitate national-level mobilization around social change issues. We approach the research question by analyzing the coevolution of the transnational and U.S. national environmental movement populations between 1945 and 2000, with particular attention to the timing of the founding of movement organizations and cumulative organizational population densities.[4]

THEORETICAL CONSIDERATIONS

SMO Population Processes. Our approach in this research draws heavily, both theoretically and empirically, upon understandings of the *dynamics of organizational populations* (Hannan and Freeman, 1989; Hannan and Carroll, 1992), the *dynamics of communities of organizational populations* (Aldrich, 1999) in general, and the application of these ideas to populations of SMOs in particular (e.g., Minkoff, 1997; Hannan and Freeman, 1987). This organizational ecology approach, which has spawned a large and vital research community, assumes that the issue focus of organizations remains quite stable, so it is the pattern of births and deaths within a population of organizations that shapes its dominant issue focus. We begin by casting the formulation with which we began into a problem of the evolution of the organizational density of communities of organizational populations (in this case, transnational and U.S. national ones) and cross-population effects within such communities.

The emergence and growth of any population of organizations occurs within a wider organizational community and institutional field composed of associated populations of organizations (Scott, 2002). A clear theoretical specification of appropriate mechanisms by which the founding of transnational populations might spur the founding of national ones, and vice versa, is embedded in conceptions of the appropriate boundaries of the institutional field in which the populations that we focus upon here are embedded (Keck and Sikkink, 1998; Carmin and Hicks, 2002). In the present case, that would necessarily include, at least, relevant international governmental organizations (IGOs), national and transnational professional associations, and foundations, as well as other populations of national and transnational SMOs in related movement families (della Porta and Rucht, 1995). In our opening effort to gain empirical purchase on this problem, the focus of this chapter, we will ignore the wider institutional field as well as mechanisms of cross-population influences. We return to the consequences of wearing this set of blinders for understanding the empirical patterns we examine in our discussion.

Organizational ecologists expect that the *density of an organizational population* will have effects upon its subsequent size, as well as upon populations within the same community. Within a single organizational population, founding rates of organizations may be enhanced through a number of mechanisms. First, increased population density initially accelerates organizational founding rates by legitimizing the domain and helping to establish viable resource niches. Related to this is the contribution each new organization makes to increased founding rates by providing templates for organizational structure and action. New organizations are more likely to be founded and persist once a model has been shown to "work," since it is easier for new organizational entrepreneurs to follow established routines and structures of action than to create them on their own.

Foundings within an organizational population are also facilitated through the provision of resources for new start-ups. Existing organizations may provide direct aid (financial, informational, human, legitimacy) to fledgling organizations, as when the National Audubon Society and Rachel Carson Fund (along with the Ford Foundation) provided grants for the founding of the Environmental Defense Fund. Alternatively, organizations may establish spin-offs as a way of addressing routines of action that are better handled by independent entities. For example, the Sierra Club established two spin-off organizations contained in our dataset of U.S. national organizations: the Sierra Club Legal Defense Fund, established in 1970 to concentrate on environmental litigation, and the Sierra Club Radioactive Waste Campaign, established in 1978.

Employees of an existing organization may also leave it to establish new spin-off organizations, either because they are dissatisfied with how their current employer operates or because they see an unmet demand in the environment that they believe they can satisfy. In the environmental movement, an example of this organizational entrepreneurship can be seen in the career of David Brower. Forced out as executive director of the Sierra Club in 1969, that same year he founded Friends of the Earth (FoE), one of the largest environmental groups in the world today. When Brower left that organization he went on to found, among others, the Earth Island Institute in 1982.

While increasing density may initially raise the rate of new foundings within an organizational population, increasing population density may also have negative effects on rates of founding. Later in a population's growth cycle, additional organizational density dampens the rate of new foundings by increasing competition for material resources. While increased density initially spurs rates of founding, as the population begins to approach the limits of its resource niche, each additional organization contributes relatively little to population legitimacy while contributing significantly more to competition over increasingly scarce resources. A majority of studies support the density dependence model and have shown *increases in organizational density that initially raise founding rates* and lower disbanding rates until, *beyond a certain point, increased density inhibits foundings* and raises rates of organizational disbanding (Singh and Lumsden, 1990; Baum and Oliver, 1996).

A few social movement researchers have explored these interorganizational processes across movement populations (Meyer and Whittier, 1994; Keck and Sikkink, 1998; Van Dyke, 1998). In particular, Deborah Minkoff (1997) has fruitfully applied the population ecology perspective to demonstrate the sequencing of social movement populations. She demonstrates how the growing density of U.S. civil rights SMOs spurred the founding of and, hence, the subsequent density of U.S. women's SMOs. This sequencing, she suggests, results from the civil rights movement having provided organizational models as well as legitimacy for implementing them, thus encouraging the founding of new women's groups. The arguments of Meyer and his colleagues suggest a similar process of increasing density among the transnational population of environmental

SMOs spurring the subsequent founding, and hence density, of national environmental SMOs.

However, the effects of density across populations of organizations linked to one another are not necessarily limited to positive ones, in which increasing densities in one population lead to increasing densities in the other. There are a number of possible relationships, ranging from fully mutual to fully competitive, that may occur among populations within the same community (Aldrich, 1999:302). Minkoff's (1997) analyses, for instance, did not show evidence of the reciprocal impact of increasing density of women's SMOs having contributed to subsequent increases in density of civil rights SMOs. Similarly, Hannan and Freeman (1987) have shown that for labor unions in the United States, the increasing density of industrial unions during the expansion of organized labor had a dampening effect upon subsequent founding of craft unions. They interpret this pattern of results as reflecting competitive processes between these two populations of organizations, the organizations within each population contending for the same scarce resources of members and financial support. Their findings suggest that we should remain alert to the possibility that the growing density of a transnational population of SMOs may dampen rather than encourage rates of founding, and hence, the organizational density of its equivalent national population, or vice versa.

CONSEQUENCES OF LIMITING OUR FOCUS TO THE UNITED STATES AND ENVIRONMENTAL MOBILIZATION

Although we are interested in the dynamics of mobilization across multiple populations of national and transnational SMOs, we have restricted our focus in this chapter to the population of transnational and U.S. national environmental SMOs only. This decision was made primarily as a practical matter. But how appropriate is it to ask our key questions for only a single movement and a single nation? We briefly address each of these questions in turn.

The environmental movement sector is large and has experienced significant growth during the period under study. With 17 percent of all TSMOs focusing on environmental issues in 2000, only the global human rights transnational population is larger, containing 26 percent of all TSMOs in 2000 (Smith, 2002b).[5] While the relative size of the transnational human rights population has remained nearly stable over recent history, however, the population of environmental TSMOs has nearly doubled as a percentage of all TSMOs since 1973. Because the questions that we are asking address movement growth and evolution over time, it made sense to start with a movement that experienced significant growth (or variance on the dependent variable) over the time period under observation.

In addition, some of the strongest claims about the sequencing of national and transnational movements have been made by John Meyer and his several colleagues, who have provided us with strong arguments and some evidence that top-down (transnational to national) mobilization processes predominate among the population of SMOs concerned with environmental issues. Meyer and his colleagues (1997) claim that the top-down method of growth should be strongest in arenas of highly rationalized "scientific/universalistic" discourse and in those most institutionalized in world society definitions of the nation-state. The environmental arena is dominated by rational-scientific discourse (Nicholson, 1987; Wright, 1992; Yearley, 1992), especially as compared to most other social movement industries, and is highly institutionalized in both world society institutions and definitions of the nation-state (Frank, 1997; Meyer et al., 1997). While they suggest that transnational mobilization of the environmental movement preceded national mobilization, they perform, in our judgment, an inadequate test of their top-down thesis of mobilization. They focus on national chapters of transnational environmental SMOs rather than national-level environmental mobilization per se. By gathering data on the entire population of national-level environmental organizations for one country, as opposed to data only on chapters of TSMOs, as they did, we hope to develop a more complete test of their top-down thesis of mobilization.

If the environmental movement is an appropriate locus of study, how appropriate is it to ask our question for a single nation (the United States)? Following Frank, Hironaka, and Schofer (2000), we expect that the United States should be an ideal location to test their theory, the nation that might be expected to most closely conform to the top-down thesis. The world polity argument predicts that in those countries with dense ties to world society, the top-down model of population growth should be strongest. "As the principle of national environmental protection has become institutionalized in world society, national activities to protect the environment have increased, *particularly among those nation-states strongly tied to world society* and those with receptor sites capable of transmitting emerging blueprints to domestic actors" (Frank, Hironaka, and Schofer, 2000:111, italics added).[6] The United States is strongly linked to world society, with many TSMO chapter memberships and a strong density of receptor sites in the form of science organizations linked to international science bodies. In the particulars too, Frank, Hironaka, and Schofer argue that United States environmentalism follows its institutionalization in world society. "By the time the United States had adopted the first legislation in 1969, the concept of environmental impact assessment laws had [already] been discussed thoroughly in the international realm" (2000:101).

There is reason to be cautious in generalizing the results obtained here to other nations, however. The process of establishing a global environmental regime has not been one of consensus; rather, definitions of environmental problems have been hotly contested. In particular, there has been persistent conflict over a range of environmental issues between developing and industrialized nations (Buttel, 2000). Absent from world polity accounts of a culturally diffused, rational-scientific logic driving the formation of global civil society is the considerable conflict and power differentials between nations (Finnemore, 1996). The United States in particular, and core nations in general, may play disproportionate roles in defining how and what values are defined as constituting world society, rather than responding to those definitions.

Further, while we do not have cross-national time-series data on the expansion of the environmental movement in other nations we suspect that the modern U.S. environmental movement was an "early riser," beginning before national environmental movements arose in most other countries.[7] In fact, the United States was the only nation to establish an environmental ministry (the Environmental Protection Agency, EPA) prior to the establishment of the United Nations Environment Program, and that event, we imagine, spurred high rates of national organizational founding.

DATA AND METHODS

In order to address our motivating question concerning the sequencing of social movement growth, we have been assembling evidence on the founding and density of transnational and U.S. national SMO populations in the environmental protection issue domain. Some of this evidence we have borrowed from other researchers; much of it we have created ourselves. We describe these several sources of evidence:

U.S. National Environmental Protection SMOs. Yearly counts of the founding of new and the total number, or density, of U.S. national environmental SMOs are drawn from the *Encyclopedia of Associations, Volume 1, National Organizations of the U.S.* (Gale Research Inc.). The *Encyclopedia* has been published annually since 1974 and intermittently before that, since 1956. Editors from the Gale Research Company, the publisher of the *Encyclopedia*, aggressively search for and conduct a yearly survey of nonprofit associations active in the United States at the national level. Those associations included in the *Encyclopedia* are likely to overrepresent the largest and most well-known groups in any category, and this should also be the case for SMOs. Nevertheless, the *Encyclopedia* does provide the most complete source available for identifying a broad range of national citizens' organizations, with data on more than twenty-five thousand national associations in the most recent edition (2003). As a result, the *Encyclopedia of Associations* has been widely used as a census for bounding populations of voluntary organizations (e.g. Baumgartner and Jones, 1993; Minkoff, 1995, 1997, 1999; Johnson, 2000).[8]

We used the 2003, 2000, 1995, 1990, 1985, 1980, 1975, 1970, and 1962 editions of the *Encyclopedia* to identify those groups to be included in our two issue domain categories. We included groups that listed environmental conservation/protection as a *primary* organizational purpose or concern. This was established through a combination of keyword headings, association name, and organizational description. The procedure followed was to first include all organizations listed under certain keywords.[9] Each entry in the entire encyclopedia was then read to determine if other groups should be included though they were not listed under one of the headings above. Finally, those organizations whose membership was drawn primarily from (1) industry, (2) governmental agencies, and (3) both industry and governmental agencies, as well as (4) professional associations whose organizational goals were primarily advancement of a professional group were deleted from the sample. When this process was complete, 657 different national environmental SMOs were identified as having been in existence at some time during the period under study.

The founding dates provided in the organizational entries were used to compile yearly counts of the number of foundings in each category. The year of founding is reported by the organization itself. For those few organizations (N = 20) that did not report a founding date, it was imputed using the first year in which the organization appears in the *Encyclopedia*.[10] Population density is calculated as the total number of organizations active during each time period. A complete time-series was constructed for each organization, indicating, for each year between 1945 and 2000, whether or not the organization was active. For each organization, the founding date (or the first year of the study if the organization was formed prior to 1945) was used to indicate the first year that an organization was present. The last year that an organization appears in the *Encyclopedia* (or 2000 if the organization persists until the end of the study period) was used as the final record for an organization. Because we project founding dates and densities back to 1945 using versions of the *Encyclopedia* published in 1962 and more recently, early estimates of population foundings and densities should be interpreted with some caution.

Transnational Environmental Protection Groups. Data on TSMOs was gathered from the *Yearbook of International Organizations*, with an initial listing of organizations provided by Jackie Smith and Kathryn Sikkink (Smith, 1997, 2002b, forthcoming; Sikkink and Smith, 2002). Published by the Union of International Associations (UIA), the *Yearbook* is the most comprehensive census of transnational organizations available, including data on more than forty thousand governmental, business, and civil society organizations in the most recent edition, and is the favored data source for research on TSMOs (Caniglia, 2002; Frank, Hironaka, and Schofer, 2000; Keck and Sikkink, 1998; Skjelsbaek, 1972; Smith, 1997, 2002b, forthcoming; Smith, Pagnucco, and Romeril, 1994; Sikkink and Smith, 2002). Clearly the *Yearbook*, along with the *Encyclopedia of Associations*, does not contain information on the entire universe of relevant organizations. But editors from both publications do attempt to identify all active organizations, and *it is reasonable to assume that the largest and the most well-known SMOs in each population are included, and that smaller and more radical organizations are less likely to be included in the sample.* Because editors of the *Yearbook* rely on United Nations (UN) and other official documents as one of the major ways to identify organizations, there may be some bias toward the more institutionally integrated organizations, although the majority of SMOs included in the *Yearbook* do not have official consultative status with the UN or other transnational governmental organizations (Caniglia, 2002).

Jackie Smith, with some help from Kathryn Sikkink, has identified all of the TSMOs (defined as those groups whose membership came from three or more countries and whose goals indicated that they work for some sort of political change) contained in the 1973, 1983, 1993, and 2000 editions of the *Yearbook*, and has kindly shared those data with us. We included in our sample all of the organizations coded as part of the environment/wildlife and environment and development SMOs. In all, 224 transnational environmental social movement organizations were identified as having been in existence at some time during the period under study.

As with the *Encyclopedia*, we used the founding dates provided to generate yearly counts of new organizational foundings. For those few organizations that did not report a founding date (N = 8), it was imputed using the first year in which the organization appeared in the *Yearbook*.[11] If the organization was "captured" by Smith and Sikkink in 2000, the organization was coded as having been present in each intervening year between the date of founding and 2000. For the remaining organizations, we relied primarily upon the 2002/3 CD-ROM version of the *Yearbook* to construct a yearly record of whether or not the organization was active. The CD-ROM version provides a record of the most recent date the *Yearbook* staff received updated information on an organization, as well as links to the *Yearbook* website that indicate whether or not an organization is still active and, for those organizations no longer active, provides information on the date of dissolution.

If an organization dissolved before 2000, the year of dissolution, as provided on the *Yearbook* website, was used as the final year of existence. If the organization was listed as no longer active and no dissolution date was provided, then the last year in which an entry was received was used as the final year of existence. For those few organizations ($N = 7$) whose disbanding dates could not be constructed using this method (i.e., the organization was no longer active and neither the date of dissolution nor the last year in which an entry was updated was available), we used the hard copies of the yearbooks to determine the last year that the organization appeared in the directory and used this as the final year of existence.

Smoothing Trends. Because we are interested in long-term trends in foundings and density, it is helpful to suppress short-run variation in the data. A moving average is the most common smoothing technique used for variables that display significant short-term fluctuation as, for example, in the analysis of changing stock prices. By smoothing values that fluctuate over time, a moving average reduces random error, increases stability, and makes long-term trends in the data clearer. In the section that follows, all counts of organizational foundings are presented as three-year moving averages. We report actual yearly densities, rather than a moving average, as this measure is relatively stable from year to year. Because the computation of each point in a three-year moving average requires three data points (i.e., the number of foundings in the current year and the year immediately preceding and following), one observation period is lost at the beginning and the end of the time series. So, while densities are reported for every year between 1945 and 2000, in the graphs that follow three-year moving averaged foundings are presented only from 1946 to 1999.

ANALYSES

In the following section, we present data on the sequencing of organizational mobilization among the transnational and U.S. national environmental movements. Temporal patterns of organizational founding and density are presented for the national and transnational movement organization populations in turn. We then compare these trends and look for indications of cross-population density effects. These trends in the founding and density of SMOs provide the underpinnings for more systematic analyses of the possible interaction between the evolution of populations of national and transnational environmental social movement organizations. In the discussion and conclusion, we discuss what is lacking from this analysis that would be needed to conduct a more thorough test of the theoretical questions that motivate this research.

Environmental national and transnational foundings and density. The annual number (three-year moving average) of new organizational foundings and the annual density for the population of *U.S. national environmental SMOs* for the period 1944–2000 is displayed in figure 4.1. The founding trend shows the inverted U-shape trajectory that population ecologists have shown characterizes the pattern of founding rates in most organizational populations. The number of new organizational foundings per year remains relatively stable and low (ranging between 1.3 and 6.7 foundings during two small cycles) from 1946 until the major period of expansion, beginning in 1966. The rate of national environmental foundings then explodes, peaking in 1971 with an average of twenty-nine new foundings per year, shortly after the National Environmental Policy Act (NEPA) was signed by then President Nixon, establishing the Environmental Protection Agency (EPA) in January of 1970. The rate of new foundings remains high (with no fewer than nineteen new foundings in any year through the early 1980s) but gradually declines from the 1971 peak to an average of 13.7 new foundings per year in 1987. This decline is temporarily reversed during the 1988–1990 period, but the rate of new national environmental SMO foundings decelerates rapidly after that point to an average of less than four foundings per year by 1993.

FIGURE 4.1
U.S. National Environmental SMO Foundings and Population Density

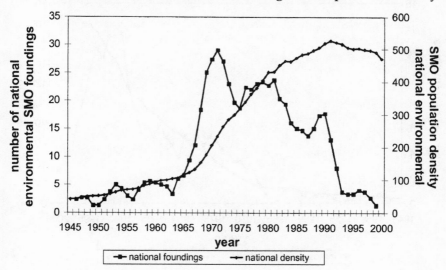

The density trend seen in figure 4.1 shows the cumulative actual number of national environmental SMOs active in each annual period. The density growth curve assumes the expected S-shaped pattern we would expect in a population experiencing a period of growth and stabilization (Carroll, 1984; Hannan and Freeman, 1987). There is very slow, but steady, growth from 1945 until 1967. From 1968 to 1973, the population experiences its most rapid period of growth, as reflected both in the steepness of the density curve and the high rates of organizational foundings during this time. Population density continues to grow at a high, but slightly reduced, rate until 1980, after which growth slows dramatically, peaking in 1991 with 527 active national environmental organizations in existence. From 1980 to 1991, the population density grows at a much reduced rate, *even though rates of new foundings remain relatively high*. This indicates that rates of organizational disbanding accelerated during this period (not shown), as the density dependence model would predict. After 1991, the population density actually begins a slow but steady decline to a total of 470 organizations remaining in 2000. Evidence of a precipitous population decline later in the period of study should be viewed somewhat skeptically, however, due to the delay before organizations typically enter the data source.

Figure 4.2 displays the number of new organizational foundings (three-

FIGURE 4.2
International Environmental SMO Foundings and Population Density

year moving average) and the annual cumulative density for the *population of transnational environmental SMOs* between 1944 and 2000. The founding rates for transnational environmental organizations are much lower than those for U.S. national organizations, never reaching more than 13.7 foundings per year, as compared to a high of twenty-nine foundings per year for national environmental SMOs. In the early period, the founding rate is very low (between 0 and 1.3 foundings per year from 1946 to 1967) before jumping to between 2.7 and 6.3 new foundings per year, a level that is sustained from 1968 until 1986. The founding rate then begins a steep ascent in 1987, peaking at thirteen or more foundings per year from 1989 until 1991, before experiencing a sharp and steady decline after 1993 that continues for the remainder of the observed period.

The density growth curve for transnational environmental SMOs, displayed in figure 4.2, assumes the expected S-shaped pattern. At the beginning of the observed period, the population density increases only very slowly, by one organization or less per year between 1945 and 1966. After 1969, the population begins to grow more quickly, experiencing steady increases over the next sixteen years until the period of most rapid growth that occurred between 1988 and 1994. After 1994, the population density curve begins to level out as fewer new organizations are founded during each time point and, presumably, rates of disbanding begin to accelerate.

As with the national population of environmental organizations, the major periods of elevated founding rates roughly correspond to the occurrence of major institutionalizing forces in the population's organizational field: the 1972 UN Conference on the Human Environment in Stockholm, Sweden, and the 1992 Rio Earth Summit in Brazil, attended by more than twenty thousand individuals representing nongovernmental organizations (NGOs) and other segments of civil society. Each of these conferences resulted in the establishment of an important new intergovernmental agency in the environmental arena: the United Nations Environment Program (UNEP) and the Commission on Sustainable Development, respectively. While both agencies have had significant institutionalizing effects on the transnational environmental field, the Commission on Sustainable Development is particularly significant in that it established a formal framework for consultation between NGOs and UN environmental bodies, representing a substantial commitment to viewing NGOs as state "partners" (Willetts, 2000). Especially important for understanding cross-population mobilization dynamics, the Commission on Sustainable Development granted consultative status to NGOs that were not transnational in structure or membership.

U.S. National and TSMO Founding Rates Compared. Figure 4.3 displays the smoothed yearly founding rates of the transnational and U.S. national environmental social movement populations in the same figure, for the purpose of comparing the timing of foundings between the two populations. Do foundings of transnational organizations appear to spur foundings of national organizations, or vice versa? The patterns seen in figure 4.3 provide a first look at one aspect of the coevolution of these interacting populations of organizations, suggesting that transnational founding rates generally seem to lag behind national founding rates early in the cycle.

Both trend lines are marked by relatively low rates of growth prior to the late 1960s. The first major increase in the rate of new organizational foundings begins in 1966 and peaks in 1971 for the national population, while rising steadily from 1968 to 1975 in the transnational population. Both populations then maintain relatively high levels of foundings until the early to mid-1980s. At this point, national organizational founding rates begin a steady decline that is temporarily reversed from 1988 to 1990. Transnational organizational founding rates, meanwhile, begin a steady increase after 1986 that peaks in the 1989–1991 period. After 1990, both organizational populations experience sharp declines in their founding rates.

What do these figures suggest as an answer to our motivating question? They suggest that the rate of founding environmental TSMOs lagged

FIGURE 4.3
International and U.S. National Environmental SMO Foundings

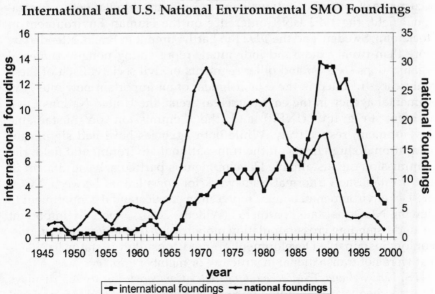

behind the U.S. national rate in the early period of growth during the late 1960s and early 1970s, but for a brief period later in the cycle, the rate of founding of U.S. national organizations lagged behind the rate of founding of environmental TSMOs. This pattern contradicts the claims of Meyer, Frank, and their colleagues, but suggests at the same time that the process of coevolution of these two populations is more complicated than our initial bottom-up/top-down imagery would imply.

National and Transnational Environmental SMO Densities Compared. The yearly population densities of the transnational and U.S. national environmental social movement populations are displayed together in figure 4.4, providing another way to look at the coevolution of these organizational populations. Does the increasing density of the transnational environmental population appear to spur increases in the national population, or vice versa? From 1967 to 1980, the U.S. national environmental SMO population experiences rapid growth, as reflected in the steepness of the population density curve, after which growth slows dramatically, peaking in 1991 with 527 active national environmental organizations in existence. Growth in the density of the transnational environmental SMO population begins later, and is most rapid between 1988 and 1994. *Clearly, expansion of the transnational environmental population comes later than growth in the population of national environmental SMOs.*

FIGURE 4.4
Yearly Density of International and U.S. National Environmental SMOs

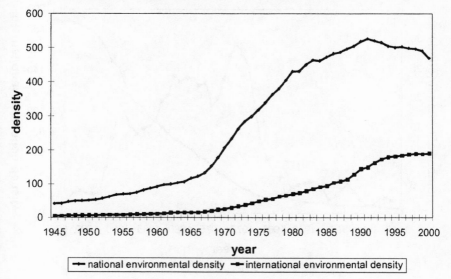

Further, rather than growth in the density of the transnational population appearing to spur national growth, the period of most rapid increase in the density of the transnational population is followed by a period of stabilization and possible decline among the national population.

Cross-Population Density Effects. We have now examined trends in the population density and rates of founding for the U.S. national and transnational populations of environmental SMOs in turn, and in comparison to one another. Recall that earlier studies of cross-population effects among movement populations argue that such effects should work through population density (Minkoff, 1999; Hannan and Freeman, 1987). What is the effect of increasing density at one level on founding rates at the other?

These cross-population effects are displayed in figures 4.5 and 4.6. Figure 4.5 shows the relationship between transnational environmental population density and U.S. national environmental founding rates. If the top-down explanation of movement mobilization is correct, we would expect increases in density at the transnational level to precede heightened rates of national foundings. Clearly, this is not the case. Transnational density does not begin to increase appreciably until after the major period of accelerated founding rates among U.S. national environmental

FIGURE 4.5
International Environmental SMO Population Density and U.S. National Foundings

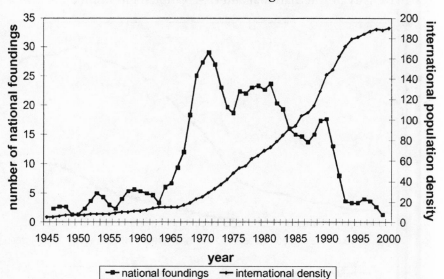

FIGURE 4.6
**National Environmental SMO Population Density and
International Foundings**

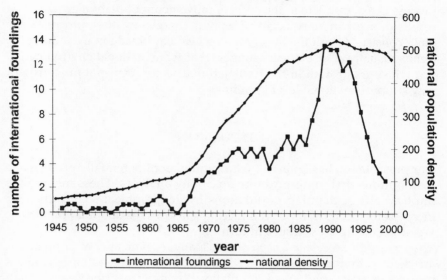

SMOs has already begun. Further, the period of most rapid growth in transnational densities occurs simultaneously with a collapse in the rate of founding of new national environmental organizations.

Figure 4.6 displays the relationship between U.S. national environmental population density and transnational founding rates. Early in the period under study, national population density was growing slowly, and transnational founding rates were low. Beginning in about 1968, both the rate of growth in the density of the national population of environmental SMOs and the rate of new transnational foundings experienced significant increases, suggesting some type of relationship. While the density of national organizations continued to increase, the rate of new transnational foundings remained relatively stable until national density began to stabilize. It is at this point, late in the growth of national densities, that transnational founding rates experience a major acceleration. This suggests that, early in the period, increasing densities at the national level did have a positive effect upon transnational rates of new organizational foundings. But later in the period, the relationship disappears, as national densities stabilize and transnational founding rates rise sharply.

The pattern of results has been consistent across our several figures. They suggest that in the early years of the rapid growth of the U.S. national population of environmental organizations, rates of founding of transnational TSMOs lagged behind, demonstrating a sequence between the two movement populations, but in the direction opposite from that predicted by the world polity model. There is some indication that this process is reversed late in the cycle of movement population growth. The results of a preliminary negative binomial model of these processes are quite consistent with the interpretations we have made in examining the trends visually. These results suggest that while national environmental growth spurs growth in the transnational sector, transnational growth may suppress national level foundings.[12]

DISCUSSION

Our presentation has ignored, so far, a number of potentially problematic assumptions that undergird our preceding analyses. These include the implications of defining populations by geographical scope, and our incomplete specification of the mechanisms of cross-population effects. We now take up these issues in turn.

Geographical Scope and Chaptering. Usually, organizational populations are defined by function (e.g., newspapers, labor unions), but movement researchers have subdivided populations by movement or issue domain (e.g., Minkoff, 1999). In the preceding analyses we defined our two populations of interest, instead, by their geographical scope. Recall that environmental TSMOs qualified for inclusion if they had chapters in at least three separate nations.[13] Defining two populations merely by geographic scope raises to prominence another mechanism of cross-population impact, the process of chaptering, or the spawning of satellite organizations, typically within narrower geographical arenas. But the development of coalitions of SMOs that, together, have wider geographical scope than any coalition member is also not uncommon. And there are hybrid forms, such as when previously independent SMOs choose to affiliate with a national or a transnational umbrella organization (e.g., Natur og Ungdom, a Norwegian environmental group that was formed in 1967, before the formation of Friends of the Earth, and is now affiliated with FoE). So affiliations between SMOs across levels of geographical scope do not necessarily reflect either top-down or bottom-up processes of mobilization, although we expect that chaptering is far more common than coalition formation.

In the process of developing affiliations of SMOs across geographical levels, typically some measure of resources and templates for action are directly exchanged. This quite direct cross-population mechanism is similar to what is seen within some organizational populations, as when new firms are "spun off" as independent firms that continue to retain ties to the "incubator" firm (Aldrich, 1999:275). There are also indications that this mechanism is reasonably common among U.S. national citizens groups, where many such groups received start-up support from other citizens groups (Walker, 1983, 1991). In fact, taking this mechanism into account in explaining the evolution of populations of organizations may be more feasible across geographical levels for SMOs than it is within a single geographical level, because the ties between organizations are usually more transparent.

The spread of national chapters of transnational environmental organizations is not new to the late twentieth century, though the evidence that Frank, Hironaka, and Schofer (2000) have generated suggests that the pace of such chaptering has accelerated during the last decades of that century. The differential impact that transnational chaptering may have on the population dynamics within the United States as compared to less-developed countries is important in explaining variation in the timing of social movement mobilization across countries. The United States has "fertile soil" in which domestic movement organizations can be expected to flourish (i.e., plentiful resources and open political opportunities), and thus a strong, dense sector of independent national organizations. No more than 15 percent of the national U.S. environmental SMOs are affiliated with environmental TSMOs, based upon our estimate from the *Encyclopedia* data.[14] It is probable that they make up a much larger percentage in less-developed countries that are more reliant upon the resources (material and human) and legitimacy provided through association with transnational SMOs (Gardner, 1995; Lewis, 2002). In such cases it seems that national mobilization would be much more likely to follow transnational mobilization, but for reasons very different than those suggested by the world polity model.[15]

Dimensions of a Fully Specified Model. Strong tests of cross-population effects, of course, require the inclusion of indicators of the several factors we have implicated as mechanisms through which the effects operate. As we noted above, without attention to these many other actors in the fields of U.S. and transnational environmental SMOs, we risk misunderstanding these cross-population effects. Nevertheless, gathering indicators of these many concepts has proven to be an incredibly labor intensive effort, which explains why we are, as yet, unable to more adequately assess the cross-population effects. At the minimum, a theoretically driven, fully specified model of cross-population influences would need to include indicators of the following concepts:[16]

1. Related social movement populations of organizations. For the environmental movement at the transnational level, this would include human rights, development, and global justice TSMOs, and at the

national level in the U.S. the civil rights, women's, peace, and consumer movements.
2. Professional and scientific associations at both the state and transnational levels.
3. Media attention to environmental issues.
4. Foundation resources available to national and transnational environmental SMOs.
5. Appropriate advocacy networks.
6. Regional and international intergovernmental organizations.
7. International triggering events.
8. Intergovernmental initiatives (e.g., treaties).
9. Transnational corporate opponents.

Debra Minkoff's work would suggest, as well, that rates of protest around environmental issues should be included in a cross-population effects model, but U.S. protests on environmental issues made up less than 1 percent of all protests reported in the *New York Times* during the 1970–1975 period.[17] And while rates were a bit higher in this period than in the previous decade, they remained extremely low, suggesting that U.S. environmental protest activity is unlikely to play any role in the founding of transnational environmental SMOs.

CONCLUSION

This work was initially motivated by the strong claims, and weak empirical tests of those claims, by that group of scholars who work with and have been inspired by John W. Meyer. Some of their claims are quite difficult to test, and this is certainly the case for the top-down versus bottom-up arguments about movement mobilization they have advanced. We reasoned, however, that a stronger, though narrower, test of those claims would be likely to go some way toward illuminating what is certainly a complex process, the cross-population effects of transnational SMO populations and national SMO populations. That process is very much worth analysis, since it can provide insight on the extent and trajectory of "infrastructures of social change" (Sikkink and Smith, 2002) at both the national and transnational levels.

Our tests of their claims about environmental mobilization make it quite clear that the U.S. case does not confirm their hypotheses of a top-down process. In fact, the evidence makes clear that U.S. environmental movement mobilization as reflected in rates of founding of SMOs and national SMO density preceded rather than followed transnational environmental mobilization, at least during the early period of the cycle.

In the process, as our previous discussion revealed, we have begun to realize how much more complex such cross-population processes may be than is reflected in the caricature of the process with which we began. Our framing of the problem has broader applicability, as well, being an appropriate one for studying similar processes between local and national populations of SMOs. As Doug McAdam (2003) has regularly remarked, we know rather little about local SMOs, let alone the dynamics of their interaction with national SMO populations.

NOTES

This research was supported with grants from the National Science Foundation, the Aspen Institute, and Pennsylvania State University. The authors would also like to thank Jennifer Schwartz, Jackie Smith, Nella Van Dyke, Sidney Tarrow, Donatella della Porta, and Kathryn Sikkink for their helpful comments on earlier drafts of this paper.

1. An organizational population refers to a group of organizations that rely upon a distinct combination of social and material resources from the environment (Aldrich, 1999). A population of social movement organizations is analogous to a "social movement industry," a term more commonly invoked in social movements literature, that includes all the SMOs "which have as their goals the attainment of the broadest preferences of a social movement" (McCarthy and Zald, 1977:1219).

2. The explication of mechanisms of "scale shift" by Tarrow and McAdam (this volume) illustrates how much this assumption is taken for granted.

3. Seidman argues that the typical, and taken for granted, empirical focus of movement researchers, which starts with local participants and moves through state-level mobilization ending with nation-state targets, constitutes a lens that narrows understanding of globalized movement processes. She says about this lens, "This bottom-up approach may limit social movement theorists' ability to explore fully the transnational side of collective action or social movement mobilization" (2002:345).

4. Density refers to the number of active organizations in a population at a given point in time, taking into account the founding of new organizations as well as the death of older ones.

5. Environmental SMOs do not, we think, so heavily dominate the social movement sector at the national level in the United States, but no similar estimate exists that would allow a comparison.

6. Receptor sites are defined by Frank, Hironaka, and Schofer as "social structures (e.g., scientific institutes) with the capacity to receive, decode, and transmit signals from world society to national actors" (2000:96).

7. Dieter Rucht says, in his description of the French and German environmental movements, "it was not until the early 1970s that genuine environmental movements emerged in Western Europe" (1989:85). And approximately 65 percent of the German national environmental groups that responded to the Trans-

formation of Environmental Activism (TEA) survey were founded after 1970 (Rucht, 2001). In addition, almost 90 percent of the Italian national environmental groups that responded to the TEA survey were founded after 1970 (della Porta and Diani, 2004b).

8. An ongoing project directed by Frank Baumgartner and John McCarthy will make this data source more accessible to a wide range of scholars in several years.

9. Conservation, wildlife conservation, environment, environmental quality, environmental protection, environmental health, toxic exposure, nuclear energy, ecology, pollution control, and hazardous waste.

10. Alternatively, these organizations could have been excluded from the founding analysis (Minkoff, 1995, 1997). This alternative made little or no difference in the results. Or, the year of first appearance minus the six-year average lag it takes to enter the *Encyclopedia* could have been imputed as the founding date for this subset of organizations. Doing so makes the spikes in foundings a bit more dramatic, but does not significantly alter the results presented.

11. We drew a random sample of one hundred organizations, from the list of 657 U.S. national environmental organizations contained in any year in the *Encyclopedia of Associations* in order to develop an estimate of the average lag between the founding of organizations and their inclusion in the *Encyclopedia*. The mean lag between an organization's founding and its inclusion in the *Encyclopedia* is 6.2 years. We do not have a similar estimate for the *Yearbook*. Such lags suggest caution in interpreting the most recent periods in the founding and density patterns we will describe.

12. The results of these analyses can be obtained by contacting the lead author at: ejohnson@pop.psu.edu.

13. In the two populations generated from the *Yearbook* and the *Encyclopedia* we use for analyses, organizations of organizations and organizations without individual members are included. We expect that the proportion of organizations that have individual members will decline as the geographical scope of an SMO expands (see McCarthy, 1997).

14. This estimate is based upon an examination of the cases contained in our dataset of U.S. national environmental SMOs. Of these, thirty-one (4.7 percent) are chapters of organizations included in our database of environmental TSMOs. Another forty-six national organizations (7 percent) include "international" in their title. While some of these organizations are undoubtedly domestically based with an international focus, we include them in our estimate of the percentage of national organizations that are chapters of TSMOs in order to err on the side of inclusion. Approximately 25 percent of local U.S. environmental SMOs are affiliated with national SMOs (Edwards and Andrews, 2002; Kempton et al., 2001). It remains to be seen whether this pattern of higher rates of affiliation at the local than at the state level will be seen in other nations.

15. Similarly, Buttel (2000) notes that many of the types of state environmental protection measured by Frank, Hironaka, and Schofer (2000) have been imposed on developing countries by the World Bank as a condition of receiving loans, suggesting a top-down process but, again, for different reasons than those provided by the world polity model.

16. This enumeration of factors draws heavily upon Keck and Sikkink (1998), Frank, Hironaka, and Schofer (2000), Carmin and Hicks (2002), and Sklair (1997).

17. This figure is a preliminary estimate based upon a coding of all protest events reported in the *New York Times* for that period (Project on the Dynamics of Collective Protest, 1960–1990; Doug McAdam, John McCarthy, Sarah Soule, and Susan Olzak, directors).

5

The Impact of Transnational Protest on Social Movement Organizations: Mass Media and the Making of ATTAC Germany

FELIX KOLB

After the riots of Gothenburg protesters and security forces alike are preparing themselves for the big battle during the world economic summit in July at Genoa. However, the violent minority distracts from the most serious problem of the free trade opponents: They don't have a concept.

—*Der Spiegel* 26/2001

A new, and for the first time truly international generation of protesters is turning the heat on politicians and the heads of multi-national corporations—and justly so. The global economy, powerful and at the same time, prone to crisis, needs new rules.

—*Der Spiegel* 30/2001

TRANSNATIONAL PROTEST AND THE GLOBAL JUSTICE MOVEMENT

Seattle, Prague, Nice, Gothenburg, Genoa, and Cancun—a few years ago these names would have been an arbitrary enumeration of towns. Today these places are widely known as synonyms for the global protest against neoliberal globalization. Moreover, these protests mark the emergence of a new transnational social movement, which represents one of the rather rare cases of transnational collective action (see della Porta and Tarrow in this volume). Erroneously, many journalists and some academics call it the "antiglobalization movement" (e.g., Ruggiero, 2002).[1] I prefer the term *global justice movement*, because it is more accurate. The global justice movement indeed opposes the current form of neoliberal globalization, but it also widely supports global political solutions—such as the Tobin tax, designed to fight the negative consequences of neoliberal globalization and achieve social and economic justice on the national as well as the international level (cf., Kolb, 2001; Aguiton, 2002). The origins of the global justice movement can be traced back to events in the early 1990s, such as the uprising of the Zapatistas in Chiapas, Mexico (Harvey, 1998), or the mass protests against the 1988 International Monetary Fund (IMF) and World Bank meetings in Berlin (Gerhards and Rucht, 1992).[2] Its overall emergence can be explained by environmental, cognitive, and relational changes, as outlined by della Porta and Tarrow in the introductory chapter of this book (see also Rucht, 2003b).

While the literature on transnational contentious politics has been growing rapidly for a number of years, the study of the global justice movement is still in its infancy as part of this new research agenda (cf., Acostavalle et al., 2003). Therefore, it is often overlooked that quite different activities, processes, and organizations are subsumed under the category *global justice movement*. Diffusion is at work when, during so-called global action days, hundreds of local groups all over the world protest the policies of the IMF and the World Bank. When national trade unions protest the reduction of corporate tax rates by their national government to meet pressures from the international financial market, we see an example of domestication. When ATTAC (Association for the Taxation of Financial Transaction for the Aid of Citizens) activists from several European countries gathered in Liege, Belgium, during a Council of Economic and Finance Ministers (ECOFIN) meeting to demand the Tobin tax, we saw an instance of transnational collective action.

Due to this complexity, studying the global justice movement as a whole is an impossible endeavor. Instead, it seems more fruitful to focus on specific processes and movement organizations. In this chapter, I will focus on two forms of transnational collective action that are not often studied together: transnational protest and transnational social movement organizations. While many aspects of the transnational protest events organized by the global justice movement have already received a considerable amount of research, most studies have not theorized on the impact of these protests on the movement's organizations (e.g., Cockburn, Clair, and Sekula, 2000; Levi and Olson, 2000; O'Connor, 2000; Thomas, 2000; Lichbach and Almeida, 2001; Andretta et al., 2003).

In order to overcome these research gaps, this chapter will analyze the emergence of the German branch of the transnational social movement organization ATTAC, and the impact of transnational protest events on its development (cf., Eskola and Kolb, 2002b). My starting point is a striking empirical puzzle in the development of ATTAC Germany. In June 2001—

after eighteen months of sustained mobilizing efforts—ATTAC Germany had only about four hundred dues-paying members and no significant national political standing with the news media, political parties, or the red–green coalition government. Beginning in July, they started attracting approximately one hundred new members per week, and local chapters began popping up like mushrooms. By the end of the year, ATTAC Germany had close to four thousand members. The organization had also gained extraordinarily strong political standing in the national debate on globalization, becoming the single most important organization in the German global justice movement (Brand and Wissen, 2002).

In order to provide a meaningful explanation for these developments, we can rely on a slightly adapted version of the political process theory of social movements (McAdam, 1982; Costain, 1994). In a nutshell, political process theory argues that the trajectory of social movements does not follow a definite series of developmental stages, but is shaped by contentious interactions with its antagonists and by factors originating from the institutionalized political process. Largely overlooked in classical formulations of the theory, two particular factors and their interplay must be included in the model, and are at the heart of my analysis of the development of ATTAC in Germany: the impact of mass media coverage and transnational protest events. Thus, the political process model is extended in a horizontal dimension to include the mass media (cf., Gitlin, 1980) and in a vertical dimension to include international politics (cf., McAdam, 1998).

The timing of the changes in ATTAC's success rate strongly suggests that its sudden increase in membership and visibility might be the consequences of the protests against the European Union (EU) summit in Gothenburg, Sweden, in June 2001 and the massive demonstrations against the G7 summit in Genoa in July (Andretta et al., 2003). In order to provide a causal mechanism for the impact of these transnational protest events, we must turn to the largely neglected role of the mass media in the creation of social movements (Rucht, 1994). I will show that the breakthrough of ATTAC Germany was a direct result of the extensive coverage of its activities and positions by all the major news media outlets, which started very suddenly in the summer of 2001 in the wake of the protests in Genoa. This explanatory approach demonstrates the advantages of setting transnational protest, the impact of news media coverage, and the emergence of social movement organizations in a triadic relationship.

The remainder of the chapter is structured as follows. *First*, I will briefly introduce the data sources and methods used in my analysis. *Second*, I will present a short narrative on the emergence of ATTAC Germany and its initially unsuccessful quest for members and publicity.

Third, I will analyze how in the summer of 2001, a sudden increase in media coverage led to a self-reinforcing process that was responsible for an increase in membership and the transformation of ATTAC Germany into a powerful political actor. *Fourth*, I will analyze the causes of the sudden increase in media coverage, showing how ATTAC Germany used the transnational protests in Gothenburg and Genoa to position itself as an authority, thus increasing media coverage. *Finally*, I will review my findings and discuss their limitations and the possibilities for further research.

METHODS AND DATA

The following analysis of the impact of transnational protest on the emergence of ATTAC Germany is mainly based on four different data sources: *First*, I use monthly data on the number of dues-paying members as an indicator of the growth of ATTAC Germany. *Second*, I use internal e-mails, meeting transcripts, and my personal firsthand experiences as a founding member of ATTAC Germany to document the discussions and decisions taken to promote the growth of the organization.[3] *Third*, I use a dataset constructed from the electronic archives of the daily newspaper *taz, die tageszeitung* to trace coverage on ATTAC Germany and its development as a political actor.[4] The *taz* was founded in 1979 because of the widespread dissatisfaction of new social movement activists with German mainstream media. Over the years, the *taz* has evolved from a mouthpiece of social movements into a professional daily newspaper (cf., Rucht, forthcoming). However, the *taz* continues to cover social movements and their activities more than other newspapers and is still mainly read by an audience very sympathetic to social movements. Therefore, it was the natural candidate to research the impact of news coverage on ATTAC membership. Using LexisNexis, I found that the overall coverage pattern in the other German daily newspapers is not very different from the *taz*.[5] In a further step, I supplemented the dataset with information on the coverage of other major organizations of the global justice movement in the *taz*. *Fourth*, to control empirically for a possible bias in the quantity of the *taz* coverage, I have also counted the number of news reports on ATTAC released by the main news agencies in Germany. The news agencies included in this dataset are the German Press Agency (DPA), the Associated Press (AP), Agence France-Presse (AFP), Reuters, the Evangelischer Pressedienst (epd), and the Inter Press Service (IPS).[6]

THE EMERGENCE OF ATTAC GERMANY AND THE UNSUCCESSFUL QUEST FOR MEMBERS AND PUBLICITY

ATTAC was started in France through an editorial called "Disarming the markets" (Désarmer les marchés), which appeared in the December 1997 issue of the leftist-intellectual monthly Le Monde diplomatique (Cassen, 2003).[7] It called for the formation of a worldwide organization to counter the destructive forces of neoliberal economic globalization. Within weeks after the publication of the editorial, Le Monde diplomatique had received thousands of letters from its readers expressing their support for the launching of a new organization. This deluge motivated the editorial board of Le Monde diplomatique to further develop the idea. In March of 1998, the newspaper organized a preparatory workshop, inviting journalists, economists, law specialists, political scientists, and trade unionists. A few months later, this forum had developed a proposal for the objectives and statutes of ATTAC. Finally, during a constituting assembly on June 3, 1998, ATTAC France was officially founded and its statutes and declaration formally adopted (for the development of ATTAC France, see Ancelovici, 2002).

As envisioned in "Disarming the markets," ATTAC quickly became a transnational social movement organization—defined as "socially mobilized groups with constituents in at least two states, engaged in sustained contentious interaction with power holders in at least one state other than their own, or against an international institution, or a multinational economic actor" (Tarrow, 2001b:11). At a meeting organized by ATTAC France, which took place in Paris on December 11 and 12, 1998, delegations from African, Asian, European, and Latin American countries approved a common declaration entitled "International movement for democratic control of financial markets and their institutions."[8] In the years to follow, ATTAC spread quickly across the globe (Eskola and Kolb, 2002a). It now has branches in more than forty countries with approximately sixty-five thousand dues-paying members worldwide.

The original initiative for ATTAC Germany came in 1999 from Peter Wahl, executive director of the development organization WEED (World Economy Ecology and Development). The preparation group for the first assembly also included representatives from Kairos Europa, a religious organization working on economic global justice issues; Pax Christi, a Christian peace organization; and Share, a small organization started by a half-dozen long-term activists with backgrounds in the environmental and antinuclear movements.[9] The Share activists would later become the first staff members of ATTAC Germany. These organizations jointly invited interested individuals and organizations from a wide range of ideological and political backgrounds to a national meeting in Frankfurt called a "Ratschlag," which took place on January 22, 2000. The one hundred participants, mainly representatives of small national and local organizations, agreed to form the "Network for the democratic control of international financial markets." It was not until the fall of 2000 that the network officially renamed itself ATTAC.

The coordination group ("Koordinierungskreis") met several times to agree on a draft of the platform, discussed at the second national meeting on April 14 and 15 in Hannover. The meeting focused around three issues: *first*, on the problems of international financial markets and the Tobin tax as a possible solution; *second*, on the problem of tax havens and the impact of tax evasion on national economies and social justice; and *third*, on the consequences of privatizing the German pension system, a measure being considered by the German government.

The next landmark was on May 31, when ATTAC organized a press conference and introduced its finalized platform, the "Declaration for the democratic control of internal financial markets"—which at that point had been signed by fifty (mostly small) organizations and a couple of rather prominent individuals. The event received only minor coverage, however; the *taz*, for example, ran only a seventy-two-word facetious piece titled "ATTAC-Alliance with Visions."[10] Very slow progress was made over the following months, and several of the organizers became frustrated. At the end of the year, the results were sobering: Only 266 individuals and organizations had signed the declaration and agreed to pay a yearly contribution. Only two local groups had been formed—one in Frankfurt and one in Hamburg—and in both cases, members of the national coordination group had taken a leading role. ATTAC was unable to influence or even enter the debate about the privatization of the German pension system. The *taz* ran only one extremely short story, "Postcards against Pension Reform," although its coverage of the overall pension reform debate was extensive.[11] No one in the German government considered ATTAC a serious political actor or an expert on globalization.

The new year brought several new developments that promised to improve the situation. *First*, the organizers of Share decided to stop working to build their own organization, which clearly had competed for members, and offered to direct their energies fully toward ATTAC. The coordination group, while cautious about the potential growth in Share's influence within the organization, nonetheless took them up on their offer. That meant that in January 2001, the equivalent of four full-time organizers started working in the ATTAC office in Verden, a small town in northern Germany where Share was based. *Second*, the coordinating group decided to focus on membership recruitment rather than mobilizing people to sign the declaration. This turned out to be the first step away from a network structure and toward the hybrid of umbrella organization and mass membership organization that ATTAC Germany would become in the years to come. *Third*, a decision was made to intensify public relations work. ATTAC started to use advertisements and direct mailings and, for the first time, designated a press spokesperson.

Although these changes improved the performance of ATTAC, they did not have the expected impact—in terms of either new members or political influence. Between January and June 2001, only 149 new members were recruited. Of particular interest were the generally unsuccessful attempts to stage protests as a means of attracting news coverage. The most spectacular action took place on April 25, when three ATTAC staff members walked into a press conference being held by the German secretary of labor to introduce a new report on wealth and poverty in Germany. Before live television cameras, they held up a banner demanding a progressive tax policy to fight poverty. Although some newspapers printed a photograph, not one article mentioned the action or ATTAC's critique, although a press release had been handed out during the action and was sent via e-mail and fax to a large number of journalists and news agencies. Further attempts were only slightly more successful. ATTAC and its claims remained largely uninteresting to journalists. The returns from direct mailings and advertisements in political magazines were equally disappointing.

MASS MEDIA AND THE MAKING
OF ATTAC GERMANY

The argument could well have stopped there, if ATTAC Germany had continued its rather unsuccessful trajectory after June 2001. Within a few months, however, everything had changed, and ATTAC was ultimately named "movement of the year" by the German weekly *Der Stern*. I will start this section by contrasting ATTAC Germany after June/July 2001 with its previous situation, described in the section above. I will show that we cannot understand these changes without considering the news media as a political actor on its own, or its role in the political process. The growth of ATTAC was a direct consequence of a very sudden increase in media coverage, which eventually became a self-reinforcing upward spiral (cf., Gitlin, 1980).

The most dramatic quantitative measure of the changes in the development of ATTAC Germany is the development of its membership, as shown in figure 5.1. From January until June 2001, approximately thirty

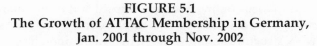

FIGURE 5.1
The Growth of ATTAC Membership in Germany,
Jan. 2001 through Nov. 2002

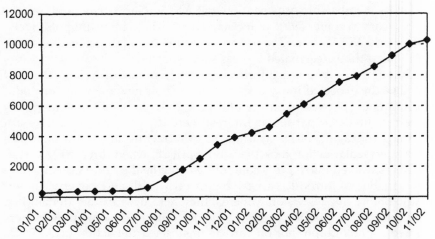

people joined ATTAC Germany each month. That was only slightly more than in the month before they intensified their PR work in the spring of 2001. Suddenly, however, the numbers went up. In June, about two hundred people enrolled, and from then on an average of 560 people joined each month—a trend that has continued to the present. Soon thereafter, starting in early August, political actors suddenly began to recognize ATTAC as a legitimate player and even as a challenger. While Germany's Green foreign minister Joschka Fischer accused ATTAC and the whole global justice movement of engaging in "stale anticapitalism" (*abgestandener Anti-Kapitalismus*), the party soon realized that it had neglected to address the negative consequences of globalization in its politics and tried to align itself with ATTAC.

For its part, ATTAC made very clear that it would not allow either the Green Party or the Social Democrats to instrumentalize it for their purposes, heavily attacking both the Green Party and the red–green coalition government (Koufen and Koch, 2001). At about this time, the Green Party had started the process of revising its decade-old party platform (the Grundsatzprogramm); ATTAC used the occasion to actively frame the debate about neoliberal globalization.[12] Representatives of ATTAC were invited to roundtable discussions with government officials, private conversations with Green Party leaders, and public discussions, which were covered in the newspapers and electronic media. Today, ATTAC Germany remains an organization that can influence the political agenda and force political parties and the government to respond to its claims. In short, ATTAC was finally able to succeed in one of the two dimensions of movement outcomes identified by William Gamson. This dimension, to use Gamson's words, "focuses on the acceptance of a challenging group by its antagonists as a valid spokesman for a legitimate set of interests" (1975:28). But what was responsible for these extraordinary changes?

The first, but—as I will argue shortly—not completely satisfactory answer is that the changes were brought about by the sudden and extremely remarkable increase in media coverage. As shown in figure 5.2, the coverage of ATTAC in the *taz* skyrocketed in the span of a few weeks.[13] It first peaked in August 2001 with eighteen articles, remaining at a fairly high level—with an average of ten articles per month—throughout the remaining time included in my dataset.[14] The *taz* had published only eight articles with a total of fifteen hundred words on ATTAC Germany in its first eighteen months of existence, but in the three-month period from July to September of 2001, it published twenty-eight articles with sixty-five hundred words. That number would likely have been even higher, but for the events of September 11. As shown in figure 5.3, the same basic pattern can be seen in the news agencies' coverage of ATTAC.[15]

FIGURE 5.2
Number of Articles on ATTAC Published in the *taz*,
Jan. 2000–Dec. 2002

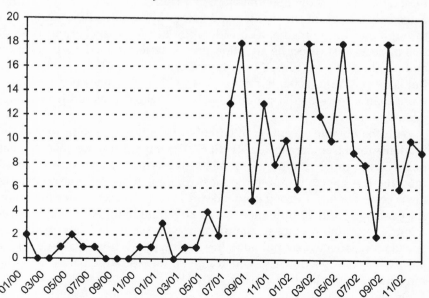

FIGURE 5.3
Number of Reports on ATTAC Generated by the Main News Agencies, by Month, Jan. 2000–Dec. 2002

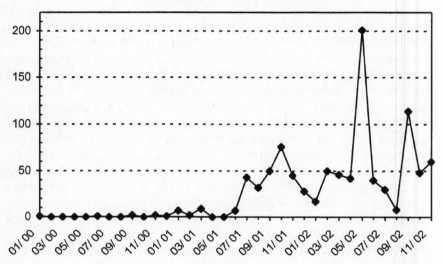

Thus, I agree with Albrecht von Lucke (2002) and others (e.g., Koufen, 2002; Rucht, 2002b) that the emergence of ATTAC Germany has to be understood as a media phenomenon. "ATTAC is thus above all one thing: a product for and of the media. And since ATTAC effectively only exists through and in the media, a consideration of the prospects and risks of this project must direct its attention primarily to the media's perception and production of ATTAC" (von Lucke, 2002:169, author's translation). But, as Peter Wahl (2002) has suggested, ATTAC has since become much more than a mere media product, or it undoubtedly would have disappeared by now.

With the notable exception of Gitlin's 1980 study on the history of the Students for a Democratic Society (SDS), the impact of news coverage has not received much attention as a factor in recruitment patterns of social movement organizations. On the most fundamental level, the content of news coverage has a strong influence on whether citizens can even imagine exerting political influence. News coverage that gives social movements a prominent place in the discourse on public policies, or depicts populations affected by public policy as potential agents, can encourage a sense of collective agency, which in turn makes participation in social movements more likely (Gamson, 2001:61f.).

On the organizational level, people are clearly more likely to join an organization they have heard of and think is important and successful, both of which are to some degree a function of news coverage. This second, more specific effect of news coverage had a smaller impact until recently, because it is a long way from reading about a social movement organization in the newspaper to becoming a member. It required that the interested party somehow find out the organization's address and then call or write to ask for a membership form. To facilitate this process, canvassing, direct mailing, and other such techniques remained the central means of getting new members. But since about the mid-1990s, widespread use of the Internet has changed the situation in a fundamental way. Using search engines like Google, it has become extremely easy and cheap to find the website of an organization and to join online. And indeed, more than 50 percent of members join ATTAC Germany through the Internet.[16] Thus, the spread of the Internet has dramatically increased the effectiveness of news coverage in recruiting new members, because to paraphrase Daniel Myers (2000), it increases the probability that information transmitted through the media will lead individuals to become members.[17]

Once the coverage started and membership began to grow, there was a consequent increase in the available resources to engage in more conventional means of recruitment, leading to more growth, which in turn became the basis of more news stories. A cycle was also triggered such that once some newspapers began covering ATTAC, others began to run stories as well, out of fear of missing a "scoop." These processes, coupled with an initial overestimation of ATTAC's political significance, led to a self-reinforcing process (Rucht, 2002b).

Outlining the mechanisms by which media coverage gained momentum once it started, however, still leaves unanswered the question of why the coverage took off so suddenly when it did. In order to answer this question, we must turn to the media studies literature. In the following, I draw on Charlotte Ryan's excellent book on the media strategies of social movements (1991). While there is as yet no unified theory about the determinants of news coverage, three partly competing and partly complementary paradigms provide helpful starting points for explaining ATTAC's sudden rise in the media.[18]

1. *The gatekeeper/organization model* is the earliest, and still very influential theoretical model used in media studies (cf., Ryan, 1991:11ff.). It attributes the determination of patterns of news coverage to the production routines of the news media and to the journalist's role as a gatekeeper who applies professional standards to decide what is newsworthy. The more an event corresponds to so-called news factors such as numbers, novelty, and violence, the more likely it is to

make the news. Because especially in their early stages, social movements lack other resources—such as prominence or expertise—they
must rely heavily on organizing protests as a way of getting media
coverage (Goldenberg, 1975; Oliver and Myers, 1999:74). But protest
by no means guarantees media attention, as ATTAC's experience
and other systematic research have shown (e.g., Oliver and Maney,
2000). Movement organizations, according to the gatekeeper model,
can also influence the likelihood of coverage by following certain
rules, such as those governing the timing and preferred format of
press releases. These factors clearly played a role in ATTAC's late
media success (Koufen, 2002), but because ATTAC was already playing by these rules before coverage spread and intensified, the *gate-
keeper/organization model* falls short of providing a satisfactory
explanation for ATTAC's sudden media breakthrough.

2. *The cultural studies model* "stresses media as an arena of ideological
struggle in which social forces contend to define an issue and its significance" (Ryan, 1991:18). The idea of *news frames* is a central concept in this tradition. The predominant *news frame* in a certain issue
area determines on a very fundamental level the ways in which real
world events are presented, which aspects are emphasized, and
which are left out. In a certain sense, they are the media's equivalent
of the master frames used by social movements (cf., Snow and Benford, 1992). A social movement can only expect to get sympathetic
or at least neutral coverage if its frame corresponds to, or at least is
not too much at odds with, the predominant news frame. This
approach might explain why ATTAC Germany was later able to gain
greater coverage than other organizations like the Peoples Global
Action (PGA) and the Bundeskoordination entwicklungspolitischer
Aktionsgruppen (BUKO) (Kleffner, Koufen, and Von Oppen, 2001).
But because ATTAC Germany has not *changed* its framing, this theory
cannot explain the sudden change in coverage.

3. *The media attention cycle* model stresses that public attention and
news coverage on certain issues are not constant, but vary greatly
over time (Hilgartner and Bosk, 1988), accounting for great differences in the selection bias with respect to protest events over time
and across issues (Oliver and Maney, 2000). In this model, social
movement organizations are thought to be unable to influence the
media attention cycle, and therefore their coverage in the news
media is partially dependent on it (McCarthy, McPhail, and Smith,
1996:494). Using this model, one could theorize that ATTAC profited
from a sudden shift in the media attention cycle toward the general
issue of globalization. To test this hypothesis, I have counted the
number of reports on globalization between 1990 and 2002 (see fig-

ure 5.4). There was a steep increase in the mid-1990s, and again around the turn of the century. The increase in stories between 2000 and 2001 suggests that the media attention cycle indeed shifted toward globalization, and that ATTAC began to receive coverage it was not able to get before. But if we look at the same change on a monthly basis (see figure 5.5), we see that the increase in coverage on ATTAC was parallel with the increase in coverage on globalization. Thus, it is impossible to determine on the basis of these data whether the changes in the media attention cycle were responsible for the increase in ATTAC coverage, or whether ATTAC contributed to the changes in the media attention cycle.

To summarize, the sudden growth of ATTAC Germany seems to have been largely the consequence of an equally sudden increase in news coverage of ATTAC, its activities, and its political positions in German mass media outlets. This increase in coverage was accompanied, but may or may not have been caused, by a shift in the media attention cycle toward the phenomenon of globalization, which made ATTAC's activities and positions more newsworthy than only a couple of months or even weeks before. The increase in coverage finally led to a self-reinforcing interaction between increased media coverage, rapid growth, increased political importance, more activity, and in turn more coverage.

FIGURE 5.4
Number of Articles on Globalization, by Year, Published in the *taz*, 1990–2002

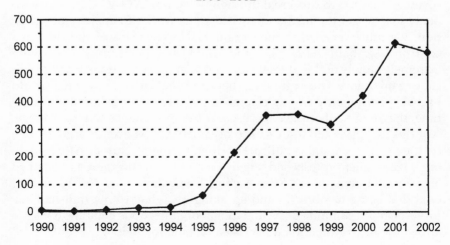

FIGURE 5.5
Number of Articles on Globalization Published in the *taz*, by Month,
November 1999–December 2001

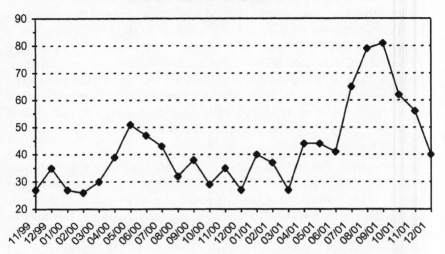

TRANSNATIONAL PROTEST EVENTS AS POLITICAL OPPORTUNITIES FOR DOMESTIC MOVEMENT ORGANIZATIONS

Although I have provided an explanation in the previous section for the sudden breakthrough of ATTAC Germany in terms of growth and political significance, I have yet to explain the extraordinary increase in media coverage that led to this breakthrough. Why was ATTAC Germany suddenly able to get the media interested in its work? To answer this question, we must recall that the organizers were aware of the dilemma confronting them. They saw that their membership was growing extremely slowly and that they were not being taken seriously as a political organization. The organizers believed that media coverage would probably be the only way to change this state of affairs; but at the same time, they had neither the expertise nor the prominence to get coverage. Nor did they have the resources to organize protest events large enough or spectacular enough to attract serious media attention. Attempts to organize smaller protests had largely failed to gain coverage, as described above. In the remainder of this section, I will show how ATTAC discovered that being involved in and speaking on behalf of big transnational protests at the summits of supranational organizations could be a way to attract the media attention it had been seeking for so long.

Although the huge protests against the World Trade Organization (WTO) ministerial meeting in Seattle had much less impact on European public opinion and the global justice movement than they did in the United States and Canada, the organizers of ATTAC Germany did regard protests targeting international summits as a valuable strategy (cf., Rucht, 2003a). Many other ATTAC branches were already actively involved in organizing counter-summit protests and activities. ATTAC France had organized protests against the EU summit in Nice in December 2000. ATTAC Switzerland was active in organizing protests against the World Economic Forum (WEF) in Davos. ATTAC was also at the forefront in organizing the World Social Forum (WSF), first held in January 2001 in Porto Alegre, Brazil, and designed as a distance counter-summit to the WEF (Kolb, 2002; Cassen, 2003). But these, as well as later protests such as those in Prague, were treated by the German news media as events unrelated to German politics and therefore granted only limited coverage. One reason for this is that the summits were covered by the papers' foreign correspondents, who were based in the cities or countries in which the protests took place and who had no knowledge of (and likely no interest in) the German global justice movement.

Unfortunately for ATTAC Germany, these protests were also not related to their movement, since in 2000 and early 2001 they were able to send only a handful of individuals to the protests in Davos, Prague, and Gothenburg—despite the fact that probably thousands of German activists participated in each of these events. These individuals were mobilized and organized by other groups within the global justice movement, including the PGA, BUKO, Linksruck (the German branch of the International Socialist Organization), and autonomous groups and networks from the radical Left.[19] At that time, ATTAC members were simply not the types of people who would take a twelve-hour bus trip to take part in a demonstration.

This situation began to change very rapidly and fundamentally after the June 2001 protests against the EU summit in Gothenburg, which drew approximately twenty-five thousand protesters from Sweden and neighboring countries, including an estimated one thousand Germans.[20] The protests were organized by a coalition of groups including ATTAC Sweden, but ATTAC Germany had not been involved in the mobilization in Germany. Although overwhelmingly nonviolent, the protests turned into riots and led to the destruction of a famous shopping mall in Gothenburg. The Gothenburg police, unused to any form of violent protest and ill-prepared to deal with it, grossly overreacted, using live ammunition and seriously injuring three demonstrators, one of them German (Wolff, 2001).[21] Among the nine hundred protesters who were arrested and the hundred or so injured by truncheons were many Germans. Police forces stormed into a school that was being used as a dormitory, injuring several people. Such an eruption of political violence was unprecedented in Sweden, and it had been decades since Europe had experienced police shooting at protesters. This violence produced several different reactions. The interior ministers of the EU met at a special summit on July 13, but could not agree on a common framework for travel restriction and thus left it to each country to decide on such measures.[22]

Suddenly, German journalists started to wonder who these "crazy guys" (*verrückte Kerle*) were, and what they could possibly want. Although only a handful of ATTAC Germany members had participated in the protests, they were ready and willing to talk to journalists whenever they got the chance, as a representative organization of the global justice movement stressing its international character. In this context, ATTAC was also immediately confronted with the violence question and had to take a position on this difficult issue. After a controversial debate, the coordination group published a discussion paper, which quickly became ATTAC Germany's position paper on protest violence.[23] The paper emphasized ATTAC's exclusive commitment to nonviolent strategies and tactics, while at the same it avoided openly condemning militant tactics by pointing to the police and neoliberal globalization as the causes of the violence. This positioning was deemed essential for the increasing and overwhelmingly positive coverage ATTAC would receive in the weeks and months to come, in which ATTAC was generally portrayed as one of the nonviolent groups within the global justice movement.

In early spring 2001, long before the Gothenburg protests, ATTAC Germany had decided for the first time in its history to take an active role in mobilizing for a transnational protest event, in this case the demonstrations being planned against the G8 meeting in Genoa, Italy, on July 20–22 (cf., Andretta et al., 2003; Ullrich, 2003). The organizing coalition, comprising around twenty groups, developed its own platform; many groups within the coalition hired their own buses, as did ATTAC. In the wake of the events in Gothenburg, there was now an unprecedented level of media interest in the preparations and likely format of the protests, which were expected to again turn violent. This trend is most clearly illustrated by the big, sensational story entitled "Auf nach Genua" ("On to Genoa"), run by the influential German weekly newsmagazine *Der Spiegel* (26/2001).

Aware of this increased media interest in the aftermath of Gothenburg, ATTAC saw a chance to establish itself as a major actor in the German global justice movement. This conclusion was primarily the result of a transnational learning process. The breakthrough of ATTAC in Sweden had been spurred by the intensive coverage of the protests against the IMF and World Bank meetings in Prague, the result of an elaborate media campaign conducted by ATTAC Sweden. Oliver Moldenhauer, one of the core organizers of ATTAC Germany, learned about this media campaign during the Prague protests and later in personal conversations, when a member of ATTAC Sweden visited its sister organization (Moldenhauer, 2003). The challenge for ATTAC Germany in using the formula was to position itself as an authoritative spokesorganization for the protests, despite the fact that ATTAC Germany was still a minor organization and unlikely to mobilize more than a busload of its own members and activists. The key to meeting this challenge would be an excellent press campaign. The press concept had several key components:[24]

- ATTAC offered to let journalists ride on the buses with the protesters on their way to Genoa, in order to make the journey itself a newsworthy event. This worked. About fifteen journalists accepted the offer, among them reporters for major newspapers like *Süddeutsche Zeitung* and *Der Spiegel*. As a result, many of these journalists covered ATTAC in their papers.
- ATTAC Germany also offered journalists the chance to sign up for special services during the Genoa protests. They could enlist to receive a daily e-mail newsletter, which ATTAC established to disseminate in-depth information, or they could be on a Short Message Service (SMS)-distribution list for frequent and up-to-date information about the exact locations of upcoming demonstrations and actions. It turned out there was great demand for these services among journalists, many of whom had not known about or ever reported on ATTAC before.
- ATTAC was prepared to provide interview partners, available for live interviews at the scenes of the protests in Genoa and in Germany. For that reason, and in order to manage the other services, the press spokesperson stayed in the national office in Germany.

The concept worked perfectly. The anticipated problems at the borders entering Switzerland and Italy in fact helped ATTAC turn "Genoa" into a newsworthy story even before the protests began. Within a couple of days, ATTAC published seven press releases. They were carefully drafted and sometimes suggested that all the German protesters were affiliated with ATTAC, even though probably only fifty of the 150 traveling in ATTAC's three buses were actually members or active in a local chapter. For example, a press release issued two weeks before the protests was entitled: "ATTAC: On to Genoa. Around 1,000 critics of globalization participate in the protests against the world economic summit."[25] Over the next several days, during which more than three hundred thousand people took part in demonstrations and actions, one protester was shot dead, and hundreds were wounded and mistreated by the police, ATTAC continued its intensive media campaign (della Porta and Tarrow, 2001).

The success of the strategy linking ATTAC with the protests in Genoa can be clearly seen in figure 5.6, which shows the weekly coverage of ATTAC from June to August 2001.[26] This was only a tiny fraction of the overall coverage of the protests in Genoa. I argue that the G7 summit and the accompanying protests in Genoa were an international political opportunity, which ATTAC Germany was able to use because it succeeded in linking itself with these protests in the mass media (Tarrow, 2001b). This explains the sudden increase of ATTAC coverage in the *taz* as well as in news agencies' reports. However, it is also important to recall two contextual factors: *first*, political violence always creates extensive coverage, but can easily backfire when initiated by the demonstrators (Kliment, 1996). In the case of Genoa, the police violence overshadowed that of the protesters; thus, coverage was generated and a backlash prevented. *Second*, the extent of media interest and coverage was also the result of the fact that the G8 summit took place during the summer ("Sommerloch"), a slow season for the German news media.

It is interesting to note that the protest coverage was a door-opener, but that afterward ATTAC became less dependent on protest events to get media attention (cf., figure 5.7). Thus, the protests in Genoa, and other transnational protests in general, functioned more to shift media attention to ATTAC and globalization issues than to provide actual occasions for

FIGURE 5.6
Number of Articles on ATTAC Published per Week in the *taz*,
June–August 2001

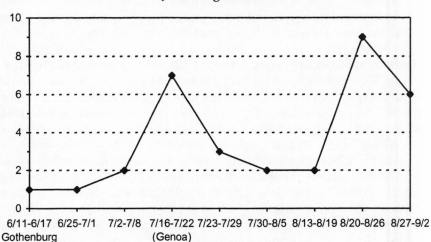

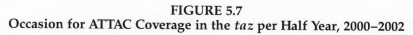

FIGURE 5.7
Occasion for ATTAC Coverage in the *taz* per Half Year, 2000–2002

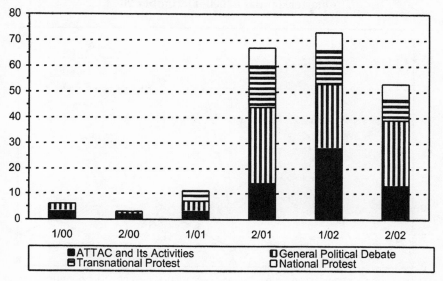

coverage. Coming back to figure 5.5 and the changes in the media attention cycle regarding globalization, it seems plausible to argue that the protests in Genoa were responsible for the observed increase in coverage.

While ATTAC Germany benefited so extraordinarily from the protests in Gothenburg and Genoa, other organizations of the German global justice movement did not, despite the fact that most were older and stronger in terms of members and active local groups, and had either been more instrumental in the mobilizations or had previously built a much greater reputation of expertise. This discrepancy was noticed by these groups as well, and led to sometimes harsh critiques of ATTAC by more radical groups like the PGA and BUKO (e.g., Stock, 2001; Habermann, 2002; Wissen, 2002). Many of the more moderate organizations and campaigns, like WEED and Jubilee 2000, were already or became members of ATTAC Germany and somehow accepted its status as the de facto umbrella organization of the German global justice movement. Figure 5.8 shows the coverage of ATTAC in comparison to five other major organizations of the global justice movement. The coverage of the PGA, BUKO, and Jubilee 2000 was so infrequent that I grouped them in the category *others*. Two facts are particularly striking. *First*, the coverage of these organizations did not increase significantly after Genoa, as ATTAC's did. *Second*, their coverage before Genoa was more extensive than ATTAC's. The following

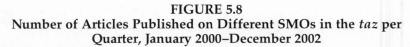

FIGURE 5.8
Number of Articles Published on Different SMOs in the *taz* per
Quarter, January 2000–December 2002

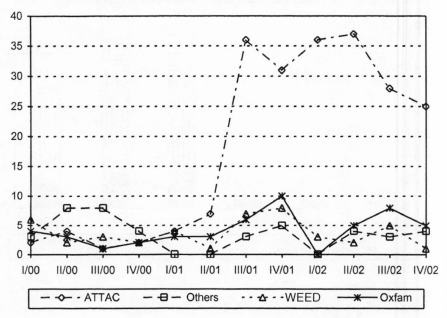

factors likely contributed to ATTAC's success and the failure of the other organizations (cf., Gamson and Wolfsfeld, 1993):

- After the protests against the EU summit in Gothenburg, German journalists were already looking for an organization they could turn into the "national champion." ATTAC's moderate agenda and specific policy proposals were more appealing to journalists and their readers than the anticapitalist rhetoric of groups like the PGA, or the neo-Marxist analyses of BUKO. "The media like ATTAC, because they can hide their own opinions behind its critical quips, because ATTAC sounds short and concise and, well like 'Attack!' And because ATTAC makes concrete demands. Not like earlier movements 'abolish capitalism' or 'build a better world,' but rather 'introduce a financial transactions tax!' That's much easier to convey to the willing reader or spectator" (Koufen, 2002, author's translation). At the same time, it was not just a normal and well-known advocacy group like WEED or Oxfam, but a new organization, which appeared to be actively involved in the mobilization of the protests.

- ATTAC Germany never had a problem with working with journalists, whereas many of the more radical groups did not seriously consider the use of the mainstream media, which they believed to be structurally disinclined to accurately portray their political perspectives.[27] Although ATTAC was not the only group with a coherent and well-implemented media strategy, it provided the most systematic and comprehensive services to journalists.
- Especially for the early reports and interviews, ATTAC Germany's credibility was strengthened by the fact that it belonged to a bigger and more important transnational social movement organization. For example, several other ATTAC branches—in particular France and Italy—had played an important role in the Genoa Social Forum (GSF), which organized the protests in Genoa (Andretta et al., 2003).

To summarize, ATTAC Germany realized that the significant increase in media attention after the protests in Gothenburg provided a window of opportunity. In response, it intensified its efforts to organize around the G7/8 meeting in Genoa and to develop a comprehensive press strategy. Due to the Gothenburg protests, German journalists were already looking desperately for a German organization they could turn into a "national champion." Thus, they were more than willing to accept ATTAC as a representative voice of the protesters. The emergence of ATTAC as the central organization for the global justice movement in Germany in the weeks and months after Genoa is the result of this convergence of interests between ATTAC and the news media.

CONCLUSION

My findings strongly support the notion that—as in the EU—international summits of supranational institutions such as the WTO, the IMF, or the G7 are of central importance for the making and mobilization of transnational social movements (see e.g., Helfferich and Kolb, 2001). They provide a forum around which social movements can organize transnational protest events and serve as visible proxies for supranational institutions, and for abstract concepts like neoliberal globalization or the global capitalist class. These protest events can become short-term windows of opportunity, especially where they become so massive or violent that they create a sense of a political crisis (Keeler, 1993:440). I have shown that the opportunities generated by the summits of the EU in Gothenburg and of the G7 in Genoa were of central importance for the successful development of ATTAC Germany, and I assume that a similar case could be made for the overall genesis of the global justice movement in many countries.

My chapter also demonstrates that we need to integrate the study of protest and the study of movement organizations to explore the impact of transnational protests on the global justice movement. Although it is not very common in social movement theory to study the two in combination, this approach provides interesting and important insights into the dynamics of social movements.[28]

Protest and organizations are linked in at least two important ways. *First*, social movement organizations are extremely important in organizing protests—especially in the case of large-scale or transnational protests, which require considerable resources and coordination (cf., Andretta et al., 2003). *Second*, protest events—especially if covered in the mass media—can have a significant impact on the development and emergence of social movement organizations (cf., Everett, 1992).

However, it is important to note that this is not meant to be a deterministic argument. The impact of transnational protest events on domestic social movements depends on the overall extent and framing of the coverage, the way the coverage of the protest is linked to certain social movement organizations, and the structure of the domestic global justice movement. My findings suggest that the impact varies along at least three different dimensions:

1. The impact of the same transnational protest event on social movements can be quite different from country to country. Whereas the protests against the IMF and World Bank meetings in Prague were important for the development of the Swedish branch of ATTAC, they were totally irrelevant for ATTAC Germany. This anecdotal evidence is supported by new research, which shows that the extent of coverage of the same transnational protests varies greatly in different countries (Rucht, 2003a).

2. The impact of transnational protest on social movement organizations is not necessarily positive. Rather, a protest event that had a positive impact on an organization in one country can have a negative impact on the same organization in another country. The protests against the EU summit in Gothenburg provide a paradigmatic case: Whereas the impact was extremely positive for the German ATTAC branch, because it brought the global justice movement onto the national political agenda, it was devastating for ATTAC Sweden. Although they were not involved in the riots that occurred during the protests, the public held them responsible for the destruction. Consequently, ATTAC Sweden lost half of its members and the government became much less open to its claims.

3. The impact of transnational protest also varies between social movement organizations within the same country. Transnational protest

events provide an opportunity for some organizations under certain circumstances. As I have shown within the German global justice movement, only ATTAC could gain significant media coverage as a consequence of Genoa.

Although further research is needed to come to strong conclusions, I suggest that the impact of transnational protest in the media depends on various factors. *First,* organizations need a clear media strategy to make use of transnational protests. *Second,* transnational organizations with well-known branches in other countries are more likely to be covered in relation to transnational protest. *Third,* on the one hand, organizations must be radical enough to plausibly claim involvement in the protests, while at the same time convincingly distancing themselves from violence. On the other hand, organizations must not have a political agenda that is so radical that it alienates journalists and the mainstream public.

My research on the emergence of ATTAC underlines the importance of the mass media in social movement politics. As I have argued, the impact of transnational protest cannot be properly understood without paying close attention to that dynamic. Unfortunately, this is still a neglected field in social movement research (Rucht, 1994; Walgrave and Manssens, 2000) and in particular in the study of transnational contention.[29] My research suggests that past judgments about the role of the mass media in fostering social movements have been too one-sided and pessimistic (e.g., Molotch, 1979). For one thing, my findings clearly contradict the claim that mass media outlets only begin to take an interest in social movements after they have already achieved legitimacy in the political sphere (Olien, Tichenor, and Donohue, 1989). At least in the case of ATTAC Germany, the reverse occurred: the extensive media coverage established ATTAC Germany as a legitimate claims maker. Although the trajectory of social movements is shaped by the mass media, among other things, they are not simply constrained by the media, nor are they merely victims of the overall media attention cycle (McCarthy, McPhail, and Smith, 1996:494). The impact of the protests in Gothenburg and Genoa as documented in this chapter suggests that social movements can also at times actively influence the media attention cycle (cf., Beyeler and Kriesi, 2003).

My findings also suggest the need for a much better understanding of the determinants of the mass media's coverage of protest and social movements. Recent studies, which have shown that media bias in reporting protest events varies over time and across issues, strongly support this claim (cf., McCarthy, McPhail, and Smith, 1996; Oliver and Maney, 2000; Hocke, 2001). Such a line of inquiry could become a starting point for addressing such questions as: Would another movement organization with similar resources, in similar political circumstances, and putting forward a similar mainstream frame, receive a similar amount of coverage? Does the reliance on protest for getting media coverage increase or decrease as a movement organization becomes more established? How much discretion do sympathetic journalists have in determining the extent and content of coverage compared to editorial policies and patterns of media ownership? Are there systematic differences between print and electronic media coverage of social movements? And how important is the level of professionalization in the public relations work of social movement organizations compared to content of the conveyed message, or the media attention cycle in determining which movement will get the coverage they seek? The transnational character of the global justice movement makes it an excellent subject for systematic comparative research, which is necessary to answer these questions.

NOTES

I would like to thank Sid Tarrow and the Institute for European Studies for the inspiration and the resources they provided me to carry out this research project. I am grateful also to Mark Anner, Sven Giegold, Marco Hauptmeier, Jai Kwan Jung, Heidi Klein, Darcy Leach, Doug McAdam, Erik Nisbet, Donatella della Porta, Silke Roth, Markus Schallhas, Dieter Rucht, and Sid Tarrow for important comments on earlier versions of this chapter, and to Cornelia Reetz for her help in coding the newspaper data. And thanks lastly to Sarah Tarrow and Darcy Leach for proofreading and editing the text for readability in English.

1. Another misnomer for the global justice movement sometimes used in the academic literature is the term *anticapitalist movement* (e.g., Desai and Said, 2001). I do not contest that some groups involved in the *global justice movement* are anticapitalist. However, the vast majority of organizations and individuals are not, or at least not explicitly, and therefore to name the whole movement "anticapitalist" is inaccurate.

2. However, until the late 1990s, the various activities and campaigns weren't widely publicized and were not seen as part of a coherent movement. The public breakthrough, at least in the United States and Canada, happened during the protests against the WTO ministerial meeting in Seattle in December 1999. The events also helped to heighten public attention in Europe, but the real public breakthrough only occurred in the summer of 2001, as the massive protests against the world economic summit in Genoa put the European global justice movement in the spotlight of the mainstream media for many weeks (cf., Rucht, 2003a).

3. I was a founding member of ATTAC Germany and worked in the ATTAC national office as the media spokesperson from January 2001 to July 2002. In this capacity, I also attended several European and worldwide ATTAC planning and coordination meetings and was able to talk to ATTAC organizers from different countries.

4. As a first step in compiling the dataset, I identified 484 articles containing the phrase "ATTAC" between 1997 and the end of 2002. I then eliminated all articles that had either appeared in one of the three local sections of the *taz*, or which contained the phrase "ATTAC" but were not at all about ATTAC, its history, positions, or activities. This left 237 articles published between 12/12/97 and 12/31/02. Next, I realized that almost all of the fifteen articles that appeared before January 2000 (when ATTAC Germany was founded) were from the *Le Monde diplomatique* (*LMD*), the German-speaking edition of which is published by the *taz*. Because the editorial policy of the *LMD* is independent from the *taz* and many of the *LMD* articles were published before ATTAC Germany was founded, I decided to exclude all twenty-three *LMD* articles from the dataset. I finally arrived at a dataset of 214 articles containing at least some substantive information on ATTAC or its history, activities, and positions. The final dataset contains all of the 213 published articles on ATTAC, its history, activities, and positions from 1/1/00 to 12/31/02.

5. In contrast, I would expect to find great differences in the kind of coverage, which, however, is not relevant to my research question.

6. I am grateful to Malte Kreutzfeld for letting me use his dataset.

7. For general literature on ATTAC, see Cassen (2003), Eskola and Kolb (2002b; 2002a), George (2002), and Ruggiero (2002). For further accounts of the emergence of ATTAC Germany, see Grefe, Greffrath, and Schumann (2002) and Leggewie (2003).

8. www.attac.org/indexen/index.html.

9. The funding for this meeting and a considerable part of the first year's budget were provided by a small Berlin-based progressive foundation.

10. *taz* nr. 6157 from June 6, 2000.

11. *taz* nr. 6323 from Dec. 15, 2000.

12. *taz* nr. 6532 from Aug. 25, 2001.

13. Although the content and the absolute volume of coverage in other major newspapers differ, a preliminary LexisNexis search, as well as my experience as the press spokesperson of ATTAC Germany during this time, have confirmed that the overall pattern of coverage was very similar.

14. The significant drop in coverage in July and August 2002 shown in figures 5.2 and 5.3 is mainly due to repeated turnover in ATTAC's spokesperson position during this period.

15. The overall number of reports is higher for several reasons. *First*, more than one news agency may cover the same event. *Second*, when covering an important event, news agencies send several updated reports on the same event. The peak in May 2002 resulted mainly from two big events. ATTAC took an active part in the protests against U.S. President Bush's visit in Berlin, and it held a national meeting where it discussed and voted on a new platform.

16. I have calculated this number by using data provided on the website of ATTAC Germany under www.attac.de/gnuplot/formmail/formmail.dat.

17. Sometimes newspapers even print the URL at the end of an article or integrate it into the article. When being visited by camera teams, ATTAC organizers also tried to produce some footage from banners or posters with the URL. For the general importance of the Internet in the work of ATTAC, see Le Grignou (2002).

18. I exclude what Charlotte Ryan (1991) has called the propaganda model of media access for social movements. Since I only focus on one newspaper, it is not helpful here. However, it could turn out to be extremely fruitful in explaining the sometimes exclusively negative tone in the coverage of ATTAC by different media outlets.

19. cf., *taz* nr. 6473 from June 18, 2001.

20. cf., *taz* nr. 6470 from June, 14, 2001.

21. Whereas fifteen thousand policemen were ordered to protect the summit in Nice, in Gothenburg the number was as low as fifteen hundred (*taz* nr. 6470 from June 14, 2001).

22. *taz* nr. 6496 from July 14, 2001.

23. ATTAC France also published a similar statement.

24. This concept was basically copied in future transnational protest events in Brussels, Barcelona, and Luxembourg.

25. www.attac.de/presse/presse_ausgabe.php?id = 21.

26. The second peak in late August was the result of the interactions between ATTAC and the Green Party, which failed in its efforts to co-opt this new movement.

27. An impression that might be actually true, because the research on the media's ownership structure and the political content of its coverage tends to support the belief that radical views on either side of the spectrum won't receive sympathetic coverage, in which case a media strategy may only really pay off for more moderate groups, regardless of their attitude or level of professionalization.

28. The study of protest and the study of organizations are virtually separate fields in social movement theory: the study of social movement organizations in the tradition of resource mobilization largely ignores the role of protest in social movements. The study of protest in the tradition of protest event analysis has almost nothing to say about the role of social movement organizations in organizing these events. For a rare exception see Tarrow (1989).

29. For two recent exceptions, see Bob (2001) and Bullert (2000).

6

Scale Shift in Transnational Contention

SIDNEY TARROW AND DOUG McADAM

The literature on globalization often makes it appear as if we are now operating in a brave new world of fading states, something approaching a mature "global civil society" or "world polity." Especially in light of the resurgence of statism in the wake of 9/11, we are skeptical of these hyperbolic claims. Nation-states remain the dominant actors and loci for all manner of politics, including contentious politics. That said, it would certainly seem as if the volume of transnational politics—including what we call "transnational contention"—has been steadily increasing in the past few decades. The growing interest of political scientists and political sociologists in transnational social movements, NGOs, international non-governmental organizations (INGOs), transnational advocacy networks, and the like reflects this general trend.

But while this growing literature has produced rich empirical studies of various movements, transnational campaigns, and advocacy networks, except for a few scholars like David Snow and Robert Benford (1999), the dynamic *processes* and constituent *mechanisms* that actually enable activists to operate transnationally have received less attention than macro-processes like globalization. Notwithstanding the technological revolution of the past twenty years or so, the coordination problems faced by actors seeking to operate transnationally remain formidable. Under what conditions does contention grow beyond its localized beginnings to become a force for transnational change? In this chapter, we focus on a single process—*scale shift*—composed of several mechanisms that we see as central to the spread of contention, intranationally no less than internationally.[1] We conceptualize this process in two broad forms—indirect and direct—and, within the latter, through two complementary but by no means identical routes—what we call "brokerage" and "diffusion." We see localized action shifting in scale in both cases through the additional mechanisms of emulation and the attribution of similarity, to produce coordinated transnational action. We utilize three important and well-studied protest campaigns—the civil rights and nuclear freeze movements in the United States, and the international solidarity movement with the Zapatista insurgency in Chiapas—to illustrate the dynamics of these two routes and some of their differences in outcomes. We close by speculating about the value added to the study of transnational contention by our process-and-mechanisms approach.

FROM THE LOCAL/NATIONAL TO THE
TRANSNATIONAL: THE "GLOBAL" CHALLENGE
TO THE STUDY OF CONTENTION

We, and others, have written so extensively about the challenge of globalization to the study of contentious politics that we limit ourselves here to a few general observations that will illustrate our point of departure:

First, the transposition of concepts: Although we agree with most observers that transnational contention has some distinct properties not found prominently in domestic social movements, we believe that findings from social movement research—albeit coming from the local and national levels—offer a battery of insights and variables that will prove useful in understanding transnational contention. For a start, much that passes for "global" in the study of transnational contention actually takes the form of "internalization" (e.g., domestic claims-making against international or foreign targets), or what we would call "global framing" (e.g., the mounting of domestic disputes in the language of globalization).

Consider the case of France in the late 1990s, where we find dramatic examples of both processes: *internalization*, in this case, the European Union's (EU) "growth and stability pact"; and *global framing* in the attacks on McDonald's and other foreign-owned firms. Both episodes were of largely domestic importance: while the 1995 strike wave closed down the French railway system and shook the foundations of the neo-gaullist government, it had virtually no international resonance. And while the burning of a McDonald's franchise created an international public relations coup and may have had an impact on sales, it was domestically organized against this global symbol of American capitalism.

In addition, we would argue that although much is new and challenging about transnational contention, some familiar processes from the social movement repertoire, like mobilization, are so essential to contentious politics that it is hard to understand these new phenomena as if they were wholly new. Transnational activists do not simply appear in great numbers at the sites of international institutions or meetings; they must be brought together, organized, and provided with common themes and forms of collective action. Finally, many of the key relationships in transnational contention start within the national arena. Consider the activists who assembled at Seattle, Genoa, Göteborg, Quebec City, and Cancun: far from being "rootless cosmopolitans" who come to life periodically at international meetings, they mainly emerge from domestic social movements, interest groups, unions, and churches, to which they return.

Second, transposition, not liquidation of local and national movements: The shift of scale from the local/national to the transnational level does not automatically cancel out national and local social movements. What we normally see in transnational contention is the *transposition* of frames, networks, and forms of collective action to the international level without a corresponding *liquidation* of the conflicts and claims that gave rise to them in their arenas of origin. The failure to recognize this difference has produced holistic thinking about transnational social movements and has led to some confusion in how they are studied.

Third, the ambiguity of "globalization": As Deborah Yashar and Sidney Tarrow have vigorously argued, no concept has created more confusion in the study of transnational contention than the umbrella term *globalization* (Yashar, 2002; Tarrow, 2002). Used indifferently to mean global economic integration, the internationalization of policymaking through international treaties, agreements, and institutions, and to indicate the homogenization of culture, the term has been used to enhance the allure of many movements that are international, but less than global. Loose usage of the term *global* has also led some analysts to characterize many movements as being "against globalization" when they are actually aimed at something else: the internationalization of policymaking, the policies of national governments, or private actors who happen to be foreign. While we heartily agree that economic integration is a crucial structural trend in the world today, we believe that social scientists (as distinct from activists) will do better to specify the distinct effects of causal variables than to lump them into one vast causal conundrum. Hence we agree with Thomas Olesen that, when it comes to social movements operating beyond their own borders, the more modest term *transnational* is preferable to the grander term *global*, which gives the false impression "of a phenomenon evenly distributed on a global scale" (Olesen, 2002:3).

Finally, from structure to process: While globalization is primarily a structural and a cultural phenomenon, we follow Snow and Benford in thinking of transnational contention as an active *process* made up of subjectively formed actors who decide to act transnationally by forging relations with one another, with third parties, and with the targets of their claims (Snow and Benford, 1999). This suggests that the most promising empirical approaches will focus not on the structural or cultural causes of globalization, but on dynamic mechanisms and processes of contention like framing, coalition formation, diffusion, and brokerage. This takes us to *scale shift*.

FROM STATIC VARIABLES TO DYNAMIC MECHANISMS: THE *DYNAMICS OF CONTENTION* (DOC) PROGRAM

Over the past three decades, research and theory on social movements have reflected the dominance of a structural approach to the study of the phenomenon. For all the narrowness inherent in this approach, it is worth noting that this structural research program has shaped the field in important and generally salutary ways. We see two especially important contributions stemming from this work. First, it had the effect of overcoming the traditional psychological conception of social movements and reoriented the field to the study of organizations, networks, power, and politics. The second significant contribution of the structural research program is that it has been a program of *research*. So, for example, at the micro level, numerous researchers have shown that prior network ties appear to mediate the process of *movement recruitment*. Similarly, at the meso level, we now know that *emergent mobilization* tends to occur, not under conditions of weak or disintegrating social organization, as some versions of collective behavior suggest, but within established social settings. And at the macro level, we have seen that collective action tends to cluster in waves or *cycles of contention*.

That said, the fact that we know very little about the dynamics accounting for these empirical regularities points up the gaps in the structural program. Motivated by these conclusions, with Charles Tilly, we coauthored the book, *Dynamics of Contention* (McAdam, Tarrow, and Tilly, 2001). In it we called for a move away from static, variable-driven structural models to a search for the dynamic *mechanisms* and concatenated or sequential *processes* that shape contentious politics. By mechanisms, we mean "a delimited class of events that alter relations among specified elements in identical or closely similar ways over a variety of situations" (2001:11). By *processes*, we mean "recurring combinations of such mechanisms that can be observed in a variety of episodes of contentious politics" (2001:11).

Thus, for example, if movements tend to develop within established social settings, that is a verified "fact"; but we still need to ask about the specific mechanisms that produce an international movement out of one that has developed intranationally. For example, that ATTAC-France produced an international movement is a "fact"; but what interactive relationships produced these "facts"? Likewise, that collective identities are "socially constructed" is by now accepted by most movement scholars, but we should try to understand that process of identity change and its outcomes as an interactive process (2001:ch. 5).

In this chapter, we turn our attention to such "how" questions as:

- How do structural propensities get translated into specific mobilization attempts?
- What are the actual dynamics by which movement activists reach decisions regarding goals and tactics?
- How concretely do social movement organizations (SMOs) seek to recruit new members?

To answer these questions, we argue, requires more precise specification of processes and their constituent mechanisms. Specifying one such process—scale shift—is the goal of this chapter.

SCALE SHIFT: A DYNAMIC
COMPONENT OF CONTENTION

In *Dynamics of Contention*, we defined the process of *scale shift* as "a change in the number and level of coordinated contentious actions leading to broader contention involving a wider range of actors and bridging their claims and identities" (2001:331). Essentially, we were talking about the spread of contention beyond its typically localized origins. Much of this book is made up of instances in which contention is designed, from the outset, as a coordinated effort over great geographic distances; in others, national or large-scale campaigns are reflected in downward scale shift. Such instances are important, but they are not our main concern here. Instead, we are interested in the dynamics by which local contentious episodes spread to other locales.

This process is familiar from episodes of contention that migrate from the local to the translocal and the national levels. For example, much of the debate about the "Swing movement" in the 1830s in England was fundamentally about scale shift and its pathways (Charlesworth, 1978). Similarly, George Rudé's analysis of the spread of disorder along French river valleys in the 1770s was fundamentally a study of scale shift (1964). And Tarrow's analysis of the Italian student movement of the 1960s traced similar processes as contention spread from the universities to the high schools (Tarrow, 1989:ch. 6). Below, we review the best-studied case of scale shift in the United States: the diffusion of the civil rights movement throughout the South and its move to the North in the 1960s, which Mc-Adam has studied in earlier work (McAdam, 1988; 1999).

Though implicated in nearly all instances of emergent contention, the concept of scale shift becomes especially important in the context of transnational social movements. This is because the obstacles, gaps, and transaction costs of mobilization are more imposing for transnational movements than for purely domestic ones (Snow and Benford, 1999; Tarrow, 1998:ch. 11). It is precisely the spread and coordination of contention across national—and even continental—boundaries that makes the phenomenon of transnational social movements so interesting and generally unexpected. But before we seek to apply the concept in relation to two instances of transnational contention, we begin with a more general discussion of the process as we see it, and follow with an example of a domestic process of scale shift.

SCALE SHIFT AS A ROBUST PROCESS IN THE DYNAMICS OF CONTENTION

Many contentious episodes begin locally but never spread beyond the settings in which they first developed. But in the case of major social movements, at least some *degree* of *scale shift* takes place (McAdam et al., 2001:ch.10). The spread of contention has not received the same level of theoretical or empirical attention as two other processes—*movement recruitment* and *emergent mobilization*—that are fixtures of the social movement literature. And although it is logically implied by the concept of *cycles of protest*, scale shift has seldom been specified theoretically except by vague concepts like "contagion" or "grass fires." In fact, much of the work that has been done on scale shift tends to reproduce the structural approach characteristic of the field as a whole. The general tendency has been to interpret the spread of contention on the basis of traditional diffusion theory, which holds that innovations or new cultural items diffuse through homophily and along established lines of interaction (Jackson et al., 1960; McAdam, 1999; McAdam and Rucht, 1993; Pinard, 1971; Strang and Meyer, 1993; Soule, 1997; see also the criticisms in Snow and Benford, 1999).

We think the inclination to model the spread of contention as no more than a specialized instance of diffusion truncates our understanding of the dynamics of the phenomenon. To say that most instances in which contention spreads will benefit from established lines of interaction between innovators and adopters is problematic as a general proposition, but it also tells us no more about the contingent dynamics of scale shift than the structural "facts" reported above do about the processes of recruitment and emergent mobilization. Although it is plausible to assume that most instances of local contention involve groups whose members are linked to others beyond their local contexts, why do so many cases of local contention *fail* to spread elsewhere? As with *mobilization, recruitment,* and *cyclicity,* certain structural conditions may be necessary to diffusion, but they are hardly sufficient to insure the process in question. The question then becomes: "What contingent social–cultural mechanisms mediate movement spread?" Drawing on *Dynamics of Contention,* we seek here to answer this question by identifying a set of linked mechanisms that constitute scale shift. We see scale shift as a robust process consisting of two distinct pathways, although both can, and frequently do, co-occur in a given contentious episode. This process is shown in figure 6.1.

Before taking up the specific mechanisms that define each of these two pathways, we first describe the process of scale shift in more general terms. Localized collective action spawns broader contention when information concerning the initial action reaches a distant group, which, having defined itself as sufficiently similar to the initial insurgents (*attribution of similarity*), engages in similar action (*emulation*), leading ultimately to *coordinated action* between the two sites.

We now turn to the three specific pathways we see as shaping the process of scale shift. Rather than describe all cases of scale shift as the result of diffusion, we posit three analytically distinct routes: *non-relational diffusion, relational diffusion,* and *brokerage.*

- By *non-relational diffusion,* we mean the transfer of information by means of impersonal carriers, such as the mass media.[2]
- By *relational diffusion,* we mean the transfer of information along established lines of interaction.
- By *brokerage* we mean information transfers that depend on the linking of two or more previously unconnected social sites.

For the balance of the chapter, we will focus most of our attention on the second and third of these pathways. This is not because we think non-relational diffusion is a rare or unimportant phenomenon. On the contrary, we think it is a common and important component of scale shift that has been woefully understudied by movement scholars. But our interest here is really in understanding the way *movement actors* facilitate scale shift. For that reason, we are principally concerned with the differences and similarities between relational diffusion and brokerage. We make this distinction to call attention to a significant difference in the nature and likely impact of scale shift, depending on whether relational diffusion or brokerage predominates as the mediating mechanism. We

FIGURE 6.1
Scale Shift; Alternative Pathways

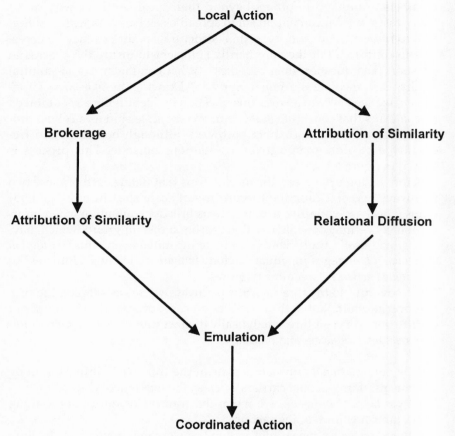

will show that movements that spread primarily through diffusion will almost certainly remain narrower in their geographic and/or institutional locus than contention that spreads through brokerage. Why? Because such movements rarely transcend the typically segmented lines of interaction that characterize most of social/political life.

While we see relational diffusion and brokerage representing different pathways to scale shift, we think both of them work through the two additional mechanisms shown in figure 6.1. The first of these, *attribution of similarity*, we define as actors in different sites identifying themselves as sufficiently similar to justify common action. The second is *emulation*, defined here simply as collective action modeled on the actions of others.

Let us spend some time explicating these two additional mechanisms, since they will both prove important in our latter discussion of diffusion and brokerage.

Attribution of Similarity. This mechanism is one that some scholars of diffusion of innovation have seen as mediating between receipt of information and emulative action (Strang and Meyer, 1993; McAdam and Rucht, 1993; Snow and Benford, 1999). The idea is simple enough. Information alone will not lead someone to adopt a new idea, cultural object, or practice. Adoption depends on at least a minimal identification between innovator and adopter. Such identification may precede the event in question, as we think happens in most instances of relational diffusion, or develop through a process of emergent social construction set in motion by the brokered transfer of information. Indeed, we suspect that brokers play an active role in this construction process in many, if not most, instances of brokered scale shift.

What factors make such identification likely? It results, first, from the deliberate attempts of agents to frame the claims and identities of influence targets as sufficiently similar to their own to justify coordinated action—what Snow and Benford call "accommodation" (1999:26). We frequently see such deliberate attempts at influence in contentious politics. Movement entrepreneurs who wish to increase their appeal to previously connected or disparate groups work tirelessly to draw parallels between the group they represent and the targets of their influence attempts. Indeed, Snow and Benford have termed this process "frame bridging" and highlighted its importance in the unfolding of a protest cycle (1988; 1992).

However, attribution of similarity need not be as purposive or strategic a process as this implies. A second factor encouraging identification among different actors is Strang and Meyer's concept of "institutional equivalence" (1993). Those authors highlight the tendency of policymakers within particular institutional domains (e.g., urban planning) to identify with their counterparts in other countries, thus facilitating the spread of policy innovations even in the absence of purposive influence attempts. In the history of contentious politics, we see such institutional equivalence in the channeling effect of mass production on industrial action: workers in mass production units with similar relations to management have historically found it much easier to join their struggles to others in similar situations than, say, to handicraft workers in isolated workshops.

Since *relational diffusion* involves the transfer of information along established lines of interaction, potential adopters can, in most cases, be expected to already identify with the initiators of movement action. To some extent, brokerage, on the other hand, connects previously unconnected people and groups, making the attribution of similarity much more of a contingent—and temporally later—process than in the case of relational diffusion. If the attribution of similarity is more difficult and more tenuous through brokerage than through a diffusion route, this would certainly make the latter a more sustainable linkage than the former, in which the links can easily disintegrate when the immediate incentive to connect has passed. We suspect that this is why so many transnational coalitions are short-lived. In fact, a plausible hypothesis is that successful brokerage promotes attribution of similarity, while unsuccessful brokerage promotes the recognition of difference.[3]

Emulation. While straightforward as a mechanism, the inclusion of emulation in figure 6.1 underscores an important point. Awareness of a prior action, even when accompanied by strong identification with the actor, does not guarantee emulative action on the part of the observing group. We can imagine groups learning of and strongly identifying with a contentious action by another group, yet refraining from action out of fear or a sensible desire to monitor the reaction of authorities before deciding whether to act themselves. Emulative action is a contingent outcome in its own right, and therefore should be regarded as a mechanism distinct from diffusion/brokerage and attribution of similarity.

Although we do not believe that every case of scale shift must of necessity involve an exact copy of the form of behavior observed by the observing group, we do believe that emulation of protest style, collective action frame, and form of organization is a solid indicator that scale shift is taking place. In fact, it is often the *only* indicator of a direct connection between prior groups and the observing group. Thus, Sarah Soule's work on the diffusion of the student divestment movement in the United States was based on the observation of a single tactic—the construction of "shantytowns" on college and university campuses (1997; 1999). The use of this tactic does not in itself demonstrate diffusion or brokerage, but it is a strong indication that the process of scale shift is occurring.

WORKING HYPOTHESES

Although relational diffusion and brokerage often combine in major movements, we see significant differences in the character and likely impact of scale shift depending on which of these two pathways predominates as the principal mediating mechanism. We offer three main hypotheses to guide the case narratives that follow.

Relational diffusion is far more likely than brokerage to be the mediating mechanism of movement spread, because actors who are connected through established lines of interaction are more likely to share information and identify with one another (e.g., attribution of similarity) than those who are less so; and also because diffusion requires a much lower investment in time and entrepreneurial energy than brokerage.

By the same line of reasoning, because contention that spreads primarily through relational diffusion works through existing channels of interaction, it will almost always remain narrower in its reach and impact than contention that spreads substantially through brokerage. It follows that scale shift through brokerage, when it does occur, is likely to be far more consequential in its effects than diffusion along segmented relational lines. First, to the extent that brokered ties succeed in encouraging previously disconnected groups to identify with one another, contention can spread beyond narrow geographic, institutional, and/or categorical boundaries to produce widespread social unrest and, potentially, enduring new ties, identities, and forms of contention. Second, whereas relational diffusion links actors already connected to one another, successful brokerage creates such connections and may even produce the attribution of similarity and new collective identities.

In the next section, we use existing research materials to illustrate the workings of *scale shift* in one of the best-studied episodes of contention in the social movement field—the American civil rights movement. Sections V and VI show how relational brokerage and diffusion operated in two more recent cases of transnational contention: the nuclear freeze movement in the United States in the 1980s, and the Zapatista Solidarity Network in the 1990s.

SCALE SHIFT AT THE INTRANATIONAL LEVEL: THE CASE OF CIVIL RIGHTS, 1955–1970

While it is in the area of transnational movements that the issue of scale shift is most starkly posed, broad national struggles are only slightly less interesting when it comes to the spread of contention. But in the attention accorded such struggles, movement scholars have tended to gloss over the complex dynamics by which episodes of contention grow beyond their typically local beginnings. Indeed, the notion of a unified *national* movement is something of a distortion. Typically, national movements more closely resemble aggregations of local struggles than they do tightly coordinated, top-down change efforts. The question is, "How are these local struggles linked, and with what consequences for the spread and impact of contention?"

The U.S. civil rights movement affords an instructive example. Though the popular view equates the movement almost exclusively with the activities of Martin Luther King, Jr., in reality the struggle involved many other groups and individuals operating in countless locales around the

United States. Nor were the dynamics of the movement the same over the course of the roughly fifteen-year period (1955–1970) that marked its heyday. With respect to scale shift, the movement can be conveniently divided into three periods. Within each of these periods, the spread of the movement was shaped by different actors adhering to different dynamics and with correspondingly different implications for the breadth and unity of the struggle.

Relational Diffusion: 1953–1959

Virtually all accounts point to the Montgomery Bus Boycott as the beginning of the mass movement phase of the civil rights struggle. It was in Montgomery, Alabama, in December 1955, that Rosa Parks was arrested for failing to give up her seat to a white bus rider, and that a coalition of local congregations mobilized to protest the arrest. Soon thereafter, Martin Luther King, Jr. was tapped to lead the organization—the Montgomery Improvement Association—formed to coordinate the boycott, and the rest, as they say, is history. But the story is actually more interesting than the popular account suggests. What is not generally known is that another minister, Theodore Jemison, in another southern town, Baton Rouge, Louisiana, had organized the same kind of bus boycott two years earlier.

We cite this earlier event, not as an interesting historical aside, but because it speaks directly to the dynamics of scale shift that characterized the earliest period of the civil rights struggle. The spread of the movement between 1953 and 1959 corresponds to a classic diffusion process, with an existing network of black ministers serving as the principal vehicle by which the innovation of the bus boycott spread from Baton Rouge to Montgomery, and then on to a host of other southern cities.

Besides inspiring other boycotts, the Montgomery campaign also served as an impetus to the development of indigenous church-based movement organizations in other southern cities. Writes Watters, "all over the South Negroes were forming organizations in imitation of the Montgomery Improvement Association" (1971:50). It was from these organizations that the Southern Christian Leadership Conference (SCLC) was forged at a meeting held in Atlanta in January 1957 (Clayton, 1964:12). As little more than the institutionalized embodiment of the preexisting ministerial network that had given birth to the boycotts, the SCLC would remain the principal vehicle of scale shift throughout this early period.

The Formation of Cross-Local Agents: 1960–1963

But for all the notoriety achieved by King and the SCLC, the truth of the matter was that the movement was essentially moribund as the 1960s dawned. It was the 1960 sit-in movement that revitalized the struggle, creating a second major diffusion vehicle that would shape the dynamics of scale shift during the early 1960s. The historical particulars of the sit-in movement are well known. It began on February 1, 1960, when four students at Greensboro A&T sat in, without incident, at a lunch counter downtown. From there, the movement spread like wildfire, as existing ties between students at proximate colleges facilitated—in classic diffusion style—the adoption of the sit-in tactic.

In the nine-day period following the Greensboro demonstration, student sit-in activity was confined to North Carolina. From there it spread to neighboring states, with sit-ins occurring in Hampton, Virginia, on the eleventh of February; Rock Hill, South Carolina, on the twelfth; and Nashville, Tennessee, on the thirteenth. In succeeding weeks, the movement surfaced in major urban centers such as Tallahassee, Florida; Atlanta; and Montgomery. That existing interpersonal ties between proximate campuses were the principal means by which the movement spread is a view supported by all contemporary chroniclers (Brooks, 1974:147; Oppenheimer, 1963:61–62; Orum, 1972:61). Reflecting its campus origins, the sit-in movement wound down as colleges adjourned for the summer.

But just as the founding of the SCLC effectively institutionalized the ministerial network that had shaped the bus boycotts, so too the creation of SNCC (Student Nonviolent Coordinating Committee), at an April conference in Raleigh, North Carolina, perpetuated an important campus-based network that would crucially affect the spread of the movement during this second period. Indeed, it is only a slight exaggeration to say that the movement's diffusion was shaped by the strategic choices made within these two organizational networks. The SCLC's characteristic approach was to organize a broad-based community movement in cities where it already had a strong organizational affiliate. The most celebrated campaigns of this period—Albany, Birmingham, Selma—owed to this strategy. For its part, the SNCC operated in a less centralized fashion, with field secretaries seeking to establish movement beachheads in countless locales in the Deep South. But it was these two contrasting approaches—highly publicized and delimited community campaigns versus largely invisible local organizing efforts—that determined where and when the movement spread during this second period.

From Relational Diffusion to Brokerage: 1964–1970

For all the great successes enjoyed by the movement between 1953 and 1963, the struggle remained confined to the South and was contained within the two organizational networks—the SNCC and the SCLC—that grew out of the bus boycotts and sit-ins. The 1964 Mississippi Freedom

Summer Project would change all of this. By connecting the southern civil rights struggle to college campuses in the north and west, Freedom Summer helped to set in motion a "revolution beyond race" in the New Left protest cycle of the 1960s. It did so by serving as a crucial catalyst for several of the other major movements of the period. In particular, a strong case can be made that the roots of the free speech movement at Berkeley (Heirich, 1968; McAdam, 1988), as well as the antiwar movement (McAdam, 1988) and women's liberation movements (Evans, 1980; Rothschild, 1979, 1982), are to be found in the Freedom Summer Project.

Three categories of brokers served to link the southern civil rights struggle to the northern college campuses. SNCC veterans did much of the work, visiting schools in the fall and winter of 1963–1964 to recruit volunteers for the project. Pioneering activists in the fledgling student Left played a key role as well. Even without visits from project recruiters, leaders of campus Friends of SNCC, Students for a Democratic Society (SDS), or other student civil rights organizations spread the word, distributed applications, and generally prevailed on their friends to sign on to the project. Finally, in a few instances, progressive faculty, administrators, or campus religious leaders brokered connections to the movement.

In conclusion, the case of the civil rights movement helps to illustrate, within one country over time, many of the hypothesized dynamics of scale shift posited above. The brokered spread of the movement, primarily through the Freedom Summer project, offers a striking contrast to the more insular and contained dynamics of diffusion that characterized the 1950s and early 1960s. But only by understanding both mechanisms of scale shift do we get a full portrait of the movement and its highly consequential spread beyond its localized beginnings in Baton Rouge and Montgomery. A full understanding of these complex dynamics is key to understanding how the movement came to be "the borning struggle" for so many other movements in the United States and, indirectly, beyond.

But the story is not simply one about the catalytic effect of the civil rights struggle on a number of other New Left movements. It is also an account of the differential impact of these forms of scale shift on the movement itself. As we will argue more generally in the next sections of the chapter, the brokered spread of contention has the capacity both to extend movements far beyond their localized origins, *and*, by doing so, to introduce new actors, new frames, and new tensions and contradictions into the original movement.

This is certainly what happened in the case of the civil rights movement. In acting on the lessons of Mississippi, the Freedom Summer volunteers carried "the movement" from the rural South to the college campuses and cities and suburbs of the north and west. The struggle was dramatically broadened in the transplantation. But it was also transformed. Though explicitly linked at the outset to race, the issues embraced by the white New Left—free speech, Vietnam, women's liberation—had the effect of shifting the focus of contention elsewhere, both substantively and geographically. Then, too, the entrance of so many white students into the movement introduced tensions and dynamics into the southern freedom struggle that, among other things, hastened the end of interracialism as a defining quality of the movement. This is not to suggest that brokerage always has such dramatic effects, but simply to say, consistent with the earlier hypotheses, that brokerage typically has far more potential to alter or transform a movement than does relational diffusion.

THE NUCLEAR FREEZE AND THE ZAPATISTA SOLIDARITY NETWORK

Before turning to our two transnational examples of scale shift, we offer two cavils. First, neither of us is an expert on these movements, and we therefore have depended heavily on the accounts of others.[4] Second, the fact that "scale shift" remained largely intranational in the case of the nuclear freeze and became transnational in the Zapatista solidarity movement does not imply that the former had no transnational resonance at all, or that the latter found supporters only outside Mexico. On the contrary, the "freeze" was contemporary with the nuclear disarmament movement in Europe (Rochon, 1988; Marullo, 1991; Cortright and Pagnucco, 1997; Snow and Benford, 1999), while the Zapatistas had an important collateral impact within Mexico (Olesen, 2002:9, 13).

We begin with two brief narratives, based on our reading of the primary literatures on the two movements. We then turn to each movement separately, to show how relational diffusion gave way to domestic political brokerage in the American freeze campaign, constraining the possibility of transnational coordinated action, while the Zapatista movement was successfully linked to a wide international solidarity movement through brokerage. We will conclude with some reflections on what our approach suggests for the study of transnational contention.

Antinuclear Movements in the Early 1980s

The nuclear freeze campaign, and the main movement organization that animated it in the United States—the Nuclear Weapons Freeze Clearinghouse (NWFC)—arose out of the decision toward the end of the Carter administration to increase America's nuclear capability, especially in Central Europe. But because, to antinuclear activists, the Democrats were preferable to any Republican administration, the goal remained "a solution in search of an opportunity" until Ronald Reagan came to power in early 1981 (Meyer, 1993:470). The new Republican administration offered an opportunity as it "repeatedly and forcefully demonstrated its commitment to policies peace activists saw as bellicose." No sooner were the Reaganites elected than they began work to provide the weapons to fight and win nuclear wars, purged moderate scientists and strategists from the State and Defense Departments, and unwittingly provided resources to the mass media and to the existing network of peace activists (Meyer, 1993:471).

The proposed Reagan missile buildup was quickly challenged by activists in both the United States and Western Europe (Marullo, 1991; Meyer, 1990; Rochon, 1988; Snow and Benford, 1999). But while the former directed their efforts mainly at a nuclear freeze "as the first step in a complicated and comprehensive program to remake world politics," the latter focused specifically on halting the North Atlantic Treaty Organization (NATO) plan to deploy intermediate range nuclear missiles in five European countries (Meyer, 1993:471). Both Europeans and Americans drew on existing and new movement organizations and engaged in a series of collective actions, culminating, in the United States, in a gathering of over a million people in Central Park in New York and in demonstrations of over a quarter of a million marchers in London and Rome and a half million in Bonn and Berlin (Rochon, 1988:5).

The American and European antinuclear campaigns arose out of the same threat and could build on a tradition of international peace activism (Snow and Benford, 1999:27), but there were sharp differences between them from the beginning. Although the American freeze activists "espoused a broad variety of ultimate goals and means, mass media grouped virtually all opponents of the Reagan administration's security policies under the bilateral strategy of the 'nuclear freeze'"; in contrast, the European campaign focused on the planned emplacement of the American Cruise and Pershing missiles and was unilateral in its central thrust. There was also a gap between the tactics of the two movements: although the American movement began with popular initiatives at the local level (Meyer and Kleidman, 1991:231, 243–45), as it gained media and popular support, it rapidly gravitated to institutional politics; conversely, as European governments showed a stolid indifference to mass pressure, a coordinated transnational protest campaign emerged (Rochon, 1988:6).

With the distance of time and the blurring of memories, the campaigns on the two sides of the Atlantic can appear as one, but there were fundamental differences and a certain diffidence between them. While both left lasting impacts on their respective sites, they never unified, except at the most general rhetorical level and through reciprocal visits and the use of the same repertoire of contention that had emerged from the common heritage of the 1960s (Snow and Benford, 1999:28–29), as we will see below.

The Zapatista Solidarity Movement

On January 1, 1994, a hitherto unknown guerilla movement in the Mexican state of Chiapas, which called itself the Ejército Zapatista de Liberación Nacional, or EZLN, attacked a number of police barracks in the city of San Cristóbal de las Casas and in surrounding towns. The rebellion broke out on the same day as the North American Free Trade Agreement treaty (NAFTA) came into effect among Canada, Mexico, and the United States. This gave the movement an international allure from the beginning, although its "spokesperson," who called himself Subcomandante Marcos, was at pains to emphasize its roots in the historical oppression of Mexico's indigenous groupings.

The epicenter of the movement remained in Chiapas, but soon it began to receive sympathetic support from both within and outside of Mexico. Thomas Olesen offers us a convenient summary of what he calls the "transnational Zapatista solidarity movement" (2002:ch. 2):

Phase 1 (January 1994–February 1995). After the Zapata rebellion broke out, international demands in solidarity with the insurgents were made against the surprised Mexican army and police forces. According to Olesen, the transnational solidarity network did not have an infrastructure at the time and activities were built on existing networks and movements (2002:3).

Phase 2 (February 1995–Summer 1996). During this phase the solidarity movement began to build its infrastructure, aimed at monitoring the Mexican army's activities against the insurgents and publicizing its abuses of human rights.

Phase 3 (Summer 1996–December 1997). In this period, the transnational solidarity movement "became more politicized and began to overlay with other transnational networks." This was largely the result of the EZLN-organized "First International Encounter for Humanity and against Neoliberalism," held in Chiapas in 1996 (Olesen, 2002:3).

Phase 4 (December 1997–mid-1998). Following a massacre of civilians by local government-inspired armed civilians in Chiapas, the transnational movement "experienced its probably most intense period of activities, organized largely around human rights violations and the militarization of the region" (Olesen, 2002:3).

Phase 5 (mid-1998–April 2001). This was a period of international demobilization as the EZLN entered a long silence that was broken only in late 2002 (Olesen, 2002:3).

Thus, we see two movements—both of which can be classified as "transnational" but with very different types and degrees of international resonance. Both, to some extent, responded to "nested" national and international opportunities and threats (Meyer, 2003); both were in touch with interlocutors beyond their borders (Keck and Sikkink, 1998); but in the first, there was little scale shift beyond the United States, while the second touched off the formation of a broad network of transnational solidarity. How that happened, and the role of diffusion and brokerage in each process, is the final part of our analysis of "scale shift."

DIFFUSION AND BROKERAGE IN THE FREEZE MOVEMENT: WITHIN THE BORDER'S EDGE

In this section, we return to the first of our international movements—the American campaign for a nuclear freeze of the early 1980s and its relationship to the simultaneous European movement against the emplacement of Pershing and Cruise missiles. We will argue that the movement spread as rapidly as it did in the United States through a combination of, first, relational diffusion, and then brokerage. But because brokerage brought the movement into contact with political groups that had their own agenda, targeting domestic political institutions and elections, the grassroots sector of the movement defected or became inactive, a bilateral, moderate program became dominant, and the movement never established operative links with its European contemporary. At the same time, the European disarmament movement was developing its own internal ties and spreading from traditional peace activists to the churches and younger left-wing activists to become a truly transnational social movement.

From Grassroots Diffusion to Political Brokerage

The campaign for a nuclear freeze in the United States began as a grassroots movement that depended on relational diffusion among newly mobilized citizens at the local level, although the work of national peace groups was also important. Diffusion occurred most dramatically via the spread of local and state referenda through New England and elsewhere (Meyer and Kleidman, 1991:243ff.). The organizers of the NWFC were clearly aiming at diffusion, shying away from brokerage, as they symbolically and concretely tried to escape the embrace of existing arms control organizations by moving their base to the center of the country, in St. Louis (246).

But brokerage was an increasingly important influence on the movement's growth. Organizations available to the campaign included, first, the "organizations that had constituted the Test Ban and anti-ABM movements . . . and the traditional pacifist or peace movement organizations." Additionally, Physicians for Social Responsibility was revived in 1979, just as the Carter administration was increasing military spending. Churches and religious communities were also potential allies, especially given Pope John Paul II's opposition to the nuclear arms race and the National Council of Churches' nuclear education project. "The nuclear disarmament, civil rights, and antiwar movements of the 1960s," writes David S. Meyer, "had established a network of organizations from which the nuclear freeze movement would draw support and also had developed an inventory of tactics" (1990:149–50).

Soon, however, the movement's growing popularity led to its co-optation by the political elite. As politicians like Senator Ted Kennedy and Representative John Markey took up the cause in Congress, and as influential figures like former CIA Director William Colby threw their support to the freeze concept, "the movement appeared to moderate its rhetoric and analysis" (Meyer and Kleidman, 1991:249). As the organization's executive director quipped, "I feel like I'm on a comet, but I don't know whether I'm leading it or on its tail" (quoted in Meyer, 1990:128). Meyer and Kleidman put it thus:

> As the nuclear freeze moved into national debate and politics, the proposal became a vehicle for expressing numerous anti-administration grievances, and provided opposition politicians with a chance to ride a wave of public support. By 1983, the freeze had catapulted into the national limelight in a more limited form. It became a vehicle to achieve Congressional action for traditional arms control measures in the face of Reagan administration hostility (233).

Once an alliance was struck with elements of the political elite, the movement's program increasingly narrowed to arms control measures that could gain a majority in Congress. Grassroots supporters dating from the movement's early diffusion began to drift away as the movement's moderate allies became more prominent and the Reagan administration gestured in the direction of arms control. Brokerage was gained at the cost of the movement's core constituency, and the NWFC eventually merged with SANE (Committee for a SANE Nuclear Policy), an older and more mainstream arms control organization.

Scale Limitation and Scale Blockage

The freeze movement was contemporary with a massive outpouring of dissent in Western Europe against the Reagan administration's goal to place Pershing and Cruise missiles in five NATO countries (countering the perceived threat of Soviet SS-20 missiles in Eastern Europe) (Rochon, 1988). This co-occurrence, as well as the traditional links between Western European and American peace groups, convinced many social movement and peace scholars that they were two wings of the same movement (Snow and Benford, 1999:27). But although campaigners like Randall Forsberg (Marullo, 1991:285) were inspired by the European protests and mutual sympathy was widespread across the Atlantic, there were four fundamental differences between the two campaigns.

First, while the freeze campaign was strategically framed around a bilateral goal, the European movement against the missile emplacement called for a unilateral shift in policy. *Second*, at least in the version sponsored by Forsberg and her allies, the freeze campaign was part of a long-term strategic plan for eventual nuclear disarmament (Forsberg, 1982), while the European campaign was aimed at stopping a particular escalation in the arms race. *Third*, mass supporters of the freeze movement in the United States saw the Euromissile controversy as a sideshow (Marullo, 1991:284), while the European movement saw the Reagan missile plan as a major threat to world peace and was part of a global opposition to American foreign policy. *Fourth*, the political co-optation of the American movement hindered its leaders' capacity to forge a close link to the Europeans. As a legislative aide to Congressman Markey later recounted, "As for Europe, we did not want the Freeze Campaign to get anywhere near the Pershing and cruise missile issue at this point" (Waller, 1987:1; quoted in Marullo, 1991:294–95).[5]

In summary, an early stage of relational diffusion expanded the scale of the freeze movement at the grass roots. Successful diffusion led to incentives to expand the movement's influence nationally through political brokerage with allied peace groups and politicians. This led to a narrowing of its goals to correspond with what would be acceptable to Cold War era Washington and made it difficult for its leaders to maintain contact with their mass base or forge mutually beneficial ties with the contemporary European movement.

BROKERING TRANSNATIONAL ZAPATISMO: BEYOND THE BORDER'S EDGE

While the historical proximity of the American and European peace movements suggested a much greater degree of transnational solidarity than in fact developed, in the Zapatista movement we see the opposite process occurring.[6] As Thomas Olesen observes, "Notwithstanding the obvious distance in both physical, social and cultural terms between the core insurgents and their supporters," the movement "won a great deal of solidarity, mainly from Western Europe and North America (2002:1). Olesen goes on to argue that "the interest and attraction generated by the EZLN beyond its national borders is matched by no other movement in the post-Cold War period." Much of this solidarity network was formed through what we see as a set of linked brokerage ties.

Transnational Brokerage Chains

Little of the success of "long-distance Zapatismo" can be understood as an outcome of direct diffusion. In fact, virtually all the transnational "scale shift" that we see in this movement can be attributed to a successful strategy of brokerage, interpreting that term, as we did earlier, to mean information transfers that depend on the linking of two or more previously unconnected sites. Olesen charts five different levels in what he calls transnational Zapatismo's "information circuit": *first*, the indigenous communities of Chiapas, which provided firsthand information to others; *second*, also at ground level, a range of Mexico- and Chiapas-based organizations, some Mexican, others international, which functioned mainly as information gatherers and information condensers. *Third*, the information gathered and condensed by the second-level organizations was often passed on to actors beyond the borders of Chiapas and Mexico. *Fourth*, there were also "periphery actors" who were dependent on core actors for their information but still devoted a significant part of their time and resources to these issues, and *fifth*, actors who had irregular and transitory ties to actors closer to the core and devoted little time to the issue of Chiapas and the EZLN (summarized from Olesen 2002:76ff.). Brokerage was the essence of the process; at different stages of the Zapatista uprising and at different points in the network, pairs of actors who would otherwise have had little or no connection to one another were connected by a third actor, with consequences for the behavior of one or both of the pair.

The most central broker was, of course, the man who calls himself Subcomandante Marcos. Coming from a traditional urban leftist intellectual background, Marcos embedded himself deeply within the Lacandón rain forest for a long period before the insurgency broke out. His words, according to Higgins, became "bridges between the Indian world of the southeast and the even-more-pervasive world of global politics" (2000:360, quoted in Olesen, 2002:10). "With a well developed sense of public relations . . . he is a mediator," writes Olesen, "translating the

EZLN indigenous struggle into a language that is understandable to a non-Mexican audience" (2002:10).

But the early mass media image of Marcos carrying his laptop through the jungle and uploading communiqués via a cellular phone assigned far too much importance to this central node of the network. Much of the Internet-based information that got out of Chiapas from the start of the insurgency came from second-level brokers, like the Mexico City left-wing newspaper *La Jornada*, which one Chiapenecan activist jokingly described as *"The Chiapas Gazette"* (quoted in Hellman, 1999:175). Other second-level nodes were listservs like Chiapas 95 and Chiapas-L, and the Ya Basta! website established in March 1994 by Justin Paulson (Olesen, 2002: ch. 3; Paulson, 2000:283). Each of these sites transmitted information from Chiapas to a wider audience, both in Mexico and abroad, and was responsible—far more than Marcos himself—for the construction of what Hellman calls a "virtual Chiapas."[7] Much information also came through interpersonal ties with people on the ground in Chiapas, for example from peace camp activists who had gone to live in Zapatista communities.

But brokers—especially information brokers—do not simply transmit information in some objective form. They select from among a wide array of information according to particular news values and ideological frames, crystallizing and condensing these images into major themes, and, at times, relaying images that can be so partial as to be downright deceptive. As Hellman writes:

> When we turn to the accounts available to this mobilized international com-munity of supporters, we find that what is generally communicated about the situation in Chiapas is a highly simplified version of a complex reality. While this picture is not intentionally distorted, it is ultimately misleading in ways that leave those who sympathize with and support the struggle in Chiapas in a very weak position to understand and analyze the events as they unfold (1999:166).

For example, while the selection of January 1, 1994, as the start of the insurrection was widely seen as evidence that it was an attack on NAFTA (which came into force on that date), Marcos later claimed that the choice of date was not as deliberate as it may have seemed from the outside (Olesen, 2002:11, citing EZLN, 1994:144). But the image of NAFTA, so widely condemned by the North American Left during the years when it was being negotiated (Ayres, 1998), was useful in the creation of an inter-national solidarity group. From the image of indigenous groups deep in the rain forest, information brokers in the Zapatista solidarity network built a bridge to the emerging "global justice" (Hellman, 1999:166–74).

Transformative Brokerage

We find three main kinds of change as outcomes of the movement's interaction with its external supporters. First, some existing groups outside of Chiapas reoriented their activities as the result of their reading of the insurgency; second, new groups were formed as a direct outcome of it; and third, the movement itself transformed its image and goals, in part in response to the overwhelming resonance of the movement outside of Mexico and in order to sustain and solidify that support.

Reorientation: An example quoted in Olesen's work will illustrate the first point. In Denver, Kerry Appel, an importer of coffee from Chiapas, describes his own experiences to Olesen:

> I started a human rights campaign as a protest against this campaign of violence against the cooperative Mut Vitz . . . so I wrote this information and put it on the Chiapas list [Chiapas-L] and I sent it to a couple of other places as well . . . and they translated it and published it on theirs. . . . now it is in four languages. . . . I have seen some writings that I had written in 1996, I have found them on Eastern European websites, Norwegian websites and Sufi websites, it is the whole life of its own the Internet has, it strikes a chord with some groups somewhere, resonates somehow with something they are doing (quoted in Olesen, 2002:71–72).

Appel himself has since become the central figure in a Denver-based solidarity organization, "practicing Zapatismo at home" (Olesen, 2002:99).

Transnational Expansion: An example of the second phenomenon was the formation of the international "global justice" group called "Peoples' Global Action." PGA was inspired by the second Zapatista *encuentro* in 1996 to call for global cooperation in the common struggle for human rights and against global corporate governance. It brought together Latin American, European, and Asian organizations in a series of "encounters" (the word was explicitly copied from the Zapatistas), and "global action" days against a variety of international meetings and organizations from the late 1990s until well into the current century. Although the original link with the EZLN has grown increasingly tenuous, its original inspiration was certainly the Zapatista struggle.[8]

Movement transformation: Third, not only did the Chiapas insurgency affect the activities of foreign activists and the formation of new movement organizations: in the weeks and months following the outbreak of the insurrection in January 1994, there was a transformation in the framing of the movement itself. While the freeze movement's transformation was due, more than anything, to its co-optation by domestic allies, the Zapatista program changed as its new international public interpreted it as a largely peaceful uprising of Chiapanecan "civil society" with symbolic military overtones (Olesen, 2002:8).

The transformation of the movement could best be seen in the framing of the two "encounters" that it held in Chiapas in 1996. The first of these, "the Continental American Encounter for Humanity and against Neoliberalism," drew about three hundred participants (Olesen, 2002:81). The second, the more ambitious "First Intercontinental Encounter for Humanity and against Neoliberalism," drew over three thousand. As Olesen found,

> new personal and organizational ties were established that would later lead to the exchange of information and experience via the computer mediated information circuit. . . . One of the direct outcomes . . . was an initiative to form an Intercontinental Network of Alternative Communications (2002:81–82).

Needless to say, not all the personal or organizational ties resulting from these two *encuentros* bore fruit in the long run. Nor is it clear that the transnational network played the most important role in the transformation of the Zapatistas and their image. After all, following brief disorientation of the Mexican army in January 1994, the movement's military weakness was quickly revealed, and its failure to trigger armed insurrections elsewhere in Mexico made patently clear. But once the Mexican government adopted a long-term dual strategy of wearing down the insurgents locally and inviting them to engage in a frustrating dialogue nationally, the choice was between retreating into armed isolation in the rain forest and engaging in some kind of appeal to a broader public. Once that decision was made, the size, the shape, and the composition of the movement's international alliance structure was an important source of the shift from a guerilla to a global civil society image.

CONCLUSION: "OUTCOMES" OF SCALE SHIFT

In concluding, let us first underscore what we have *not* claimed in this chapter.

We do not claim to have provided a causal account of any of the three episodes of contention that we have examined. As in the case of the civil rights movement with which we began, we drew selectively from well-studied cases to focus on one dynamic process that we think has been underspecified in the literatures on a wide variety of contentious politics. Researchers will return to these episodes for many years to find theoretical insights that were not apparent, or were considered unimportant during these movements' emergence; we hope they will find our partial and provisional analysis helpful in understanding the "how" of the movements' dynamics.

Second, we give scale shift particular attention, first, because it has often been taken for granted or reduced to metaphors like "contagion"; second, because it is logically important in episodes of transnational contention; and third, because we think we have found an important variation in the two principal paths we have specified, with important consequences for movement dynamics. (Non-relational diffusion may have distinctive consequences as well, but for reasons of space we have chosen to focus on the two paths that depend on the active effort of movement actors.)

We can only speculate about the long-term impacts of these different routes of scale shift. We think the brokerage pathway may produce more discord and disintegration than diffusion as contention spreads. But we have only hints of evidence to support this hunch: in civil rights, where the evidence is most extensive, the later "brokered" phase was marked by deep splits, both within the movement, and between it and its liberal white support groups. In the nuclear freeze campaign, cleavages with its grassroots sector were experienced as the movement shifted to alliances in the congressional and electoral arenas. And in the Zapatista movement, "there are significant differences within the network in terms of the understanding of solidarity," in part relating to the inequalities in the relationship between the providers and the beneficiaries in the solidarity relationship (Olesen, 2002).

Finally, we do not claim to have "explained" either short-term movement success or long-term failure—nor do we expect to. The mechanisms we specify are "nuts and bolts" of a more complex process that includes other mechanisms, only some of which we have examined here, and the particular conditions of each episode that play an important role in the episodes' outcomes. Our aim has been to better specify the "how" of transnational scale shift; outcomes are far more difficult to explain.

What follows is a recapitulation of what we *do* claim. *First,* we maintain that transnational movements do not automatically emerge from global consciousness or economic integration: they have to be built up through agentic processes like coalition-building, identity formation, and a shift in scale from the local/national to the international level. Focusing on one of these processes, we tried to disaggregate it into specific mechanisms such as localized action, emulation, attribution of similarity, and coordinated transnational action.

Second, within the process of scale shift, we posited two major routes. We use the term *relational diffusion* to refer to the transfer of information along established lines of interaction, while *brokerage* entails information transfers that depend on the linking of two or more previously unconnected social sites. We argue that while diffusion is the more common route because it uses existing identities and ties and facilitates emulation, when borders are to be crossed and distant social actors brought together, brokerage is the more likely mechanism of scale shift.

Third, this distinction calls attention to significant differences in the nature and likely impact of scale shift. In the case of the civil rights movement, we saw a process initiated through relational diffusion involving black ministers and college students in the South give way to scale shift brokered by civil rights organizers and northern campus sympathizers. In the nuclear freeze movement, we saw a movement that began locally through relational diffusion give way to a national coalition that reached into the political elite but stopped at the water's edge. And in the case of the indigenous Zapatista movement, we saw a remarkable international solidarity movement that operated largely through brokerage.

A final thought: When we ask how so widespread a solidarity network developed in the Zapatista solidarity movement despite its geographic distance, a possible answer emerges. An important characteristic of transnational contention that was often missed in early accounts is that a domestic movement that shifts in scale to the international level does not, as a result, automatically *become* a transnational or a global movement. *Transposition* of part of the movement's activities, rather than its *transformation,* is a far more common pattern. While this may disappoint advocates of a global civil society, it has two important implications: first, a movement may embrace transnational commitments without abandoning its primarily domestic ones; and, second, as a result, a movement can spread faster through the relatively weak ties of a brokerage chain than through the more intense ties typical of diffusion. Transnational transposition involves not transformation, but partial commitments, verbal compromises, and organizational drift from one issue to another as priorities and agendas change. Although what results is far less than a "global" movement, the major strength of the current campaign against neoliberal globalization is that it retains considerable local, regional, and national roots.

These implications—like the process of scale shift itself—have indeterminate implications for transnational social movements. On the one hand, social movements can increasingly identify with a movement elsewhere in the world, like the Italian Ya Basta! group whose members' knowledge of the culture and ethnic divisions of Chiapas developed only after they arrived in the region (Hellman, 1999; Vanderford, 2003). On the other hand, a movement like Global Exchange can make important contributions to Chiapas and to the Zapatista cause without, as a result, abandoning its other domestic or international commitments.

"Scale shift" is just that—and no more than that. To understand its dynamics in each case requires both theoretical specification and an ethnographic engagement with each case in question. As we urged in *Dynamics of Contention*,

> Analysts who seek to explain particular episodes actually do so by identifying explanatory principles that extend beyond those episodes. We propose mechanisms and processes as just such principles. . . . [But] to embrace the idea of robust mechanisms and processes across contentious episodes, countries, and periods of history is not to propose a strategy for their reconciliation in-between the celebration of particularism and the laying down of general laws (McAdam, Tarrow, and Tilly, 2001:345, 347).

By embedding their analytical categories in the historical and cultural particulars of each episode we study, we would venture that analysts can discern the more general, dynamic processes that typically fuel contention. In this chapter, we hope to have contributed to this outcome.[9]

NOTES

1. This effort is an extension of a brief discussion of scale shift in chapter 10 of Doug McAdam, Sidney Tarrow, and Charles Tilly, *Dynamics of Contention* (2001).
2. For a complete discussion of the distinction between "relational" and "non-relational diffusion," see Rogers, 1983. For an example of the distinction applied to the spread of movement activity, see McAdam and Rucht, 1993.
3. We are grateful to Charles Tilly for this observation.
4. Needless to say, none of the authors on whose work we have depended is in any way responsible for our interpretations.
5. This American diffidence was widely reciprocated: when Randall Forsberg took a batch of "freeze" handouts to a European disarmament conference and asked her hosts to distribute them, she later found them discreetly dumped in an alleyway outside the hall.
6. More than usual, this paper is heavily dependent on the research of other scholars. In the case of the Zapatista movement, we were helped by the research and the advice of Judy Hellman (see Hellman, 1999) and of Thomas Olesen (2002). With respect to the nuclear freeze movement, we were helped a great deal by the research and the advice of David S. Meyer.
7. For the complexity of the network and its reliance on a few key sources on the ground and in the United States, see Olesen, 2002:67–68. For the working of the information links from a key participant, see Paulson, 2000.
8. We are grateful to Dana Perls for collecting the information on the PGA for this paper. For original documents, see www.nadir.org/nadir/initiativ/agp/en/PGAInfos.
9. For works subsequent to *DOC* that advance our program, see McAdam and Su, 2001; McAdam, 2003; Tarrow, 2002 and 2003; and Tilly, 2001 and 2003.

Part III

INTERNATIONALIZATION

7

Patterns of Dynamic Multilevel Governance and the Insider–Outsider Coalition

KATHRYN SIKKINK

As a sustained subfield of social movement studies devoted to theorizing transnational campaigning develops, there could be some mutual benefit from ongoing exchanges with international relations theory (IR).[1] In particular, two theoretical dialogues are potentially fruitful: first, the debates about norms and ideas in IR could benefit from engagement with debates over framing and collective beliefs in the social movements literature. Second, the political opportunity structure debates in social movement theory could be usefully informed by IR literatures that explore the dynamic interaction of domestic politics and the international system. This chapter will focus on the second of these two dialogues.[2]

Social movement theorists are increasingly aware that social movements operate in both a domestic and an international environment: they speak of "multilayered" opportunity structure including a "supranational" layer, or a "multilevel polity," or highlight how international pressures influence domestic opportunity structures (Oberschall, 1996; Klandermans, 1997; Marks and McAdam, 1996; McAdam, 1996; Tarrow, 2002; della Porta, Kriesi, and Rucht, 1999; Meyer, 2003). In this volume, Tarrow and McAdam use the term *scale shift* to describe this move of contention from the national to the transnational level, and identify the mechanisms and paths through which it occurs. McCarthy and Johnson discuss the sequencing of transnational and national mobilization. The conclusions to this volume also highlight multilevel opportunity structures.

Most authors writing about transnational opportunity structures see international institutions as targets or constraints, not as opportunities or arenas for social movement activity. Most of the chapters in this volume focus on transnational collective action *against* international actors and international institutions. From a theoretical point of view, and thinking about the whole universe of possible transnational contention, however, transnational opportunity structures, just like domestic opportunity structures, need to be seen as presenting both threats *and* opportunities. Some forms of transnational contention, like those on human rights issues discussed in this chapter, use opportunities available in international institutions in campaigns against states.

Few social movement theorists do research that looks inside of international institutions to understand how social movements work there and what kinds of impact they have had. As studies of transnational campaigning increase, I believe that social movement theorists will find it useful to take international institutions more seriously as actual arenas for social movement activity, not just as targets. Social movements may sometimes be capable of transforming opportunity structures at the international level and of using international institutions to change domestic opportunity structures, what Imig and Tarrow (2001) call "domestification." As social movement theorists explore how national mobilization and transnational mobilization interact, they may find it useful to consider the IR literature on transnationalism.

Since the mid-1990s, there has been a flurry of academic activity in the international relations field around a reemergent transnationalist research agenda, alternatively focused on "new transnationalism," transnational networks, global civil society, transnational social movements, or world polity. Despite their differences, these diverse literatures all make the common point that transnational relations in which nonstate actors play a prominent role are an increasingly significant part of international relations. The transnationalist research program is intrinsically linked to broader concerns within constructivist IR theory (and some neoliberal institutionalism) with the influence of ideas, norms, and identity on world politics (Katzenstein, 1996; Finnemore and Sikkink, 1998; Goldstein and Keohane, 1993; Lumsdaine, 1993; Finnemore, 1993; 1996). But this literature also engages an older debate in IR theory about how domestic politics and the international system interact. This older debate may be particularly useful as social movement theorists contemplate the interaction of domestic and international opportunity structures.

IR LITERATURES ON DOMESTIC POLITICS AND THE INTERNATIONAL SYSTEM

We can classify the IR literatures into three categories in terms of how they address the relation of domestic politics and the international system: (1) theories that grant primacy to the international level; (2) theories that grant primacy to domestic politics within constraints imposed by the international system, and (3) more genuinely interactive theories.[3] Most literatures grant primacy to either the international or the domestic, and then hold constant the other for the purposes of their research. Peter Gourevitch recognizes that the body of research that explores the interactions of levels is "the least well developed, and that place that particularly requires further analysis" (2002:310). For many research puzzles, it is entirely appropriate to focus on either a domestic or an international problem, and hold the other constant. But I will argue that for some international issues, including the study of transnational social movements, an interactive approach is necessary to understand the potential for change and innovation in the international system.

Among the more interactive IR work, I would include work by Thomas Risse that focuses on the importance of "domestic structures" for understanding international outcomes. In a 1995 volume, Risse argues that domestic structures mediate transnational interactions. By domestic structures, he means state structure (centralized vs. fragmented), societal structure (weak vs. strong), and policy networks (consensual vs. polarized) (Risse-Kappen, 1995). Risse argues that the impact of transnational actors on outcomes "depends on the domestic structures of the policy to be affected and the extent to which transnational actors operate in an environment regulated by international institutions" (2002:258). Transnational actors must gain access to the political systems of their target state and contribute to the winning coalitions in order to change decisions. Risse now recognizes that this argument to some extent resembles the social movement argument that political opportunity structures are an important factor for explaining the success of movements (2002). In recent work, Brysk also argues that globalization offers both constraints and opportunities, and that the impact of globalization at the domestic level varies in different types of states (2002). This is a promising line of argument, but we still need to more closely examine how particular global constraints or opportunities interact with different kinds of domestic structures to produce different characteristic patterns of interaction.

One sophisticated vision of domestic/international interaction is the two-level game model, first proposed by Robert Putnam (1988), and later developed by Evans, Jacobson, and Putnam in the edited volume *Double-Edged Diplomacy: Bargaining and Domestic Politics* (1993). This model has the virtue of being truly interactive and dynamic. For many international issues, the two-level game continues to be a useful model of how the international and the domestic interact. Della Porta and Kriesi (1999) have adapted the two-level model to study the interactions of social movements in a globalizing world. For many issues, however, the two-level game's concentration on a chief negotiator or head of government as the linchpin mediating between the international and the domestic simply misses what is most important theoretically and empirically. Social movements interacting in the domestic and international realm often bypass heads of governments and engage directly in cross-table lobbying. In other words, the *metaphor* of the two-level game may be useful to social movement theorists, but the actual mechanisms the theory proposes are less so.[4]

In *Activists beyond Borders*, Margaret Keck and I developed one type of alternative to the two-level game that we called the "boomerang effect," where nonstate actors, faced with repression and blockage at home, seek out state and nonstate allies in the international arena, and in some cases are able to bring pressure to bear from above on their government to carry out domestic political change (Keck and Sikkink, 1998). The major dynamic of the boomerang is a form of international collective action where domestic social movements and nongovernmental organizations (NGOs) provide most of the initial impetus and information for getting issues in their country onto the international agenda. Once on the international agenda, however, the issue develops an international constituency of its own. While state-to-state negotiation can be a part of the boomerang, to focus solely on this, as Putnam's two-level game model does, misses much that is most interesting about the interaction.

Thomas Risse and I later expanded the boomerang effect into what we called the spiral model (Risse and Sikkink, 1999). The spiral model integrated the boomerang into a more dynamic five-phase conceptualization of the effects of domestic–transnational linkages on *domestic* political change. The idea of a boomerang suggested that social movements engaged in a single move, while the spiral model recognized that this was a longer-term process that involved a series of different kinds of political moves.

In the short term, one can analyze the dynamics of social movement activity as groups operating rationally within international and domestic contexts of opportunities and constraints (Finnemore and Sikkink, 1998). But social movement theorists have long recognized that social movements not only operate within existing domestic opportunity structures, but they can also make or expand existing opportunity structures (Tarrow, 1996; Gamson and Meyer, 1996). The same is the case at the international level. Over a longer term, the goal of many transnational activists is to transform or recreate the very opportunity structures within which they work.

The boomerang effect and spiral model are useful to describe many forms of international and domestic interactions. But other patterns of international–domestic interactions do not fit the boomerang or spiral.

Many labor and environmental activists do not seek out international allies because they face repression or blockage at home. To the contrary, they believe that key legislation and protections in their home countries risk being eroded by the transfer of decision-making powers to international institutions. This is what scholars of the European Union have called the problem of the democratic deficit. The idea of a democratic deficit is not limited to regional integration schemes, and is one of the main arguments in many neoliberal globalization protests.

As opposed to the boomerang model, where activists seek out international institutions as *more open* arenas to pursue their agendas, in the democratic deficit model activists are forced defensively into the international arena, and the brunt of their activity is aimed at protecting gains made within their domestic polities. So, for example, antiglobalization protesters oppose the power of the World Trade Organization (WTO) or the North American Free Trade Agreement (NAFTA) to overturn domestic environmental or labor legislation. They believe that these international institutions represent a democratic deficit when compared to domestic politics. Activists initially worked to defeat the treaties that set up the institutions, and when that failed, they continued to pressure global trade institutions to open to more democratic participation. How can we explain these two very different dynamics?

INTERACTION OF DOMESTIC AND INTERNATIONAL OPPORTUNITY STRUCTURES

To explore these characteristic patterns of interactions, I focus on an essential aspect of political opportunity structure at both the domestic and the international level—access to institutions, or how open or closed domestic and international institutions are to network or social movement pressures and participation. Although repression is often seen as a separate aspect of political opportunity structure, I see it as an aspect of access, since repression can be an extreme form of closing domestic institutions to political participation. Though less relevant internationally, repression can also be used to keep international institutions closed. When police used force against protesters at the WTO meeting in Seattle, local police were used to enforce the closure of an international institution. I recognize that social movement theorists conceive of political opportunity structure as a more multifaceted construct than just "access" and "repression," but these elements appear in most discussions of the concept (McAdam, 1996). In order to develop a typology of the interactions of domestic and international opportunity structures, I limit myself to focusing only on openness and closure. This is related to della Porta's argument that a single variable like protest policing can serve as a barometer for political opportunities (della Porta, 1996).

Using the basic idea of closed and open structures at the domestic and international level as an analytical starting point, one can think of at least four different characteristic patterns of activism (see figure 7.1). This notion will help us explain what may appear as a paradox in social movement activism and scholarship: why for some activists, international institutions are part of the solution, and for others, they *are* the problem.

Here, *international* opportunity structure refers mainly to the degree of openness of international institutions to the participation of transnational NGOs, networks, and coalitions. Many IR scholars think there is a single international structure that can be defined by a predominant characteristic such as international anarchy or unipolarity.[5] Neoliberal institutionalists also see anarchy as the defining characteristic of the international order, but believe that the nature of the "game" in certain issue areas created greater possibilities for international cooperation than realists would admit (Keohane, 1984). In this sense, we might say that neoliberal institutionalists see different international opportunity structures in different issue areas. But they do not systematically study how opportunity structures might vary at both the international and domestic levels. Both neorealism and neoliberal institutionalism fit in what I call "category one" above, as theories that grant primacy to the international level.

The way I use international opportunity structure here implies that there is not a single international opportunity structure, but that opportunities vary over time and across intergovernmental institutions, which in turn is related to variation across issues, and across regions. So, for example, international institutions were considerably more open in the 1990s

FIGURE 7.1
Dynamic Multilevel Governance

International Opportunity Structure

		Closed	Open
Domestic Opportunity Structure	Closed	A. Diminished chances of activism	B. Boomerang pattern and "spiral model"
	Open	D. Democratic deficit/defensive transnationalization	C. Insider/outsider coalition model

than in the 1960s; international institutions dealing with human rights are more open to transnational activists than those that deal with trade; and regional institutions in Europe are more open than those in Asia. Thus, for a particular network around a particular issue at a particular moment in time, one can specify how open or closed we expect international institutions to be. We can operationalize this understanding of international opportunity structure by looking at the formal and informal mechanisms or procedures for inclusions and participation in different international institutions. For example, the institutions connected to United Nations Economic and Social Council (ECOSOC) not only have provisions for NGOs to seek and be granted consultative status, but many have also developed practices that permit some NGOs to speak at meetings and present written materials for inclusion in the record. The WTO or the International Monetary Fund (IMF), for example, have no such provisions for NGO participation.

Domestic opportunity structure here refers primarily to how open or closed domestic political institutions are to domestic social movement or NGO influence. It varies primarily across countries, but it also varies over time and across issues within countries. As in the case of international opportunity structures, we can operationalize it by looking at the formal and informal mechanisms or procedures for participation on different issues. So, for example, domestic political opportunity structures are "closed" if social movements experience repression or exclusion in authoritarian regimes. But knowing if a country is democratic or authoritarian is only a starting point for understanding how open domestic institutions may be. As della Porta and her colleagues have demonstrated, protest policing varies dramatically across countries and may be a useful proxy for how open or closed countries are to social movements (della Porta and Reiter, 1998). But there may also be significant differences across issues within a single country.[6] Sometimes we can find specific laws or institutions (or note the absence of these) that determine the degree of openness or closure on particular issues. So, for example, amnesty laws close off the issue of legal accountability for past human rights abuses. Democratic countries with amnesty laws thus may still be "closed" opportunity structures around issues of such legal accountability. Likewise, laws or practices of Central Bank autonomy and insulation essentially "close" off decisions about domestic monetary policy from societal actors.

This issue of variation on closure helps address the main critique of the domestic structures argument in IR. Critics point out that domestic structures are not as useful to explain outcomes, because some movements have been much more effective than others within the same political opportunity structure (Keck and Sikkink, 1998; Risse, 2002). But this is only the case if a domestic opportunity structure is seen as static or permanent across issues. Domestic opportunity structures that vary across issues could help explain differences in movement effectiveness.

Likewise, the issue of openness or closure is relative, in the sense that activists compare the openness of domestic institutions to that of international institutions. Here I adopt the position of McAdam, Tarrow, and Tilly (2001) that opportunities and threats are not objective structural factors, but are perceived by activists. Thus, both opportunities and threats need to be visible to potential challengers. Activists need to perceive and compare opportunities and threats at both the international and the domestic levels. Some social movement theorists have tended to assume that most international institutions are "relatively inaccessible" (della Porta and Kriesi, 1999). This may be the case if we compare international institutions to the quite open political opportunity structures of Western democracies (in other words, if we focus mainly on box D). But if we take the whole range of domestic political opportunity structures—including quite authoritarian countries—and the whole range of international institutions, there are frequently situations where international institutions may be more accessible than domestic polities. In some international institutions, NGOs are not only consulted, they can speak and help draft resolutions and treaties. This is still much less than the participation of social movements in democratic societies, but may look attractive to social movement activists likely to be imprisoned for speaking in their home countries. Once activists become familiar with international institutions, and thus the opportunities they offer become visible, they may perceive more opportunities at the international level than at the domestic. Or, through a process of "attribution of similarity," activists may watch other social movements that act internationally, and identify them as sufficiently alike to justify using similar actions (McAdam, Tarrow, and Tilly, 2001:334).

This figure yields four different characteristic types of activism. While in practice these certainly come in mixed forms, it may be useful to begin to specify the nature of each of the pure forms. These categories tell us something about (1) the probability of international and domestic activism; (2) the type or focus of such activism, and (3) to a lesser degree, the likelihood of effectiveness of such activism.

The combined types of domestic–international interactions in figure 7.1 provide a way of thinking about multilevel governance that is neither "top-down" nor "bottom-up," but a complex and dynamic process of interaction of domestic politics and international politics. A two-level interacting political opportunity structure produces outcomes that would be counterintuitive for those looking only at domestic political opportunity structure. For example, it is generally assumed that a state's capacity or propensity for repression will diminish domestic social movement activity (Tarrow, 1995; McAdam, 1996). But the boomerang model suggests that repression may simultaneously move actors into international arenas to pursue their activities. Some movement activists conceive of maps of political opportunities at both the domestic and international levels, where a blockage at the domestic level could lead to a move at the international level (sometimes with the object of opening space domestically). Repression is the most obvious form of blockage, but lack of responsiveness may also project groups internationally. For example, feminist groups and groups of indigenous peoples have often found the international arena more receptive to their demands than are domestic political institutions. This dynamic is not unlike the dynamic of some social movements in federal systems. So, for example, civil rights activists in the U.S. South, lacking the necessary power to defeat their segregationist opponents in a local conflict, used tactics designed to provoke the intervention of the federal government on behalf of integration (McAdam, 1982).

It is important to keep in mind that the figure doesn't describe a set of static conditions. First, the opportunities and resources are "perceived and constructed by activists" (della Porta and Tarrow, this volume). Even when international institutions would potentially be open to social movement demands, if the social movements do not perceive them as open, they will not be used. Second, once using international institutions has become part of the repertoires of action of some domestic social movements, other domestic social movements are more likely to perceive international institutions as open to their participation.

Finally, social movements are not "stuck" indefinitely in one box or another. Much of the most interesting bi-level social movement activity aims to move from one box to another. Activists in box A strive to move into box B or D by transforming either domestic or international opportunity structures to make them more open on these issues. With these points in mind, let us look at each of the individual boxes.

Box A: Diminished Opportunities for Activism

In box A, where activists perceive that they face closed opportunity structures both nationally and internationally, we would expect to see the least activism, and thus fewer chances of success. Examples could include such diverse issues as monetary policy or the situation of abortion rights activists in Latin America.

Advocates of careful monetary policy have made one of their institutional goals to secure closed opportunity structures both domestically and internationally for monetary issues. So, for example, the very idea of

Central Bank autonomy essentially is concerned with limiting access of domestic social and political groups to decisions about monetary policy. At the same time, the IMF has been one of the least open of the international institutions to pressures of NGOs and transnational networks. No formal mechanisms exist, like consultative status in ECOSOC, for NGOs or social movements to participate in any deliberation within the institution. Informal mechanisms for such participation are very weak, and run counter to the dominant ideology of the institutions, which sees all forms of such participation as some type of undesirable rent seeking behavior (O'Brien et al., 2000). We would expect less activism and less effectiveness in this area, and I believe that has been the case. The most successful activism in this area has been in the area of debt forgiveness, not monetary policy per se (see Donnelly, 2002). In this volume, also see Kolb's discussion of ATTAC's work on fiscal policy.

Campaigns for abortion rights in Latin America face related problems. Because of the political and moral power and influence of the Catholic Church, domestic polities in Latin America have been closed to activism on this issue. But efforts to move internationally have proved difficult, because although international institutions have been relatively open to women's rights issues, a coalition of the Vatican, some Muslim states, and the U.S. government under conservative Republicans with antiabortion agendas have closed international institutions on the issue of abortion rights. For example, this coalition held the Cairo population conference hostage for days arguing over minor language issues in the conference declarations, because they might have implications for abortion politics.

Activism is not absent or impossible for issues in box A; it just faces a more serious set of obstacles. In these cases, we would expect to see attempts to open both domestic and international opportunity structures on these issues. Where domestic actors face the most severe repression, they may be less likely to form transnational coalitions and use brokerage strategies, because domestic opportunity structures are so closed that it is difficult to maintain transnational linkages. This was the case in Guatemala in the 1980s, for example, where repression was so severe that domestic NGOs were unable to function, and international linkages were weak. The closure on international institutions, in turn, makes it difficult to attempt boomerang strategies, and gives activists few chances of finding international institutional footholds to advance their causes.

Nevertheless, change is possible in some cases. Human rights activists in the 1960s and early 1970s in the Soviet Union, Eastern Europe, and authoritarian regimes in Latin America initially faced this kind of "box A" situation. Their domestic political contexts were essentially closed to human rights activism. But international institutions were not yet open on the issue of addressing human rights violations in specific countries.

United Nations procedures prohibited the institutions from acting in the case of a specific country unless there was a clear threat to international peace and security. Protocol prohibited even the naming aloud of a specific country engaged in human rights violations in the meetings of the Human Rights Commission. The basic human rights treaties, the Covenants on Civil and Political Rights, and on Economic, Social, and Cultural Rights, had been completed and opened for ratification but had not yet entered into force.

Resolution 1503 in 1970 empowered the United Nations (UN) to receive communications and refer particular situations of gross violations of human rights to the commission for its consideration. This opened important space in the UN because it allowed human rights NGOs, both domestic and international, access to the UN to file petitions about specific human rights violations in their country. After 1977, a series of "special procedures" were subsequently developed in the UN Human Rights Commission to enhance its ability to look into specific human rights situations, including the use of special rapporteurs and working groups. Human rights NGOs and their state allies pushed for the adoption of these special procedures, which later provided more points of access to the institution, since NGOs could send them information and lobby, and in some cases, members of NGOs were named as rapporteurs or working group members. Likewise, as states ratified human rights treaties and those treaties went into effect, new mechanisms for access were created in the form of the treaty-monitoring bodies that received reports from countries. Human rights activists succeeded in transforming the international opportunity structure in which they worked, and thus moved human rights issues from box A to box B in the early 1970s and early 1980s.

Box B: Boomerangs and Spirals

Box B is where the boomerang pattern or the spiral model has been most prevalent. When domestic structures are perceived as closed and international structures as open, activists will seek international allies and attempt to bring pressure to bear from above on their governments to implement changes. The mechanisms they use usually include coalition formation and brokerage (McAdam, Tarrow, and Tilly, 2001). That is, for boomerangs to work, it is usually not sufficient for domestic activists to simply transfer information and emulate tactics they have seen other activists use in the international arenas. Instead, they almost always link to other activists abroad.

The case of justice for human rights violations in Chile and the arrest of Pinochet in London, for example, can be explained using a boomerang or spiral model. Even after democratization in Chile, the amnesty law effectively blocked human rights activists from seeking justice for past human rights violations in domestic courts. In turn, they sought out allies and alternative institutions abroad to pursue their justice claims, most importantly the Spanish National Audience Court, which was empowered to hear cases involving international crimes. Note that in this case the "open international opportunity structure" was not an international or regional organization. Rather, activists were "borrowing" domestic courts in other countries that are empowered by universal jurisdiction to hear human rights cases from abroad. Chilean activists emulated a tactic used initially by Argentine human rights activists in Spain, and introduced a case against Pinochet and other Chilean military officers before the Spanish National Audience Court. In doing so, they also formed new coalitions with groups in Spain, including members of the Progressive Prosecutors Association and the United Left Political Party (Lutz and Sikkink, 2001; Roht-Arriaza, 2004).

The cases in Spain led to the arrest of Pinochet in Britain in 1998. The British Law Lords eventually determined that Pinochet could be extradited to Spain to stand trial because international institutions (in this case the Torture Convention that had been ratified by Chile, Spain, and the United Kingdom) provided for universal jurisdiction in the case of torture. So, the "open political opportunity structure" was provided by an international institution (a treaty) as interpreted and implemented in domestic courts. This makes the quite important point that while international opportunity structures are often found in international organizations and spaces like the United Nations, they can also be found in domestic spaces where the opportunities or constraints are made possible by international institutions like treaties. The Pinochet case also makes clear that international opportunities are not only found, they are also constructed. Until Argentine and Chilean human rights activists brought their cases before the Spanish court, it was not at all clear that the Spanish legal system could provide an open international opportunity. It was through the process of presenting the cases that the opportunity structure was perceived and created.

Although Pinochet was eventually released and allowed to return to Chile for health and political reasons, his detention led to important changes in the political opportunity structure in Chile. Specifically, it opened previously blocked space in the Chilean judicial system for victims of human rights violations to pursue their claims.[7] In the context of Pinochet's detention in the United Kingdom, the Chilean Supreme Court decided that past disappearances were ongoing crimes, and thus not covered by the amnesty law. This helped persuade the British government that justice for human rights violations was possible in Chile, and thus may have contributed to Pinochet's return. But it had the additional effect of making it possible for Chilean human rights victims to reopen hundreds of cases that had been previously closed. While the domestic opportunity structure in Chile as regards justice for past human rights abuses is not yet fully open, it is considerably more open than it was before Pinochet's arrest. Chile has not yet moved to box C, but it is moving in that direction.

The international/domestic dynamics here fit the boomerang pattern well, and illustrate that while the boomerang has been used primarily to describe political change under authoritarian regimes, even formally democratic regimes may have the kinds of domestic political blockages that lead domestic actors to seek international help to pressure for domestic change. As the spiral model points out, however, one of the goals of boomerang activism is to open domestic space for political activism. The interesting point is that if the spiral is truly successful, it will move the case from box B to box C. The spiral model moved beyond the boomerang effect exactly because it theorized the processes through which countries move from a closed to a more open domestic opportunity structure, and how those processes would affect that nature of transnational activism. This is, in fact, the case for much human rights activism in Latin America and also in some other parts of the world. Primarily through a process of redemocratization, previously closed domestic political institutions are opened for domestic human rights activism.

Part of what makes this model of multilevel governance *dynamic* is that the goal of social movement activity is very often to change or transform both domestic and international opportunity structures. The goal of many human rights movements was both to improve human rights and to push for democracy, thus transforming the domestic structure from a closed to a more open one: from box B to box C. To open domestic opportunity structures, activists have used multiple tactics, some novel, and others emulated or brokered from other similar cases. They pushed for plebiscites to spearhead a transition from authoritarian rule, urged other states to condition economic aid on progress made toward the restoration of democracy, and encouraged involvement of multilateral institutions like the Organization of American States (OAS) in election monitoring. Activists in the last two decades have had considerable success in moving from box B to C. The success in moving from box B to C may be the result of the wave of democratization in the region in the 1980s and 1990s.

Box D: Democratic Deficit and Defensive Transnationalization

Activists in box D engage in the characteristic form of activism that I call defensive transnationalization. These activists have not sought out international organizations but rather have been forced to work internationally, because their governments have made international agreements that move significant decision-making power into international institutions. Because such activists operate in domestic opportunity structures that they perceive as open relative to international institutions, they organize transnationally to minimize losses rather than to seek gains.

Defensive transnational activists, despite other differences with boomerangers, are also pushing to move into box C. Their efforts often focus on democratizing international institutions, and making them more open. Although some activists in this category are trying simply to block international institutional activities (the slogan of the "Fifty years is enough" campaign, for example, suggested that activists would be most satisfied if the international financial institutions simply shut down), most are attempting to make decision making in international institutions more responsive. But, once again, the essential question is democratic relative to what? Democratic deficit theorists and activists usually see international institutions as exhibiting deficits relative to their very democratic domestic polities. But implicit in every situation in box A, B, and D, there can be gains in democracy. We could argue that activists working in box D already live in more democratic situations than activists working in box A and box B, and are only in deficit (in an international sense) to those in box C.

Because activists in box D situations operate in relatively open domestic opportunity structures, they are more likely to use a wide range of domestic protest and political pressure activities. They also lobby their governments to try to block particular international commitments or to open up international organizations. So, for example, neoliberal globalization activists in the United States worked hard to try to convince members of Congress to vote against both NAFTA and the WTO. They also worked to get Congress to condition financial replenishment legislation for the IMF and the World Bank to contain provisions for more transparency and consultation within international financial institutions. Scholars attribute World Bank efforts to ensure more transparency and accountability in governance to such lobbying (Nelson, 2002). Because neoliberal globalization activists perceive international opportunity structures as closed, they are less likely to lobby or network within international institutions, and more likely to bring pressure to bear from outside. The majority of the chapters in this volume look at this form of transnational organizing.

Box C: Activists within and beyond Borders: Insider–Outsider Coalitions

Box C is the least studied, and thus of particular interest. What happens when both international and domestic opportunity structures are relatively open? Domestic activists will, I believe, privilege domestic political change, but will keep international activism as a complementary and compensatory option. Domestic political change is closer to home and more directly addresses the problems activists face, so they will concentrate their attention there. However, activists who have learned how to use international institutions in an earlier boomerang phase will keep this avenue open in case of need. I'll call box C the insider–outsider coalition category. The term *inside–outside coalition* has been used by Jonathan Fox and L. David Brown (1998) to discuss relations among the World Bank, northern NGOs, and southern grassroots movements. In the introduction to this volume, della Porta and Tarrow use the term *insider–outsider coalition* to describe one type of externalization strategy. Although my use is related to these, I use the term to refer to the specific types of coalitions that emerge when activists operate in open domestic and international opportunity structures.

This is the current situation of groups working on the topic of transitional justice in Argentina, which will be the topic of the rest of the article. However, I believe that the insider–outsider model is of particular importance because it is not limited to cases like Argentina but may be a key dynamic to explain how many protest movements located in democratic countries relate to the international. So, for example, this model of insider–outsider coalitions may be useful to help think about the emergence and dynamics of the global antiwar movement against the war in Iraq, with active participation of a U.S. antiwar movement. Domestic political opportunity structures are not formally closed to the U.S. movement, although they have been rather deaf to its demands. International institutions, on the other hand, have been more open to the concerns of the peace movement, and alliances have emerged between governments, movements, and international organizations to block international support for the war.

THE ARGENTINE CASE: INSIDER–OUTSIDER COALITIONS IN THE DEMAND FOR JUSTICE AND ACCOUNTABILITY

Argentine human rights groups displayed virtuosity in playing the boomerang game when their domestic opportunity structures were blocked during the dictatorship of the period 1976–1983. They formed coalitions with like-minded human rights organizations abroad to carry out boomerangs. With the return to democracy, these groups returned to focus their attention on the now much more open domestic polity, pressuring for and securing a path-breaking Truth Commission, trials of the nine top leaders of the military juntas, reparations for victims of human rights violations, and other significant domestic changes. This could be seen as an example of what McAdam, Tarrow, and Tilly call "downward scale shift" (2001:331–32). In this case, coordinated international action did not fragment until it achieved its goal of regime change and human rights improvement. But the domestic space for securing justice for past human rights violations narrowed when the Argentine government passed two laws that were effectively amnesty laws (Punto Final and Obediencia Debida), and when President Carlos Menem issued pardons for already convicted and imprisoned military commanders.

Human rights organizations, recognizing that there was still some important openness in the relevant domestic institutions (especially the judicial system), implemented a two-track strategy. They launched a series of innovative legal challenges to attempt an end run around the amnesty laws, and they cooperated with and initiated some international and regional tactics as well. Specifically, they reactivated coalitions formed during the boomerang and spiral phase, and formed new transnational coalitions to further new goals. In other words, Argentine human rights groups were able to selectively scale shift up and down as required by the demands of the particular situations they faced.

One innovative domestic legal challenge was initiated by the legal team of the Grandmothers of the Plaza de Mayo to hold military officers responsible for the kidnapping and identity change of the children of the disappeared, who in many cases had been given for adoption to allies of the military regime. The Grandmothers' lawyers argued that because the crime of kidnapping had not been covered in the amnesty laws, they were not blocked from pursuing justice for these crimes. Their legal strategy began to succeed by the mid-1990s, but initially most of those found guilty were lower-level military and the adoptive families.[8]

But on June 9, 1998, Federal Judge Roberto Marquevich ordered preventative prison for ex-president General Rafael Videla for the crimes of kidnapping babies and falsifying public documents. It is often overlooked that when Pinochet was detained in London three months later, Argentine courts had already done the equivalent by ordering the preventive detention of an ex-president for human rights violations. And they had done it using domestic political institutions. But, even in this case, the international was also involved. Videla had been tried for human rights violations during the trials of the juntas in 1985, convicted, and sentenced to life in prison, but he had been released in 1990 under President Menem's pardon. Why, all of a sudden, was Videla back under arrest?

At the end of May 1998, President Menem came back from a diplomatic trip to Scandinavian countries. Instead of the economic contacts he had been seeking, both the Finnish and the Swedish governments asked for an investigation of the cases of two disappearances: those of the Swede Dagmar Hagelin and the Finn Hanna Hietala. European human rights activists and family members of the disappeared had made these cases causes célèbres in their respective countries and had recruited allies at the highest levels of the relevant European governments. The European press focused its coverage of the Menem visit on these two cases. These two cases, in turn, are connected to two other cases of disappearances, those of two French nuns, Alice Domon and Leonie Duquet, because all were kidnapped by a navy group in which the notorious Captain Alfredo Astiz had participated. Menem realized that in his upcoming visit to Paris a week later, he would also face demands for the extradition of Astiz to France, where he had been condemned in absentia for the kidnapping of the nuns. Menem was scheduled to meet with French president Jacques Chirac, who had publicly stated that he wanted Astiz to be extradited to France. Just a few hours before the Chirac–Menem meeting, Judge Marquevich decided to detain Videla. In his meeting with the French press, instead of facing criticism, Menem was greeted as a human rights hero. Menem told reporters that "this is one more sign that we have one of the best justice systems in the world."[9]

This is an excellent example of an insider–outsider coalition. Domestic human rights organizations using innovative legal strategies had done all the preliminary legal and political work to secure Videla's arrest. They still needed some help from their international allies, however, for the final push to put a top-level military leader in jail. The judge who ordered Videla's arrest was not known for his commitment to human rights, but for his intense loyalty to President Menem, who had appointed him. There is strong reason to believe that Judge Marquevich was responding to Menem's political agenda in his trip to France when he ordered the detention.[10]

Four months later, after Pinochet had been detained in London and the Spanish court had issued arrest warrants for a wide range of Argentine military officers, another Menem loyalist on the bench ordered the preventive detention of Admiral Emilio Massera, ex-head of the navy and junta member, and, after Videla, the second most powerful leader in Argentina during the most intense period of repression. The context and timing of Massera's arrest suggests that the decision by another Argentine judge to imprison him was apparently a preemptive measure in response to Spanish international arrest warrants for Argentine military officers.[11] On November 2, 1998, Judge Garzon in Spain issued indictments of ninety-eight members of the Argentine military for genocide and terrorism. Three weeks later, the Argentine judge ordered the preventative imprisonment of Massera for kidnapping babies.

Why would international arrest warrants lead local judges to order arrests in Argentina? The warrants for Argentine military officers created international and domestic pressure to extradite the officers to Spain to stand trial. The Argentine military was adamantly opposed to extradition, and nationalist sentiment in Argentine political parties resisted the idea of extradition. But the relevant international legal precept was that a state must either extradite or try the accused domestically. To fend off political pressures to extradite many officers, the Argentine government apparently decided to place under preventative prison a few high-profile, but now politically marginalized officers like Videla and Massera. In 2003, however, the new president of Argentina, Nestor Kirchner, announced that he was prepared to reconsider the extradition requests that previous governments had denied. His position has support within the Ministry of Justice and the Foreign Ministry, but is still opposed by the Ministry of Defense, which reflects continued unease in the armed forces.[12]

Perhaps the most challenging of the legal battles was the case led by Centro de Estudios de Estado y Sociedad (CELS) to have the amnesty laws declared null, or unconstitutional. Once again, using the case of a kidnapped child of the disappeared, CELS argued that amnesty laws put the Argentine judicial system in the unusual position of being able to find people criminally responsible for kidnapping a child and falsely changing her identity (more minor crimes), but not for the more serious original crime of murder and disappearance of the parents that later gave rise to the crime of kidnapping. Additionally, they argued that the amnesty laws were a violation of international and regional human rights treaties to which Argentina was party, and which were directly incorporated into Argentine law. A judge of the first instance found the arguments compelling, and wrote a judgment that was a 185-page treatise on the significance of international human rights law in Argentine criminal law.[13] The appeals courts supported the decision, and the case is now before the Argentine Supreme Court. Previously, it seemed unlikely that the Supreme Court would support the decision of the appeals court, but the election of President Kirchner and his initial support for the idea of accountability for past human rights violations may change the climate for the Supreme Court decision.

But while pursuing these domestic judicial strategies, Argentine activists did not neglect the international realm. Once a case against members of the Argentine military was initiated in the Spanish National Audience Court, many Argentine family members of the disappeared traveled to Spain to present testimony and add their cases. Argentine human rights organizations cooperated actively with requests from the Spanish courts and from human rights organizations based in Spain to provide documentation and case material. In most cases, this cooperation between Spanish-based groups and groups in Argentina was brokered by a handful of individuals such as Carlos Slepoy, a lawyer who worked with the Argentine Association for Human Rights in Madrid and traveled frequently back and forth between Argentina and Spain.[14]

Likewise, the Grandmothers of the Plaza de Mayo pursued an insider–outsider coalition strategy. During the international process of drafting the Convention on the Rights of the Child, the Grandmothers lobbied the Argentine government to include specific provisions in the convention that they believed would enhance the success of their domestic trials. Specifically, they realized that domestic law did not provide a legal basis for arguing that the kidnapped children had standing in court. So the Grandmothers convinced the Argentine foreign ministry to press for provisions on the "right to identity" in the Convention on the Rights of the Child. They are included as articles 7 and 8 of the final convention, and are informally called the "Argentine articles." Because the Argentine constitution incorporates international law directly into domestic law, once Argentina had ratified the convention, these articles provided the Grandmothers with the legal bases to argue that children had a right to identity, and thus to permit judges to order blood tests (even though they were opposed by the adoptive parents) to establish whether or not the children were the sons and daughters of the disappeared.[15] In this case, the Grandmothers of the Plaza de Mayo, a domestic Argentine human rights movement, helped to change the international opportunity structure by changing the wording of a treaty, which in turn changed their domestic opportunity structure and made it easier to get convictions.

CELS solicited international groups they had worked with before to write amicus briefs for their cases, and succeeded in establishing for the first time in the Argentine judicial system the practice of using foreign amicus briefs. Local groups stayed in close contact with the Inter-American Commission on Human Rights, and at one point when progress on the truth trials broke down, they brought a case before that body. The commission, in negotiations with the Argentine government, was able to secure a commitment to allow the trials to continue.[16] The human rights groups also are poised, should the Supreme Court uphold the validity of the amnesty laws, to reopen a case before the Inter-American Commission, which has already found such laws to be a violation of the Inter-American Convention on Human Rights. In other words, domestic groups are concentrating primarily on their very active domestic judicial agenda, but moving with relative ease and fluidity in foreign, international, and regional institutions as a complement and/or backup to their domestic work. This is neither the boomerang nor an example of defensive transnationalization, but an example of a mixed coalition of insiders and outsiders, or box C. International and regional activism remains one of the tactics in the repertoires of these groups. At times it is more latent than others, but always there. But it is not a privileged sphere, largely because there has been so much domestic space in which to participate.

The Argentine case also illustrates a point frequently made by social movement theorists that political opportunities are not only perceived and taken advantage of, but they are also created by social actors. Argentine political actors faced a more open political opportunity structure for their human rights demands after the transition to democracy, in part because the failure of the military in the Malvinas/Falklands war led to an abrupt transition where the military had little bargaining power. This is in contrast to the situation in Chile and Uruguay, where negotiated transitions gave the military more veto power and more control over the agenda. And yet, the tactics groups chose also made a difference. Uruguayan groups chose an electoral strategy against the amnesty law, and when they lost the vote, they almost gave up looking for innovative judicial strategies to limit impunity until just recently. Argentine activists felt no such compulsion to respect majoritarian sentiment on human rights issues, and pursued legal strategies in the face of political opposition.

These social movement and legal strategies are so extensive that I consider Argentine social movement activists, and at times even members of the Argentine government, to be among the most innovative protagonists in the area of domestic human rights activism. They are not emulating tactics they discovered elsewhere, but developing new tactics. On a number of occasions, they have then exported or diffused their institutional and tactical innovations abroad. This model is in contrast to the expectations of the world polity school that sees institutional and normative innovation as emanating primarily from politically and economically powerful Western countries (Meyer et al., 1997). Argentina, which was never a passive recipient of international human rights action but was a classic case of the boomerang effect, has gone well "beyond the boomerang," to become an important international protagonist in the human rights realm, involved in actively modifying the international structure of political opportunities for human rights activism. For example, Argentina was one of the four or five most active countries in the development of the International Criminal Court (ICC), and an Argentine activist has been named the new prosecutor for the ICC, perhaps the most important position in the court.[17] This dynamism of the Argentine human rights sector is even more interesting and important in the context of active U.S. hegemonic opposition to the expansion of international human rights law, because it suggests that the advancement of human rights institutions may proceed even in the face of opposition from the United States, as has been the case with the ICC.

What does this say about the future of the boomerang? Am I suggesting that the boomerang is likely to disappear and be replaced by insider–

outsider coalitions? The boomerang was never an optimum form of political activism. It was a particular set of tactics derived in less than desirable political circumstances: when activists faced repression or blockage in their home country. At least in many parts of Latin America, redemocratization has reopened previously closed domestic polities, and activists have understandably redirected their energies into the closer and more responsive process of domestic politics. This is a positive political development, and we expect to see fewer boomerangs in Latin America in the future than in the past. But in much of the world, and even in Latin America on many issues, the boomerang is still alive and well. In particular, actors who used boomerangs in earlier stages of activism keep transnational network linkages active and are able to reinvigorate them if need be.

CONCLUSION

In this chapter, I have attempted to sketch out a framework for understanding the interaction of domestic and international politics in influencing the emergence and success of transnational collective action. International institutions offer international opportunity structures, which interact with domestic political opportunity structures to produce particular types of environments for transnational collective action (Khagram and Sikkink, 2002; Tarrow, 2002). Activists, both domestic and international, aware of the possibilities created by this dynamic interaction, choose strategies attuned to opportunities at both the international and domestic levels. Different combinations of domestic and international political opportunity structures thus may produce characteristic patterns of activism.

The framework presented does not replace some existing models, but complements and in some cases subsumes them as specific examples of particular dynamics. Both the boomerang effect and the spiral model are examples of a characteristic pattern of action that develops when activists, operating in domestic opportunity structures closed by repression or exclusion, seek international allies in more open international opportunity structures to bring pressure to bear on their governments "from above." But there are other characteristic patterns of activism deriving from different types of interactions of domestic and international opportunity structures. The defensive transnationalism identified in much of the globalization literature is yet another characteristic form of activism when activists operate primarily in open domestic structures and face closed international institutions.

This framework aims to provide a dynamic and interactive understanding of how the international and the domestic relate to influence the choices and outcomes of transnational networks activity. In a recent essay on domestic politics and international relations, Gourevitch argues that building such interactive frameworks is "[t]he great challenge confronting the domestic political research agenda. We have developed strong research traditions which hold either system or country constant. We do not have very good theories to handle what happens when both are in play, when each influences the other, . . . an interaction which itself helps define a system that reverberates back on the parts. We have good metaphors, but not clear research programs" (2002:321). In the area of social movement and transnational networks, I propose that the interaction of groups in the context of the relative access to domestic and international institutions may help us think about and explain the emergence of new forms of dynamic multilevel governance.

NOTES

For their assistance or comments on earlier versions of this chapter, I wish to thank Donatella della Porta and Sidney Tarrow, and other participants in the Bellagio Conference, as well as Catalina Smulovitz, Enrique Peruzzotti, Elizabeth Jelin, Roberto Russell, Ellen Lutz, Naomi Roht-Arriaza, Raymond Duvall, and other members of the University of Minnesota International Relations Colloquium.

1. Examples of this dialogue include Tarrow, 2001b and 2002; della Porta and Kriesi, 1999; Smith, Chatfield, and Pagnucco, 1997; and Meyer, 2003.

2. Sanjeev Khagram and I have addressed both of these theoretical dialogues in the introduction to *Restructuring World Politics* (2002). Here I draw on and develop further some arguments initially presented there.

3. This discussion draws on a chapter by Peter Gourevitch surveying the literature on domestic political and international relations, 2002.

4. Where legislatures or narrow policymaking bodies continue to dominate policy and exercise vetoes, the two-level game emphasis on how narrow win sets influence international negotiations continues to be a useful tool. But for a range of other issues, where legislatures have a less central role, and where the chief of government neither attempts nor is able to monopolize negotiations among players, the model is less useful. Lisa Martin and I signaled these concerns as regards human rights issues in our 1993 chapter in *Double-Edged Diplomacy*.

5. Realists refer to international structure as anarchical, and characterized by a particular balance of power. Constructivists have pointed to the importance of ideational structures, or structures of social purpose.

6. On issue specific political opportunity structure, also see Meyer, 1993.

7. Ellen Lutz and I develop this argument in "The Justice Cascade: The Evolution and Impact of Foreign Human Rights Trials in Latin America," *Chicago Journal of International Law* 2(1) (Spring 2001); see also: Brian Loveman and Elizabeth

Lira, *El Espejismo de la Reconciliacion: Chile 1990–2002* (Santiago, Chile: LOM Ediciones, 2002), and Giselle Munizaga, "Augusto Pinochet en Londres: El Caso Pinochet en los Noticiarios de Television," en *Nuevo Gobierno: Desafios de la Reconciliacion: Chile 1999–2000* (Santiago, Chile: FLACSO-Chile, 2000).

8. Interview with Alcira Rios, Buenos Aires, December 2002.

9. *Clarin*, Dec. 22, 2002: "Cuatro historias escandalosas en el legajo del juez Marquevich."

10. Interview with Luis Moreno Ocampo, December 21, 2002, Buenos Aires, Argentina.

11. Interview with Martin Abregu, Buenos Aires, July 1999.

12. *La Nacion*, June 20, 2003.

13. Resolucion del Juez Gabriel Cavallo, Juzgado Federal No. 4, 6 de marzo, 2001, Caso Poblete-Hlaczik.

14. Interviews with Carlos Slepoy, Madrid, May 7, 2003, and with Maria Jose Guembe, Buenos Aires, December 2002.

15. *Abuelas de la Plaza de Mayo, Juventud e Identidad, Tomo II* (Buenos Aires, Argentina: Espacio Editorial, 2001). Interview with Alcira Rios, December 2, 2002, Buenos Aires.

16. Interview with Victor Abramovitz, Buenos Aires, November 13, 2002.

17. Luis Moreno Ocampo, the new prosecutor of the ICC, was the assistant prosecutor of the trials against the military juntas in Argentina. He later resigned from the judicial branch, and founded an important NGO in Argentina called "Poder Ciudadano" (Citizen Power). He was a member of the board of Transparency International.

8

Multiple Belongings, Tolerant Identities, and the Construction of "Another Politics": Between the European Social Forum and the Local Social Fora

DONATELLA DELLA PORTA

I come from the old twentieth-century militancy of the Fifties, Sixties and Seventies, but then came the yuppie years, the Eighties and then the terrible Nineties where there was no room for political action except what was decided by political bureaucracies of varying kinds . . . so for me it was a reopening of a public space of confrontation, debate, initiative, which certainly . . . may also be the beginning of a new politics, no longer delegated or entrusted to the competent, to technicians, but taken on by people as their own prime responsibility (6E:143).[1]

On November 6–9, 2002, Florence hosted the European Social Forum (ESF). After the violent repression of the anti-G8 counter-summit in Genoa, Italy, in July 2001, many demonstrations followed in Italy as well as in other European countries. Unsuccessful attempts were made by center-Right governments and by some center-Left politicians to stigmatize the Genoa Social Forum, a network of groups that had organized the protest, as violent and "antipolitical." Since the events in Genoa, although there have been ups and downs, local social fora have mushroomed in many Italian cities, networking organizations and individuals who criticized "neoliberal globalization" and advocated "global justice." These networks have coordinated national demonstrations on issues such as the rights of migrants and the defense of public schools, but also on protection of labor rights as well as opposition to wars and terrorism. In particular, three hundred thousand took part in a special version of the annual March for Peace between Assisi and Perugia, called after the terrorist attacks of September 11. After Genoa, the Italian local social fora were indeed able to increase support for what started out as a "movement for global justice" (or "a globalization of rights," or "a globalization from below"). It was, in fact, in recognition of the strength of the Italian social fora that the coalition of European associations present at the annual World Social Forum in Porto Alegre decided to hold the first European Social Forum in Italy.

Notwithstanding the tensions before the meeting—with center-Right politicians but also many opinion leaders expressing a strong fear of violence in a city considered particularly delicate because of its artistic value (to the point of suggesting limitations to the right of demonstration in the "città d'arte")—the ESF in Florence was a success. Not only was there not a single act of violence, but participation went beyond the most optimistic expectations. Sixty thousand participants—more than three times the expected number—took part in the 30 plenary sessions, 160 seminars, and 180 workshops organized at the Fortezza da Basso; *even more attended the 75 cultural events in various parts of the city. About one million took part in the march that closed the forum. The international nature of the event is not disputable. More than 20,000 delegates of 426 associations arrived from 105 countries—among others, 24 buses from Barcelona; a special train from France and another from Austria; and a special ship from Greece. Up to four hundred interpreters worked without charge in order to ensure simultaneous translations. A year later, as many as a thousand Florentines went to Paris for the second ESF.*

The protests in Florence were greeted as a moment of consolidation of a social movement. The document approved by the assembly of the ESF stated, "We, the European social movements, are struggling for social rights and social justice, for democracy, against all forms of oppression. We want a World of differences, freedom and reciprocal respect."[2] The press described the events as the expression of "A movement, with various souls and no recognized leader" (La stampa 17/10/02:8): the Noglobal, for the critical observers; the New Global for the more sympathetic ones. After the ESF, opinion polls signaled growing support for the movement's demands, but also the expectation that the movement would produce a split in the main center-Left party, the Democratici di sinistra (DS) (Corriere della sera 11/11/02:6). Fulvio Bertinotti, general secretary of the "neocommunist" party Rifondazione Comunista, stated that "the movement of movements" "irrupted in the Left," "putting in circulation an enormous quantity of politics" (Avvenire 7/11/02).

SOCIAL MOVEMENT THEORY AND THE "GLOBAL MOVEMENT"

The ESF in Florence was one of the many increasingly massive international counter-summits that developed in the world's North and the South, especially after the World Trade Organization (WTO) protests in

Seattle, demanding "global justice" and "democratization from below" (Pianta and Silva, 2003). Given these unexpected developments, a general, central question has been asked more and more often by both scholars and activists: Is there a new global movement? Although we still have no definitive answer, we can reach a greater degree of clarity if we break down the "big" question into some "smaller" ones: Is there a movement? Is it global? Does it have new features? Social movements have been defined as movements composed of networks of groups and activists, with an emerging identity, involved in conflictual issues, using mainly nonconventional forms of participation (della Porta and Diani, 1999:ch. 1). Transnational social movements are "socially mobilized groups with constituents in at least two states, engaged in sustained contentious inter-actions with power-holders in at least one state other than their own, or against an international institution, or a multinational economic actor" (Tarrow 2001b:11).

If we look at the movement *identities*, recent research indicates that a large majority of the activists taking part in recent demonstrations against international summits identify themselves with a movement critical of globalization (della Porta, 2003c). The presence of such a movement is moreover acknowledged by opponents and sympathizers, as well as by the press. The semantic conflicts over the definition of the movement as "no global," and the plurality of names proposed for it (from "the Seattle people" to the movement for a globalization from below, or for global justice, or for a globalization of rights, etc.), testify to a still uncertain spec-ification of the movement's core goals, a fate that has been shared by sev-eral movements in the past (for example, the "68th movement").

If we look at the dimension of unconventional *actions*, the activities of transnational social movement organizations have expanded since Seattle from lobbying to protest. While research on protest events confirms that only a tiny percentage of protests address supranational institutions and are organized supranationally, these types of events seem to have increased dramatically in number and salience since 1999. However, par-ticipation in these supranational protests is still dominated by local activ-ists—this was true in Seattle, but also in Europe.[3]

The complex interaction between local and supranational activism is reflected in terms of *organizational* structures: in the emergence of more transnational SMOs and, especially, transnational coalitions of SMOs; but also in the growing presence of locally rooted networks structured around global issues (see chapter 3 in this volume). These groups occa-sionally participate in transnational protest events, but their activities remain strongly rooted at the local level.

Finally, looking at the definition of the *conflict*, if local, national, and transnational organizations agree in defining the scope of the movement as "global"—addressing as main enemies multinational corporations as well as international governmental organizations (IGOs)—transnational aims are articulated at the national and even local levels. Not by chance, national political opportunities continue to have a relevant influence on "global" movements, which are also active nationally (see chapter 2 in this volume).

On all these dimensions, the emerging movement on global issues seems to present a blend of path dependency and learning processes. Protest combines the traditional repertoires built up during previous cycles of protest (especially in the consolidation of nonviolent forms of action), with some innovations (in particular, "consumerist" forms of protest, but also new tactics of civil disobedience). The crux of the conflict is a blend of Old Left attention to issues of social justice and new social movements' focus on differential rights and positive freedom, which goes beyond mere frame bridging. As in the past, the movement is formed by "networks of networks," but the new definition as a "movement of movements" stresses the preference for even more flexible organizational formats.

In this chapter, I intend to focus on the way in which the movement mobilizes, but also on how it *constructs* its own resources and opportunities. As McAdam, Tarrow, and Tilly put it, in fact, "participants in contentious politics constantly manipulate, strategize, modify and reinterpret the identities of parties to their contention, including themselves" (2001:56). Addressing their environment, activists engage in cognitive mechanisms of identity shift and attribution of threats and opportunities. Along these lines, I will first reflect upon the way in which the movement exploits a social capital that is vast, but very heterogeneous in nature, as well as an individualistic Zeitgeist that tends to discourage traditional forms of militantism. Activists develop *tolerant identities*, framing differences as an enriching characteristic of the movement and emphasizing the role of "subjectivity." Emerging frames are not just cognitive devices, instrumentally managed by the movement organizations; tolerant identities derive from long-lasting experiences of common mobilization— through a process of "contamination in action." A challenge for the movement is sustaining this apparently weak form of commitment over the long term.

Second, as traditional opportunities appear limited at both the supranational and national levels, the movement engages in a discursive struggle over the very definition of politics. At the supranational level, the institutional structures of IGOs leave little opportunity for control, or even participation, by outsiders. At the national level, the dynamics of economic globalization and the hegemony of the neoliberal doctrine have weakened the potential support for issues of global justice in the party system. Facing these limited opportunities, the movement challenges the dominant definition of politics, enlarging the scope of its criticism from policy decisions to institutional assets and the understanding of democracy. The political activities are (again) located within the society with a new definition of the *polis,* and an expressed interest in addressing citizens rather than power-holders. The challenge appears to be the ability to combine consciousness-raising with the capacity to affect political decisions, translating the growing sympathies in public opinion into influence on the process of public deliberation.

In order to reconstruct the movement's identity and politics as conceived by the activists, I rely mainly upon two types of data, both collected at the individual level: a) a survey with activists of the ESF, held in Florence in November 2002; and b) six focus groups, held with members of the Florence Social Forum, on their conception of politics and democracy. During the ESF, the Gruppo di Ricerca sull'Azione Collettiva in Europa (GRACE) interviewed 2,384 (1668 Italians, 124 French, 77 Germans, 88 Spanish, 118 British, and 309 from other countries) activists using a semistructured questionnaire. The different sizes of the country samples are proportionate to national presence at the supranational meeting. However, for cross-national comparisons, I have weighted the responses in order to control for the oversampling of the Italian population—randomly extracting a subsample of the Italian activists.[4] Moreover, in order to take into account the differences in the degrees of commitment of the subgroups of local participants vis-à-vis the others, I have contrasted the Tuscan respondents with those living in other regions. These data will be compared with those collected at the demonstrations against the G8 in Genoa in July 2001 (Andretta et al., 2002; della Porta and Mosca, 2003); at the Perugia–Assisi Peace March in the fall of the same year (della Porta, Andretta, and Mosca, 2003); and at the International Day of Protest against the Iraq War on February 15, 2003, in Rome (della Porta and Diani, 2004a).[5]

In all these cases, questionnaires have primarily been distributed face-to-face. In Genoa, we distributed them at the various meeting points of the networks that co-organized the protest within the Genoa Social Forum, weighting them according to organizers' estimates of the number of participants, subdivided by political coalitions. At the Perugia–Assisi March, we distributed questionnaires randomly during the demonstration, which lasted several hours. For the February 15 demonstration, we covered the special trains coming from different regions, controlling for possible bias with a subsample of questionnaires distributed in Rome to local activists, who were asked to return them in a prepaid envelope.

The six focus groups were conducted after the ESF, with generationally homogeneous groupings of participants at the Firenze Social Forum, the local organizational net of individuals and groups involved in the "new global" movement. Each group included activists of both genders, with different political backgrounds. The groups met with a researcher for about two hours in a university seminar room, responding to general questions about the movement and its environment. The meetings were taped and integrally transcribed for qualitative analysis.

With both types of sources, the research aim was to study the behaviors and attitudes of the movement's activists. Taking into account all the richness and limitations of individual data, I focus especially on the activists' perceptions of the external reality and their role in it. The responses to the questionnaires provide information about the general characteristics of the activists' experiences with politics and social life, as well as their opinions on various political and social institutions. The focus groups, as group interviews, were allowed to go beyond the aggregate of individuals, and to look instead at the interactions between different actors.[6] For the interpretation of my data, I rely upon a secondary analysis of the growing amount of existing research on the movement for global justice in various countries (della Porta, 2003c).

In what follows, after presenting the complex nature of the "movement of movements," I focus on two mechanisms of mobilization. The first is a sort of identity shift, with the construction of tolerant identities; the second refers to the attribution of threats and opportunities, and focuses on the reinterpretation of politics around the idea of a participatory polis. I conclude with some reflections on the potential strengths and weaknesses of these processes for the sustainability of the mobilization and its effects.

THE HETEROGENEOUS BASES OF THE "MOVEMENT OF MOVEMENTS"

Social movement theory has stressed the role of the availability of resources for collective mobilization. In particular, mobilization processes are facilitated for groups with a high degree of *catnetness*—that is, structural similarities (category) and dense relationships (network) (Tilly 1978). If research on the labor movement stressed the homogeneity of the "working class" (in particular in the Fordist factory) as a facilitative factor, for more recent movements generational or gender homogeneity have been more notable, together with high levels of education and the overwhelming presence of a "new middle class" background.

After Seattle, one of the points highlighted in comments on the global protest is, instead, its *composite nature*, with variable-geometry convergence of varying social and political actors who in the past had often opposed each other. While the literature on social movements had noted a strong representation of the new middle class, the protest against neo-liberal globalization also increasingly involved workers and employees, especially from public service. From the generational viewpoint, too, these mobilizations have been highly heterogeneous, with the return of the youngest group to be particularly noted. For if social movements had long been dominated, at least in the North, by the '68 generation—and research on young people had stressed, if anything, their political apathy—the prominent presence of youth was noted in Seattle (Burbach, 2001:9–10) and repeated in Washington, D.C. (where among the more surprising aspects was "the large number of young people, a level of participation never seen in the United States since the end of the Vietnam war" [Aguiton 2001:9]).

Our data (see table 8.1) confirm the presence of a heterogeneous background. In all the demonstrations we studied, participants were balanced by gender, with a slight overrepresentation of male participants (especially in Genoa, and, to a lesser extent, in Florence). They included young and "less young" people, with a high percentage of participants born after 1977, especially in Genoa and Florence; the average age was about twenty-eight, but closer to thirty-five in Rome. There were a large number of students, but also a number of dependent workers (up to 41 percent in Rome), as well as unemployed and underemployed (especially in Genoa and Florence).

Moreover, the activists come from various political and social backgrounds. A broad area of the movement links globalization with environmental disasters. Calls for mobilization against globalization have, in fact, often come from such transnational *ecological* organizations as the WWF (World Wide Fund for Nature) and Friends of the Earth, or national ones like Legambiente (the League for the Environment) and the Anti-Vivisection League in Italy or Bund in Germany. Environmentalists' chief criticism of globalization is that it favors production and trade over the defense of nature and health. Also numerous are *feminist* groups that stress the "gender" consequences of globalization: cuts in social services that constrain women into increasingly burdensome "double jobs," as well as the ghettoization of women in unprotected positions.

Globalization protests have also (re)mobilized *youth* movements. In Britain, young people have formed Reclaim the Street, an organization that has since 1995 organized improvised street parties (with the slogan "Free the City—Kill the Car") against the pollution associated with abuse of private transport and the privatization of public transport. In American universities, the United Students against Sweatshops are active on many campuses, denouncing the wretched conditions of workers in the "sweatshops" where T-shirts and publicity souvenirs are manufactured for their colleges. In Spain and Italy, a youth counterculture has grown up in the

TABLE 8.1
Sociographic Characteristics of Participants in Italian Demonstrations

| Year of Birth | Demonstration | | | |
	Genoa	Perugia–Assisi	ESF (only Italians)	February 15th
Up to 1956	10.3	13.3	9.1	23.2
1957–1966	8.0	13.3	8.3	18.4
1967–1976	37.6	34.9	27.1	24.9
After 1977	44.1	38.5	55.5	33.5
	100.0	100.0	100.0	100.0
Total	(758)	(413)	(1788)	(1004)

| Gender | Demonstration | | | |
	Genoa	Perugia–Assisi	ESF (only Italians)	February 15th
Men	57.1	48.9	53.7	49.8
Women	42.9	51.1	46.3	50.2
	100.0	100.0	100.0	100.0
Total	(760)	(419)	(1798)	(996)

| Position in the Labor Market | Demonstration | | | |
	Genoa	Perugia–Assisi	ESF (only Italians)	February 15th
Unemployed/Underemployed	9.7	5.2	11.1	5.3
Dependent Worker	24.5	31.5	24.5	40.7
Autonomous Worker	9.7	14.6	7.0	21.4
Student	56.1	48.6	57.3	32.6
	100.0	100.0	100.0	100.0
Total	(660)	(362)	(1692)	(990)

autonomous social centers, stressing both the defense of the most marginalized groups, and the need to reappropriate space and construct identities (Dines, 1999).

In differing ways in the various countries, moreover, many *trade union organizations* in the North have joined in protest against neoliberal globalization, accused of subordinating citizens' rights to the free market, thus increasing the inequalities both between the North and South and within their own countries. The forerunners of the Seattle protests can in fact be found, at least in part, in the world of work. In various ways, depending on the prevailing patterns of interest representation in various countries, the 1990s saw a transformation of labor action. While, in general terms, the union federations in European countries supported privatization, deregulation, and the "flexibilization" of labor, opposition grew both inside and outside unions. In France, Italy, and Germany, for example, protest extended particularly to public services, aimed against privatization and its effects on domestic work conditions and the global efficiency of services. Accused of supporting old privileges, the public-sector unions often sought consensus in public opinion by claiming to defend public against private values, service against goods.

Apart from public transport, opposition to neoliberal economic policies extended particularly to schools and health. In these areas, in countries with pluralist patterns of industrial relations (with various representative organizations competing with each other), new unions highly critical of the various forms of privatization arose and expanded—from Coordonner, Rassembler, Construire (CRC) and Solidaire, Unitaire, Démocratique (SUD-PTT) in France (Béroud, Mouriaux, and Vakaloulis, 1998:49) to Cobas in Italy. In the so-called neocorporative countries, with occupational representation confined to a single union, public-sector unionists took the most radical positions (for instance, first the OETV and then Ver.di in Germany). It was no coincidence that these unions were the most involved in the protest campaigns against neoliberal globalization. Alongside them were often the traditionally most combative occupations from big industry, from the IG-Metall metalworkers in Germany or FIOM (Federazione impiegati operai metallurgici) in Italy (who had already taken part in, for instance, the G8 demonstrations in Genoa), to the dockworkers of Seattle, a city known for a militant trade-union tradition since the nineteenth century (Levi and Olson, 2000).

Another component in the movement for globalization from below was born out of the *voluntary work and international cooperation* area. Experience of interaction among social volunteer groups (many of religious origin) and social-movement activists developed particularly in the Jubilee 2000 campaign to cut poor countries' foreign debt (after 2000 Drop the Debt and Jubilee South). In solidarity operations in the developing countries, in humanitarian emergencies, and even on the peripheries of cities in the North, volunteers from lay and religious NGOs had often worked together, jointly denouncing increased poverty following cuts in public expenditure.

Demonstrators interviewed in Italy—in Genoa, and afterwards—had previous or current experience of participation in associations of various types, often overlapping: from NGOs to voluntary work, from trade unions to religious groups, from parties to social movements (see table 8.2). This rich, varied "social capital" does not seem to have been affected by the Genoa events—not by the repression or the ensuing debate inside

TABLE 8.2
Participation (Present and Past) in Associations by Demonstration

Participation in:	Percentage of Demonstrators			
	Genoa	Perugia/ Assisi	ESF (only Italians)	February 15th
Nongovernmental organizations	32.0	31.8	32.1	—
Unions	19.0	22.0	26.3	40.5
Parties	32.2	29.0	30.3	33.5
New social movement organizations	37.7	38.5	46.5	—
Pacifist associations			—	22.4
Antiracist associations			27.0	19.9
Third world associations			—	20.2
Women's rights associations			16.2	13.4
New global associations			—	18.8
Neighborhood groups			18.1	16.1
Human rights associations				22.6
Student groups	52.0	48.6	55.6	40.2
Autonomous social centers	35.0	46.0	36.9	8.7
Religious movements	17.6	23.9	20.2	30.9
Environmental associations	24.2	30.6	42.8	27.9
Voluntary associations	41.4	47.5	49.2	30.0
Recreational associations	34.4	39.5	51.7	44.9
Cultural associations				34.0
Other organizations				22.0

and outside the movement on forms of action. Nor were they impacted by the terrorist attacks of September 11, 2001, which led to talk—especially in the United States, which was caught between terrorist threats and the blasts of war—of an early end to mobilization against neoliberal globalization. Over time, between the anti-G8 protests in Genoa and the ESF in Florence (and especially at the peace march in Rome), the movement seems to have extended its capacity to persuade and involve not only trade-union activists and even their leaders, but also religious groups and environmental associations, while not losing its younger student groups and more radical youth components. There remains a stable presence of participants who are or have been members of political parties—who are, as we shall see, quite critical of those parties.

The same associational density of the movement that we found among Italian activists can be observed in activists coming to Florence from different countries (see table 8.3). The origins of the movement, in Italy and elsewhere, are found in platforms bringing together trade unions and sol-

TABLE 8.3
Participation (Present and Past) at the ESF by Nationality
(Weighted Sample)

Participation in:					Percentage of Demonstrators			
	Italy	France	Germany	Spain	Great Britain	Total	Cr.'s V	Sig.
Unions	28.3	48.2	28.8	28.1	77.2	44.3	.40	***
Parties	35.2	32.1	27.5	27.2	78.5	42.4	.41	***
Student groups	58.6	45.7	46.3	51.3	82.6	58.5	.29	***
Youth social centers	45.5	27.5	22.4	20.5	14.8	26.8	.25	***
Religious groups	17.9	12.2	20.0	12.4	18.1	16.0	.08	Ns.
Environmental associations	47.3	12.9	48.1	46.9	55.0	41.5	.32	***
New social movements (in general)	57.6	56.8	68.8	40.7	89.3	63.4	.34	***
Voluntary groups (charities)	46.6	53.6	40.7	52.6	57.1	51.0	.11	Ns.
Recreational associations	49.3	48.6	56.8	44.2	54.7	50.5	.08	Ns.
NGOs	38.0	46.8	65.8	56.1	63.5	52.9	.21	***
Total cases	142	139	79	114	148	622	—	—

* significant at 0.05 level; ** significant at 0.01 level; *** significant at 0.001 level

idarity groups, Catholics and feminists, ecologists and the radical Left, in a critique of neoliberal globalization. Yet, there is no lack of specific national features to confirm the role of the political resources and opportunities peculiar to each country. For instance, the greater heterogeneity of social capital for protest in Italy or Spain by comparison with, for example, Britain (where the bulk of those interviewed belong to the Socialist Workers' Party), seems to point to the movement's greater appeal in countries marked by a particularly closed structure of internal political opportunities—with center-Right governments committed to neoliberal positions, so that a broad front is created for opposition.

Relevance also seems to attach to the traditions of the national sectors of social movements, albeit with great similarities among the various countries. A comparison of Germany and France, for instance, confirms the greater presence among German Globalisierungskritiker of "new social movement" and "ecological" activists—in contrast with the trade-union component in the French case, which particularly through the new unions has had a strong influence on the development of the *altermondialist* movement. Activists with backgrounds in religious-type groups are more strongly represented in Italy and Germany, where the pacifist movement had already seen intense collaboration between lay and religious people.

Tolerant Identities

Many observers, even those sympathetic to the movement, have stressed the potential risks of this fragmentation, to the point of proposing a concept of *"movements* of globalization critics" in the plural (Rucht, 2001). On the other hand, the heterogeneity of the movement was highlighted as an innovative feature or an enhancement by comparison to movements of the past (Epstein, 2000; Gill, 2000). The self-definition as a "movement of movements," particularly successful in Italy, emphasizes the positive aspects of heterogeneous, multiply faceted identities that reflect social complexity while, as activists often stress, respecting their "subjectivity." I suggest here that the identity shift from single-movement identity to multiple, *tolerant identities* has helped the movement in dealing with its heterogeneous bases. As we shall see, tolerant identities are characterized by inclusiveness and positive emphasis upon diversity and cross-fertilization, with limited identification. They develop especially around common campaigns on objects perceived as "concrete" and nurtured by an "evangelical" search for dialogue.

The first characteristic of the activists' identities is their emphasis upon *diversity*, presented by the activists as a positive value—"a great novelty and a huge asset, because it brings together men and women, from twenty to sixty, who discuss with each other, opposing the logic of the old Leftist parties of separating women, young people and so on" (4E:101). The various generations present in the movement seem to agree that "the fine thing about this movement is its *variety* and its capacity to bring together the most varied individuals, on objectives common to them" (1D:10). Diversity is in fact interwoven with the search for joint action, but also for joint identity.

Something seen as "kind of epoch making" is the *inclusiveness* of the movement: the fact that "there really is belonging . . . yet they're actually not exclusive, that's the novelty." The action itself reflects and promotes overlapping membership, with simultaneous expression of multiple identities. Telling is the following dialogue which took place during a focus group:

4G: we are going to the demonstration, what part of the demonstration will we be with? What banner do we parade under? . . . identity as a social forum is taking roots from the identity viewpoint. . . . those who belong to bigger organizations, according to me they feel belonging to the social forum as something that matters . . .

4B: and try to shift the banner as close as possible . . .

4G: yes, that's true. . . . at the European Social Forum demonstration there was some wonderful dancing around this sort of thing . . . you wanted to be in four or five places at once. . . .

4C: I think it's a kind of sign of the times too . . . as well as the fact that today you can even experience belonging in a different way. . . . there's no longer political belonging in a strong sense, but you can experience belonging in a different way (pp. 89–93).

In joint actions—especially when it comes to smaller scales, such as small working groups—the capacity is seen for building common values, for being *"contaminated,"* or as one activist says, "fluidifying." The various organizational solutions adopted are thus often defined in pragmatic fashion as experimentations, efforts to get as close as possible to the participatory model: "there's a *new willingness to really fluidify*, to confront ideas without wanting to pull this way or that" (3C:66). Building a common organizational network thus does not rule out other membership—indeed, the co-presence of organizational memberships and identities is seen as an enrichment, enabling a specific nature to be kept while building common identities. As one activist explains, there is participation *"as long as I can manage to find myself"* (2D:46).

The interviews confirm that, in fact, the multiplicity of reference bases in terms of class, gender, generation, race, and religion has not prevented the emergence of a sense of belonging to a movement. According to information on perceptions of the movement by the Italian activists themselves (table 8.4), only a minority cast doubt on the existence of a single move-

TABLE 8.4

Relationship with the Movement for Global Justice, per Demonstration

Organizational membership	Genoa	Perugia/ Assisi	ESF (only Italians)	February 15th
Members of movement organizations	44.6	31.4	34.0	32.2
Sympathizers of the movement	—	94.7	—	92.7
Identification with the movement				
Little/none	14.7	12.5	24.3	37.9
Some	57.9	47.7	55.4	33.7
A lot	27.4	39.8	20.3	28.4
Total	763	502	1668	910

ment with which to identify. While another, larger component believes strongly in the existence of a movement, identifying themselves with it "a lot," most of the activists seem to prefer a "limited" identification. Moreover, the percentage of demonstrators not affiliated with the organizations calling for the demonstrations increased from slightly more than half in Genoa to about two-thirds in Florence. A cross-national comparison of the activists at the ESF (table 8.5) shows that while it is true that greater homogeneity of the reference basis leads (as in the British case) to stronger identification, greater heterogeneity does not prevent levels, even if less intense, of identification with the movement.[7] Indeed, the presence of very high percentages of demonstrators (in all countries except Britain) stating they do not belong to an organization responsible for the ESF points to the capacity of the movement to spread beyond organizational networks.

The movement's strength is thus seen as its capacity to "network" associations and "individuals," bringing together "many situations . . . that in previous years, especially the last ten, did not come together enough, . . . while instead this is, I feel, the first experience I have had in such an alive way of contact and networking where the fact of being in contact and in a network is one of the most important factors. . . . this is the positive thing . . . the value of the Social Forums" (4G:89). The network is defined as more than a sum of groups, for it is in the network that the activist "gets to know people, forms relationships, becomes a commu-

TABLE 8.5
Identification with the European Social Forum by Nationality
(Equilibrated Sample)

Identification with the movement	Italy	France	Germany	Spain	Great Britain	Total*
Little/none	25.5	16.7	29.5	15.1	11.2	18.8
Some	54.1	53.9	48.7	53.8	32.2	30.0
A lot	20.4	29.4	21.8	31.1	56.6	33.2
N	137	126	78	106	143	590

Organizational membership	Italy	France	Germany	Spain	Great Britain	Total**
No membership in the organization that prepared the ESF	38.4	63.3	50.0	34.8	81.8	54.9
N	146	144	84	115	148	637

* Cramer's V = .20 significant at 0.001 level.
** Cramer's V = .36 significant at 0.001 level.

nity" (4A:92). The search for "another possible world" is contrasted with the specialized, fragmented action of foregoing decades. While the activists share previous experience in associations, the focus groups show that the movement also arises from a critique of life in associations in the 1990s—defined, indeed, as "the coming together of people who were no longer finding answers to the everyday problems they had to face, day after day, in the various associations they were members of, or else people who weren't in any association because they didn't trust any" (3A:62). The added value of the movement is seen as the capacity to bring together single-issue knowledge and mobilizations, fitting them all into a more general framework.

The very cross-fertilization among the "various souls of the movement" is seen as being made possible by *concrete initiatives*, daily conduct, and interaction among individuals rather than organizations. During common campaigns, tolerant identities developed from the direct experience of acting together with different people and groups. The movement originated in mobilizations of diverse, initially barely related groups that had turned against a number of international organizations. Contacts among the various affiliations have been built up over time, during previous mobilizations. In Canada, a mid-1980s protest campaign against the Canada–U.S. Free Trade Agreement (CUSFTA) had included churches and feminist associations, trade unions, and aboriginal populations in the Pro-Canada Network, which subsequently remobilized against NAFTA and then the Multilateral Agreement on Investments (MAI). In North America, trade unions had mobilized alongside ecologists (in what was defined as a "strange alliance"), first against the signing of NAFTA, and then in 1997 and 1998 against President Clinton's request for fast-track authorization for agreements to liberalize trade (Shoch, 2000). Bové's Confédération Paysanne and the Greens had protested together in France against GMOs and in defense of quality products. Together with environmentalists, agricultural workers' associations and aboriginal populations demonstrated against the destruction of tropical rain forests in connection with highway projects funded by the World Bank in India and Brazil.[8] NGOs of the North came together in the South with the "global civil society" they themselves had helped to nurture, and from which they now absorbed not only information on the local situation, but also new ideas. Religious, feminist, and ecologist groups had participated jointly in the campaign to abolish the poorest countries' external debt.

In the focus groups, in fact, the movement was defined as "a big building site" (1E:26), its strength "coming just from all those people working in their own *little* way in their own *little* associations" (1D:24). Agreement among different kinds of people can be found around concrete action, because a strongly felt common aim helps in overcoming ideological differences: "one person maybe has a photo of Stalin, and another a photo of Jesus over his bed, all in all it doesn't matter too much, if both believe that Nestlé has to be boycotted . . . because with ideologies, extreme objectives, dogmatism, you can't ever get anywhere" (2G:42). The movements' emphasis is on "regaining universal categories of politics, in short, a much higher level of politics" than in the specialization of the 1980s and 1990s. As one activist remarks, "I feel my generation's growing up in the second half of the Eighties and in the Nineties . . . had to do with a sort of specialization of politics, with no general vision of politics, and especially no direction to aim at: this movement has instead regained universal categories, as shown by the basic slogan, 'another possible world.' For me this is a very important fact, that has given me enthusiasm and passion in politics" (3E:63). The strength of the movement comes, indeed, "from the fact that various experiences intersect, so that if I was concerned until yesterday more with human rights, I have been able to interweave my experience with someone more concerned with economics, with work, or so many other things, and the overall interpretation of modern society cannot be partial along one line" (3E:63).

Interaction around concrete objectives helps, in the activists' view, to build an ever more solid common base. A "strength of the movement," "its richness," "a strategically winning choice" is "to go forward for a long time coming together around particular points, leaving aside more systematic discussions, theoretical ones and so on." From an initially instrumental impetus to act as a coalition, there ensues the start of a process of building a collective identification—albeit partial, given that "the relationship with any organization ought properly to be to take a critical position but try to form part of a general scheme *even not taking totally on board everything that's offered to you, but at any rate belonging to something*" (IG:19).

Common solidarity develops, indeed, in concrete actions or, as the activists say, in the search for a new style of activism founded on *immediately gratifying action* rather than on sacrifice for the sake of a distant future.[9] The search for a new type of activist, oriented to immediate transformation in everyday life, brings together the new generations with the old, building in both cases upon experiences with voluntary associations. In the words of a member of the '68 generation, voluntary work "doing politics because it was doing society, doing action in society, in the neighborhoods etc.," is contrasted with "the endurance of the old-style militancy, sort of . . . today I'm busting my ass, sacrificing myself, so that tomorrow I can shift political equilibria, get into government, and through government change society and make it better. In the present, sacrifice is the mode of politics, happiness is for after the victory when things can be changed" (5E:122–23).

The search for a deliberative element emerges particularly in the acknowledged higher capacity for *dialogue*: "the Forum has something evangelical, that is, something new, something we were waiting for, something there was a need of. . . . how is it new? It's new particularly . . . in the way of arguing, the way of confronting each other, in its caution, its different mode of approach, avoiding oppositions: it's bringing together components that are very far from each other and very different, that see each other a different way today" (6G:144). The movement is therefore described as a discursive arena: "a network bringing into communication a whole series of environments, of people with a common sense of things they want to change, even if among them the differences are profound." And the movement is praised for building up from the "common substrate among all these identities inside it . . . for a moment setting aside for the sake of the movement the more specific objectives each identity has and certainly must maintain as its own" and "nonetheless realizing the strength to be found from unity in diversity" (2C:38).

DEFINING "LEFT" AND "POLITICS": (RE)FORGING A POLIS

Social movement theory stressed the role of political opportunities in triggering mobilization: in particular, an opening up in institutional politics makes protest potentially more rewarding, and therefore more likely. This does not mean that movement activists allied easily with potential supporters in the party system. If we look, for instance, at the protest cycle of the late 1960s and early 1970s, there is evidence of a strong critique of the institutional Left, considered as too open to compromises. The alternative was expressed in the New Left especially in terms of a more "pure" attachment to the revolutionary goals, and interpreted as a refusal of consociational practices (Pizzorno, 1996). With the development of "new" social movements, there was then a de facto acceptance of a division of labor—with movements "retreating" in the social sphere and political parties "representing" them in political institutions. In the 1980s and 1990s, SMOs in fact seemed to transform themselves into lobbies and voluntary groups, countercultural communities, and neighborhood associations. The attempts at influencing the political system via the traditional forms of protest apparently declined (della Porta, 2003d). At the same time, the transformations in representative democracy mentioned in the introduction to this volume—the increasing power of the market over the state, of the executive over the legislative, of global institutions over national ones—all converged in closing channels of political influence to movements. Due to the crisis of Keynesian economic politics and the hegemonic neoliberal ideology, the potential for finding alliances in the party system also diminished, at least in the Western democracies (della Porta, 2003c).

Our data seems to indicate, however, that instead of choosing radical ideologies or retreating to the private (or social) sphere, activists addressed the political challenges via an attempt to redefine politics. The search for a "polis," which political parties and institutions are accused of betraying, is expressed as the need for a reappropriation of political activities by "the citizens" (versus professionals), the emphasis of participation (versus bureaucratization), the attempt to construct values and identities (versus managing existing ones).

The responses to our questionnaires confirm, first, that while respecting differences, the activists are quite homogeneous in locating themselves to the left of the political spectrum. While doubts about the liberalization of markets and cultural homogenization are also expressed in religious fundamentalism or conservative protectionism, these particular expressions of antiglobalization are not present in the movement, which has a clearly left-wing profile. Our data on self-location on the Left–Right continuum reveal a consistent majority of demonstrators defining themselves as "leftist," with only a minority considering themselves "radical leftists" (see table 8.6). In Italy, from Genoa to Florence, the movement seems to have extended its reach toward the more moderate Left—but those who declare themselves as "center-Right" are still an exception, while more than 12 percent refuse to locate on the Left–Right axis. In a cross-national comparison, we can observe that activists interviewed at the ESF also generally defined themselves as "Left," with a significant component saying

TABLE 8.6
Self-Location on the Left–Right Axis by Demonstrations and by Nationality (for the ESF)

Full Samples	Extreme Left	Left	Center-Left	Center	Center-Right and Right	Refuse to locate	Total
Genoa	37.5	54.2	7.3	0.6	0.4	—	683
Perugia/Assisi	22.2	50.3	15.4	3.5	2.4	13.0	463
Italy-FSE	24.9	49.1	10.1	0.4	0.4	15.1	1683
FSE-weighted sample*							
Italy	28.9	50.7	4.9	0.7	0.7	14.1	142
France	37.3	44.8	4.5	0.7	0.0	12.7	134
Germany	25.0	43.8	13.8	0.0	0.0	17.5	80
Spain	23.6	52.8	5.7	0.9	0.9	16.0	106
Great Britain	68.1	26.4	2.1	0.7	0.7	2.1	144

*Cramer's V = .19 significant at 0.001.

"extreme Left," and a limited number at the "center-Left." With the exception of British activists, the great majority of whom were extreme Left (68 percent, followed at a distance by the French at 37.3 percent) placement on the Left ranges from 44.9 percent (Germans) to 52.8 percent (Spaniards), with Italians around the average of 50 percent. Many activists also refuse to commit on the Left–Right axis—with highest percentages among "postmaterialist" Germans and Spanish ethno-nationalists. From this viewpoint, the movement emerges in various countries from a critique of the policy choices of national governments—including left-wing governments—as well as those of intergovernmental organizations.

However, the experience of participation in associations forges a conception of politics alternative to the institutional one. While disappointment with "ordinary" politics was expressed in the 1990s in a return, if not to private life, at least to social life (joining the voluntary sector, as opposed to politics), the current movement is seen as based upon the interaction between society and politics. As one activist of the 1990s generation ("the years without movements") puts it: "I never went in for politics, but before I always did voluntary stuff. . . . according to me there's now this merger between voluntary work and politics in the strict sense . . . and this is maybe the novelty that gives the impetus, the fuel that makes the forces of two worlds that were perhaps a bit separate before come together" (3I:77).

In seeking a different politics, one central motivation is *mistrust* for parties and representative institutions. The common identification with the Left is blended with high interest in politics, defined as politics "from below," but mistrust in the actors of institutional politics. In Italy, notwithstanding increasing contacts with the unions and center-Left parties (della Porta, 2003c:ch. 5), mistrust in political parties does not decline with time (see table 8.7). On the contrary, between Genoa and Florence there is a decline in trust in political parties (from 26.2 to 21.4 percent, with an even lower 14.7 percent at the February 15 demonstration). A similar decline can be noticed for trust in parliaments (from 19.5 to 14.9 percent), replaced by growing trust in local governments, the United Nations (UN), and the European Union, and very high trust in social movements.

In a European comparison (see table 8.8), there is significant, spatially fairly homogeneous trust in social movements and voluntary associations as actors of a "different" politics (ranging from some 85 percent among the Germans and British to 95.6 percent of the French). By contrast, there is little trust in political parties: a bare 17.8 percent of interviewees from the ESF have fair or great trust (even less than in the Genoa survey), with extreme expression of Parteiverdrossenheit (disillusionment with parties) among German activists, attributable to the heavy critique of the national Red–Green government that underlay the formation of ATTAC-Germany.

TABLE 8.7
Trust in Actors of Political Participation and Representative Institutions by Demonstration

	Percentage of Demonstrators			
Enough or much trust in	*Genoa*	*Perugia/ Assisi*	*ESF (only Italians)*	*February 15th*
Parties	26.2	21.3	21.4	14.7
Unions	43.7	40.2	—	56.5
Social movements	87.0	88.5	89.7	78.8
Local governments	40.3	39.8	50.6	24.9
Parliament	19.5	24.1	14.9	8.8
European Union	26.3	39.1	33.9	38.2
United Nations	25.2	41.3	32.0	22.4

Significantly, trust in parties increases with age: only 18 percent of ESF participants between the ages of nineteen and twenty-five trust parties "enough" or "a lot."

Focus groups confirmed activists' mistrust of the institutions of representative democracy—since, as one activist says, "for better or worse, many of us who believed we were living in a democracy have woken up. We've realized we were not even valued properly, we were not even really electors, we were no use to anything or anyone, since these agreements did without government bodies or especially parliaments, so there was nothing to be got out of us even in that" (5B:127). This perception applies not only to national governments—even left-wing governments obtained the trust of not more than 15 percent of interviewees (with barely 2.7 percent of activists expressing at least fair trust in Britain, followed by Italy with 11.8 percent, and even among Germans only 14.6 percent). Not even parliaments, the main instrument of representative democracy, are regarded with trust (with a deterioration for the Italians in comparison with Genoa). There is significantly greater trust in local bodies (especially in Italy, France, or Spain), and, to a lesser extent, in the UN (especially in Germany); whereas the European Union scores a trust level barely higher than for the national government (except, in this case, for the more trustful Italian activists).

The comparison with Eurobarometer figures highlights some special features of activists in the various countries. While trust in parties sees limited swings around low values in the overall population, among activists opinions seem to vary more, with percentages a little above the average for the population in Italy, France, and Britain, and lower in Spain and Germany, by many percentage points. Also highly varied are atti-

TABLE 8.8
Trust in Actors of Political Participation and Representative Institutions by Nationality (Data in Italics Refer to Entire Population)

Trust much or enough	Percentage of Demonstrators							
	Italy	France	Germany	Spain	Great Britain	Total	Cr.'s V	Sig.
Parties	18.9	22.7	6.0	14.4	22.1	17.8	.15	*
Parties-Eurobarometer	*15*	*13*	*17*	*24*	*15*	—		
Unions		67.4	37.7	45.3	71.9	58.5[1]	.29	***
Cisl/Uil	*8.7*							
Cgil	*58.2*							
Sindacati di base	*62.6*							
Unions-Eurobarometer	*34*	*36*	*34*	*37*	*39*	—		
Movements	86.1	95.6	85.2	92.7	84.4	88.9	.15	*
NGOs-Eurobarometer	*39*	*42*	*30*	*69*	*30*	—		
Voluntary-Eurobarometer	*57*	*63*	*48*	*68*	*63*	—		
Local governments	50.0	46.0	28.9	34.5	18.4	36.0	.25	***
National government	3.4	9.3	8.5	1.8	2.7	4.9	.14	*
Nat. Gov.-Eurobarometer	*33*	*30*	*37*	*48*	*33*	—		
National Parliament	11.8	20.2	14.6	18.2	2.8	13.0	.19	***
European Union	22.3	12.5	10.0	10.2	3.4	11.8	.20	***
United Nations	17.7	27.7	37.0	17.4	8.2	20.1	.23	***
UN-Eurobarometer	*57*	*44*	*48*	*58*	*55*	—		

*significant at 0.05 level; ** significant at 0.01 level; *** significant at 0.001 level
[1]Without Italians.
Source: for data on entire population. Eurobarometer 57, spring 2002

tudes to the unions: here, too, while the populations show very similar figures, activists report higher levels of trust not only in Italy (where the figure differs according to the type of trade union), but also in France, Spain, Britain, and (less) in Germany.

As regards governments and parliaments, activists everywhere express much less trust than citizens of their countries as a whole, with the lowest figures for the Spanish (conservative) government or Britain's New Labour. Confirming the figure for parties, activists also express heavy criticism of majorities on the Left (which one participant in the focus groups significantly defined not as "favorable" but instead as "less averse"). Similarly more varied for activists than for the population as a whole are the figures for trust in the UN. Everywhere, by contrast, activists show much higher trust in movements than found by the Eurobarometer survey for NGOs and voluntary associations: on this point, ESF participation seems to have a homogenizing effect, whereas figures found in the Eurobarometer survey are more varied, with Spanish and British activists proportionally much more skeptical than their fellow citizens, but French and Germans by contrast relatively more trusting.

By contrast with the movements of the 1970s, the "Left" critique largely avoids ideologism. If the New Left was fascinated by a possible revolutionary seizure of power, current activists instead present their action as *pragmatic, concrete, and gradualist*. The movement's objective is in fact to "make the world aware": it "does not have the objective of taking power, but of changing society in its relationships, in feelings, in relations with people, of building a different world; and a different world is built from below" (5B:128). In the words of one participant in the focus group, the movement is a river, and

> the broader the river, the slower it flows. . . . sometimes it even seems as if it flows underground, just because it's so broad, every time it has to redefine its way of doing things in relation to what's happening around too, and fortunately it does so in the broadest possible way, and perhaps the most democratic and mixed up. . . . the movement is like water permeating and flowing everywhere, so that when it knocks the wall down it already owns the field (3C:66).

The critique of parties—especially those potentially closest—concerns the conception of politics as an activity for professionals, even more than opposition to specific policy choices. The gap in ways of conceiving and doing politics is perfectly summed up in this dialogue during a focus group:

> 4B: I think the parties feel threatened by this type of [movement] participation. . . .
> 4A: I don't think they understand it at all. . . .
> 4B: because they're all going through a crisis of representation too. . . . they are not representative of anyone, as things are. . . .
> 4B: on the one hand there's also a completely different model of self-representation, etc., that doesn't fit, doesn't gel with a party's way of selection from above. . . .
> 4G: they don't even let themselves be called in question. . . .
> 4F: well, anyway, without denying the function of parties, we have to assert the fully political character of this movement, and the fact that at any rate it represents a very advanced experiment in political action, something that absolutely has to be preserved. . . .
> 4E: I, in the last analysis, it's not that I believed the parties could themselves adopt the Forum's way of working, but perhaps I'd at least have expected from the left-wing parties a minimum of attention, whereas instead they

looked down on it: now it's clear that the Forum has brought so many people together, so many people that had stopped doing politics because they were sick of the parties on the left, so instead of being looked down on I'd have expected a minimum of attention for a movement that, for better or worse, manages to mobilize a whole lot of people, and are active on themes that are important . . . but it didn't happen (p. 94).

As emerges from the focus groups, the demand for politics coincides with a demand for participation; one criticism of the parties is that by now they have become *bureaucracies* founded upon delegation. In one activist's words, the movement marks "the passage from representation to participation: what the movement is looking for is not to involve people through delegation" (2C:42). It's the discovery that "I don't have to be represented but represent myself, so that I myself have to participate in something and don't have to feel locked out" (4A:88). Participation is seen as an antidote to the "aridity" of politics in the 1980s and 1990s:

in these recent decades, politics had become dried up. . . . every so often someone says politics never takes jumps; in fact politics almost always goes by jumps, a little like earthquakes: those plates pushing day after day, until finally the earthquake happens instantaneously. It was a little like that, then . . . [the movement] exploded partly because of the desire to express your own condition, express it yourself, not necessarily delegating it. . . . the purely representative machinery of politics has more or less broken down or gone off the rails, since the individuals that in various ways underwent the neo-liberal offensive felt the desire to express this condition of theirs them-selves, and simply by expressing it get over the first level of their own diffi-culties (3F:63–4).

Parties are stigmatized as bearers of the wrong idea: of politics as done by *professionals*, interested at most in electorally exploiting the movement, while still denying its political nature. It is particularly the "senior" activ-ists who perceive, and criticize, the defense by parties and public admin-istrators of a sort of monopoly of political knowledge:

there are two attitudes towards the Forum, and the parties manage to have them both at the same time: one is seeking to put their hat on the Forum by attempting to identify with it, even if for intrinsic reasons this movement can never identify with a party; the other aspect, instead, is more or less crypti-cally to downgrade what the Forum tries to say: "they're kids; yes, their enthusiasm is important, but the big issues are discussed elsewhere" . . . that's very serious, yes. . . . I'm reminded of a great e-mail that came on the mailing list: "I'm fed up with being called a kid" (4D:94).

In the activists' perception, politics involves the search, through con-frontation, for an emerging conception of the common good. The politics of parties, even left-wing ones, is seen by the activists as administering what exists, as opposed to searching "in the movement" ("that's why it's called a movement: the ideas and therefore the practices are moving too"). Party politicians are stigmatized for referring to a *"prepolitical movement* asking to be heard and then translated into a project and a political programme by those who do politics in the institutional sense of the word. . . . I remember an interview with the Florence mayor after the Social Forum when he said 'you can't ask these young people to express political projects, it's we who have to interpret them'" (6E:143).

For all the difficulties the activists acknowledge and discuss, politics is experienced as an involvement of citizens (even "individuals") in developing "demands" and "responses":

> the movement of movements has also the ability to bring organized structures (even old ones, with ideologies etc.) into relation with individuals, and hence with the movement in the truest sense. . . . *it's no longer the way it was, with the movement on the one hand with its spontaneity, asking questions, and on the other the politicians giving answers or trying to . . . in this case the answers come along with the questions, and the questions come along with the answers.* . . . Parties, associations, organized groups, were historically set up as the ones that gave answers (from an ideological, institutional, existential viewpoint). Today it's not that way, today there's this movement that is first and foremost building a spirit . . . building a surplus, an added value which neither the individuals nor the organizations have by themselves, but by putting themselves together, looking in this way for a sort of alchemy (2A:42–43).

The pluralism of the reference base is bound up with an assertion of equality, ruling out delegation in the name of everyone's equal right to speak for him or herself. The movement is in fact defined as "a form of relations among forces, political movements, organizations etc., that have not previously worked together; it manages to hold so many approaches together by endeavoring—and I think this is the great effort—not to compel them, basically, in this way broadening the fights" (2B:38). For older activists, the movement reopens a public sphere that had been shut off in previous decades.

The very essence of the movement, its "constant becoming," is also seen as the search for values, involving the activist in the wealth of his/ her "subjectivity": "politics is also a struggle of ideas, not just organizing something, it's also choosing what to organize around, since otherwise we risk falling into a logic that I feel is old, for which politics is organization, is the bureaucratic thing, is coordination, is you having one job and him another, is him being up top and you down below" (2A:48). Particularly the new generations are acknowledged to have a sensitivity toward a politics based on confrontation and searching, rather than demand and delegation. In the observations by "fathers" and "mothers," sons and daughters convey a vision of politics as the building of values—as "making the *polis*," in the words of one focus group participant. The encounter between new and old generations of activists is perceived as being based upon

> the same desire for something different, but something very instinctive, joyous, celebratory, practical (not just theorized but practiced). So this encounter was really something great for me, the possibility of a way of doing politics which is immediately a building of public places, building the *polis*, not organizing in order to gain votes, become a majority, govern, change the world, but immediately, on the spot, because you manage to build relationships, set up contacts, do concrete things, no? Doing politics straight away in this sense, making society, *making the polis*, has for me been the most exhilarating aspect (5E:123).

CONCLUSION: POLITICS, ANTIPOLITICS, OR OTHER POLITICS?

To conclude, the movement for global justice seems to bring out the conception of democracy as a search for a common good, starting from a pluralist confrontation among equals. These features seem linked with internal and external resources for the movement, yet they also create new challenges.

The literature on social movements has asked what conditions favor the bringing together of the weakest interests. Charles Tilly (1978) maintained that the mobilization of groups is influenced by their *catnet* level, a synthesis of features associated with social *category* and the density of social *networks*. In fact, the move from category (as an aggregate of individuals sharing particular traits) to social group (as a community capable of collective action) is facilitated by the simultaneous presence of specific category features and networks of relationships linking the individuals who share those traits. For the workers' movement, the presence of socially homogeneous networks marked by intense social relations is seen as having created favorable conditions for cooperation; collective action then strengthened the awareness of common interests—nurturing what Karl Marx called class consciousness.

The movement we have analyzed is typified by a very different reference basis from the workers' movement: as we have seen, it is heterogeneous not just socially, but also generationally, as well as seeking to bring differing and remote national cultures together. The weakness in terms of category homogeneity is counterbalanced, more than in other recent movements, by the presence of high associational density. Joining a movement is favored by the incorporation into informal networks of individuals and organizations sharing an interest in certain causes.

Social heterogeneity interacts with particular forms of collective identities. In the past, movements based on homogeneous social groups—in particular, specific social classes or ethnic groups—often, especially in the initial stages of their mobilization, developed strong, totalizing exclusive identities. The need to build a "we," often by reversing the sign of a stigmatized identity into a positive one (for instance in the case of workers, African Americans, or even women), led to clear contrasts in relation to the outside, the other. The search for recognition of an emergent collective identity often happened through the development of great utopias. In the case of the movement for globalization from below, the multiplicity of reference bases in terms of class, gender, generation, race, and religion seems instead to have pushed in the direction of identities that are, if not weak, certainly composite. Through continual work of "frame-bridging," the fragments of diverse cultures—lay and Catholic, radical and reformist, youth or "mature"—have been brought together into a more complex discourse that has chosen the theme of social justice as an adhesive, while leaving broad margins for autonomous developments. At the cost of leaving margins of ambiguity as to the movement's proposals—in particular, oscillating between antiliberalism and anticapitalism, between a return to a "pure, hard" Old Left discourse and the innovative development of themes of freedom emphasized by the women's and ecological movements in past decades—the development of a collective identity that is "open" and many-faceted makes it possible to hold together very different spirits, in part combining them, however gradually, and producing a high degree of identification among activists and sympathizers.

Since, in the past, movements relied upon strong forms of commitment with clear symbolic incentives and elaborated ideology, it remains to be seen to what extent "tolerant identities" are able to produce continuous mobilization. In fact, the activists emphasize as positive values inclusiveness, diversity, cross-fertilization, multiple identification—stressing the positive effects of collaboration during "concrete" campaigns and the continuous search for dialogue.

The movement bears dense social capital—made up of rich associational memberships and experiences—but it is certainly also very critical. The protest is not only developing largely outside parties, but also producing strong criticism of the forms of representative democracy. The demand for "Left" policies intersects with rejection of the conception of politics as a specialized activity for a few professionals occupying elective posts in the public administration. In fact, demands for "Left content" and more participatory politics combine in the criticism of the main political parties on the Left. These parties are seen as emphasizing their function of running institutions over the building of collective identities, tending to approach the potential electorate directly and regarding it as predominantly centrist and moderate, thereby discouraging the activist circles by definition more bound up with organizational identities and sensitive to ideological incentives (della Porta, 2001). Mutual mistrust thus grows between the parties seeking to replace the activists by surveys and promotion campaigns, emphasizing legitimation of a representative-delegate type, and the activists who instead stress politics as participation—and in particular between center-Left parties looking for the floating voter in the "center" and the demonstrators who criticize bipartisan agreement around neoliberal policies. If the search for new forms of democracy thus resonates with the demand for growing participation—and increasing dissatisfaction with the political parties—the important theme of representation of the movement's demands in the institutions nonetheless remains open. To those who accuse them of being "antipolitical"—or at best "nonpolitical"—the activists respond with a concept of politics as an activity based upon "strong" forms of participation of all citizens, rather than delegation to a few professionals. Moreover, the essence of politics is considered the elaboration of "demands and responses"—constructing identities rather than "occupying power."

In the face of challenges to old models of representation coming from the assertion of "multilevel governance," however, the movement for globalization from below finds itself tackling the difficult search for democratic institutions that are not just participatory, but also effective in influencing public policies in the direction of principles of social justice. One "older generation" activist asks, in fact, if "this indispensable networking that constitutes the vitality of this movement . . . is it enough to fully express political projects?" (6E:161). And the political efficacy of the movement is at any rate regarded as a problem even by the youngest—"the great strength is that there are big issues around which there is strong convergence: now the problem is the next move, that is, giving answers, doing actions" (2E:39). The problem of building political alliances within the institutions is indeed perceived by the activists, but certainly far from solved.

NOTES

1. This chapter reports the results of a research project on Deliberative Democracy, coordinated by Massimo Bonanni, which has been financed by the Italian Ministry for the University and Research (MIUR, 2002). Quotes from focus groups (the number refers to the focus group, the letter to the participant) refer to the

internal research report "I figli dei fori," edited by Elena Del Giorgio. A previous version of this chapter was translated by Iain L. Fraser.

2. www.fse-esf.org/article.php3?id_article = 328.

3. For instance, at the December 14, 2001, international march protesting the EU summit in Brussels, more than 60 percent of the participants were Belgians, and another 20 percent came from neighboring France and The Netherlands (Bédoyan, van Aelst, and Walgrave, 2003).

4. Although the distribution of most sociodemographic characteristics (education, age, and social situation, such as student status or not) was significantly different between the Italian sample and the population (Likelihood ratio chi square test), the Italian sample was not stratified for these conditions, because the distributions of some other countries also differed from the population. Varying the Italian sample would have meant reducing the Italian sample to a median category and giving up variation. However, the gender distribution was equal among all the other countries; only the Italian gender distribution deviated from this (males dominating). Therefore, a stratified subsample was drawn from the Italian sample, which respected the equal distribution of men and women in the population. Furthermore, the Italian subsample was reduced in numbers, as an overrepresentation of Italians would have biased the results and made some types of statistical analysis even less applicable.

5. The Genoa, Perugia-Assisi and ESF surveys were coordinated by Massimiliano Andretta and Lorenzo Mosca; Maria Fabbri was responsible for most of the data entry. The data on the February 15, 2003, demonstration have been collected within a cross-national comparative project coordinated by Stefaan Walgrave; with Mario Diani and Carlo Ruzza I have been responsible for the Italian survey. I am grateful to Claudius Wagemann for his help with data analysis. The focus groups were run by Elena Del Giorgio with the supervision of Fiammetta Benati, psychologist.

6. On the use of group interviews in social movement research, see Touraine, 1981; Melucci, 1989; della Porta 2004.

7. The rate of identification with the movement is particularly high, not only among those who declared a "global identity," but also among those (as many as 73 percent) who declared feelings of identification at both the global and the local (subnational) levels.

8. As in the late 1980s, coalitions of environmentalists, development associations, human rights activists and churches, aboriginal populations and agricultural workers' organizations had formed against the construction of dams in the Philippines, Indonesia, or, again, India (Fox and Brown, 1998).

9. Research on ATTAC-France local groups highlighted rejection of the idea of sacrifice for the sake of the cause: activists do not wish to conform to the group but to make available their own diversity, seen as a specific individuality that brings resources (Szczepanski, 2002).

9

Social Movements beyond Borders: Understanding Two Eras of Transnational Activism

W. LANCE BENNETT

As I write these words, the now-familiar stream of protests around the world continues. Three stories from the recent period illustrate three properties of emerging transnational protest that I would like to put in theoretical context here: *inclusive organization models* that favor diversity and issue-linking through distributed network designs; *social technologies* that facilitate these relatively decentralized, "leaderless" networks and help explain shifts in the scale of coordinated transnational activism; and the *political capacities* of members of these technology-rich networks to communicate their issues and form effective political relationships with targets of protest. These theoretical formulations rest on observations about an emerging global social justice movement (as it is increasingly termed by activists) and its intersection with protests against the U.S. war and occupation of Iraq. Following the introduction of these defining elements of recent-generation transnational activism, I offer a framework for understanding the tensions between these so-called direct action networks and the more centralized nongovernmental organizations (NGO) and social movement coalitions that continue to hold sway from the earlier era of transnational activism described by Keck and Sikkink (1998) and Smith (1997), among others.

AN ANTIWAR DEMONSTRATION IN
WASHINGTON, D.C.: INCLUSIVE
ORGANIZATION

The first story introduces a theoretical discussion of protest organization in inclusive, distributed networks, which I will later contrast with a more familiar (and still evident) model of organizationally brokered, ideological, and issue-driven coalitions. The scene is a demonstration against the war in Iraq on October 25, 2003, in Washington, D.C. Organizers estimated the crowd at one hundred thousand people and disputed the police figures of twenty thousand.[1] A reporter who went into the crowd discovered a great diversity of positions among demonstrators, many of which seemed to contradict the messages on the signs they waved. According to the report, the signs were provided by ANSWER (Act Now to Stop War and End Racism), one of the cosponsoring organizations of the "End the Occupation" rally. ANSWER is described by the reporter as a front organization for the Stalinist Workers Party and as advocating immediate U.S. troop withdrawal and public support for the Iraqi popular resistance.

Whether or not ANSWER is a Stalinist front, its positions do seem at odds with more popular alternatives present in the anti-Iraq War movement, such as bringing in the United Nations to coordinate a more gradual transition. This discrepancy raises questions about how ANSWER built such a diverse list of endorsers and how it mobilized such a large demonstration.[2] Evidently unperturbed by these questions, the reporter hinted at confusion in the ranks by doubting that many members of the crowd shared the organization's position of immediate withdrawal from Iraq. The reporter asked a demonstrator carrying a "US Troops Out" sign provided by ANSWER if he agreed with its sentiments. He replied, "I didn't even look at it. I was just waving it," and then offered fairly sophisticated ideas about a more gradual transition. With members of military families, the global social justice movement, and ANSWER sharing the same stage, the reporter concluded that "It was a day full of purposeful misunderstandings" (Goldberg, 2003:2).

Although the reporter's framing may be questioned, the idea of *purposeful misunderstandings* gets at what I detect as a trend toward relaxing the ideological framing commitments for common participation in many transnational protest activities. In their introduction to this volume, della Porta and Tarrow refer to this tendency as a redefinition of political involvement in an era in which progressive politics emphasize diversity and subjectivity over ideology and conformity. The problem of achieving common framing (frame bridging) has been a common source of tensions and fragmentation in social movements. Studies of protest movements in the past suggested that coordination was difficult, in part because core positions were not shared. For example, as Tarrow and McAdam point out in their chapter, efforts to join antinuclear movements across the Atlantic failed in the 1980s because the U.S. movement generally settled on the common position of a nuclear *freeze*, while European counterparts generally advocated nuclear *disarmament*.

This problem appears to be eased among many contemporary antiwar and global social justice activists through diffusion of an organizing code (often termed "relationship-building") based on metaframes such as diversity, inclusiveness, and social justice. This "relaxed framing" (part of what della Porta's chapter describes as "flexible identities") enables people with diverse positions to join in impressively large actions, often bringing multiple issues into the same protest event. A reasonable question here is whether such protest activities display enough organizational coherence to be sustainable, much less to qualify as social movements.

ANTIWAR DEMONSTRATIONS ON A GLOBAL SCALE: SOCIAL TECHNOLOGY, ORGANIZATIONAL DYNAMICS, AND SCALE SHIFT

My second story circles back to matters of sustainability, coherence, and definitions of social movements by starting with a far simpler question: What made the antiwar demonstration above more than just an isolated domestic protest event? In particular, what qualifies it as an example of transnational activism? Exploring this question takes us to the second set of factors underlying my claim that there are some things new and worth paying attention to in the current generation of transnational activism: *applications of communication technology* that generally favor the kinds of organizational structure alluded to in the first story, loosely linked "distributed" networks that are minimally dependent on central coordination, leaders, or ideological commitment.[3] These social technologies generally combine online and offline relationship-building aimed at achieving trust, credibility, and commitment as defined at the individual rather than the collective level. The relationship between technology and social organization is crucial to understanding the scale of recent antiwar and social justice protests.

The technology story behind the Washington demonstration is thus a *social* technology story. This point cannot be overemphasized: it is not the technology alone that creates rapidly expanding action networks—it is the capacity to move easily between on- and offline relationships that makes the scale shift to transnational activism possible. The innovative design and diffusion of communication and information technologies increasingly embeds those technologies in face-to-face experiences such as organizing, meeting, talking with friends, scheduling future protests, remembering and learning from past events, coordinating local protest actions in real time as they happen, and reporting them back through digital media channels so they can be recognized by activists themselves, as part of larger-scale developments.

The lesson here is that technologies contribute various mechanisms that help explain the scale shift in transnational activism discussed by Tarrow and McAdam in this volume: *virtual brokerage* (e.g., information archives, automated affiliation and membership, and automated, affinity-based choices of action repertoires), *hyperlinked diffusion* (e.g., news, icons, messages, and protest calendars that become densely linked across multiple activist sites and can be retrieved quickly through searches defined by individuals), and *virtual emulation* (e.g., the personal forwarding of pleasing stories, images, and artifacts).

The story begins by stepping back from what may seem to be just a routine national protest event, and finding that both ANSWER and United for Peace and Justice, the other primary organizing coalition of the Washington demonstration, were involved in coordinating the internationalization of the war protests. Social justice activists from dozens of countries built relationships at meetings of the European Social Forum (ESF) in Florence, Italy, in November 2002, and of the World Social Forum (WSF) in Porto Alegre, Brazil, in January of 2003. According to the account of Walgrave and Verhulst (2003) and our own documentation, the call for an international protest on February 15 was issued in Florence and punctuated by the first large antiwar demonstration that drew hundreds of thousands of people into the streets, including most global social justice activists at the forum (indicating once again, the relaxation of issue and ideological divides in these protests). Representatives of some seventy U.S. peace and social justice groups operating under the name of United for Peace and Justice met with ESF organizers in Copenhagen shortly after the Florence meeting and made plans to coordinate the European and North American protests scheduled for February 15, 2003. Planning for the full internationalization of the February 15 demonstrations continued at the WSF meetings attended by some five thousand groups and one hundred thousand individuals from countries around the world, including members of ANSWER, United for Peace and Justice, and other U.S. groups involved with coordinating North American activities.

Beyond agreeing to simultaneous protests, deeper levels of coordination involved sharing open-source communication technologies, establishing web links, and agreeing on common messages that would encourage inclusiveness and maximize turnout. One of the symbols that could be downloaded from nearly every transnational coalition website for further diffusion through e-mail and printed posters was the image of a missile crossed out by the words "Stop the War."[4] Demonstrators the world over used much the same set of slogans translated into dozens of languages: "No War in Iraq," "Not in My Name," and "No Blood for Oil," among others (Walgrave and Verhulst, 2003:12). The technological links and social software common to many sites facilitated the diffusion of posters, banners, slogans, information about gathering points, transportation, computer matching of socially comfortable (affinity) groups for different types of people to join, guides to protest tactics, and information and Internet news reports on the war and the pending protests. The result of this combination of on- and offline networking may well stand as the largest simultaneous multinational demonstration in recorded history. Depending on the sources of estimates, somewhere between seven and thirty million people took to the streets, in three hundred to six hundred cities and countless small towns. BBC (2003a) reports based on conservative police estimates put the figure as high as ten million.

The campaign did not end with protests; it was followed by a number of commitment-building exercises, one of which occurred shortly after the February 15 events, when MoveOn (www.moveon.org) in the United States drew on its virtual membership to send hundreds of thousands of messages to Congress. The organization then helped its members find each other offline to hold local candlelight vigils aimed at building social capital for future actions. Another impressive display of the capacity of digitally mediated networks to continue to mobilize protest occurred in London, some eight months after the February 15 turnout. The Stop the War UK network (not really an organization, but a network of thousands of organizations and individuals) facilitated what the BBC described as the largest weekday demonstration in the history of London to mark a visit by George W. Bush (BBC, 2003b). Unity at this demonstration was enhanced by such technological features as distributed digital swarms (see Rheingold, 2002). In one example, downloadable street posters with tear-off instructions and e-mail lists alerted demonstrators with cell phones and other communication platforms to spread the word when they spotted Bush motorcades in London, drawing swarms of people to those locations, "Chasing Bush."[5]

By some measures, these transnational antiwar protests seem to fall under Tilly's definition of a social movement:

> We are looking for times and places in which people making collective claims on authorities frequently form special-purpose associations or named coalitions, hold public meetings, communicate their programs to available media, stage processions, rallies, or demonstrations, and through all these

activities offer concerted displays of worthiness, unity, numbers, and commitment. If the complex occurs together regularly outside of electoral campaigns and management-labor struggles, we become more confident that the
social movement has arrived on its own terms (Tilly, 2004:29).

And yet, both the antiwar and the globalization protests seem alien in
other social movement terms. The proclivities of activists to switch easily
among issues, targets, and messages seem to raise questions about the
stability of membership and the terms of unity. Tilly (in a personal communication) raises important questions about whether such loose, multi-
issue networks are likely to generate the commitment and focus required
for movements to develop credible political positions and forge the kinds
of political relationships with their targets that might actually produce
change. These questions get to our final concern about the current generation of transnational activism: the *political capacity* of these distributed,
loosely linked, technologically constituted networks that, Coopman
argues, are distinctive enough to be given their own name: *dissentworks*
(2003). Are these networks limited—by their shifting composition, leaderless tendencies, and "opt-in/opt-out" memberships—in their capacities
to influence larger publics and establish effective political relationships
with the targets of their protest?

POLITICAL RELATIONSHIPS IN A TRADE
PROTEST: HOW STRENGTHS AND
VULNERABILITIES OF WEAK TIES
AFFECT POLITICAL CAPACITY

Our third story illustrates why the organizational and technological features of contemporary transnational activist networks cannot easily be
separated from questions about their political capacity, which I define
along two dimensions: being able to shape public debate about the issues
in contention, and developing effective political relations with protest targets to influence political change on those issues. (A third aspect of political capacity—the exclusion of potential members due to restrictive
technologies—will be addressed later).

On the same day in November 2003, as record numbers of Londoners
took to the streets to protest against an American president, U.S. activists
across the Atlantic gathered in Miami to register their opposition to an
expanded Free Trade Area of the Americas (FTAA). One indicator of their
commitment was the advance notice that they would face a formidable
police response with enhanced paramilitary and surveillance operations,
funded through the Bush administration's domestication of the war on

terror. The FTAA had been a target of past contention, as is well documented in activist web archives that offer a historical record of the global social justice movement as it has evolved through the chain of G8, WTO, European Union, World Economic Forum (WEF), or World Bank protests from Genoa to Prague to Montreal to Davos to Washington to Seattle.[6]

Our first question about public influence illustrates the ties between organizational structure, technological infrastructure, and capacity. Beyond their capacity to consistently turn out large numbers of demonstrators, were these so-called direct action networks able to generate enough internal dialogue to achieve the message unity required to focus broader public discussion? Or do weak ties also produce a weakness of core ideas? The latter view appears in the accounts of many mainstream journalists, who seem to dismiss the multi-issue, leaderless, direct action networks as largely chaotic and hard to summarize. Consider this (*New York Times*) journalist's attempt to describe the activists on their own terms:

> There are no leaders or spokesmen or women, just clusters of voices acting in coordination, though not necessarily in concert. The politics of the global social justice movement are as fragmented and postmodern as the technologies that helped give it life. "That's the nice thing about being a hydra," one eco-activist told me. "They can't assassinate our leaders" (Bunn, 2003:61).

The reporter went on to dispute the claim about "no leaders" by focusing on an organizer named Lisa Fithian who spends most of each year traveling from one demonstration to the next, renting meeting facilities, coordinating affinity groups, and offering training in march tactics and police responses. Yet the reporter acknowledged that she was a different kind of leader—less a spokesperson for a movement than a stylist of abstracted confrontation rituals, nicely orchestrated, but removed from meaningful messages or much dialogue with the targets of protest on the other side of the police barricades. As for Fithian, she admitted that there were leaders in this movement, but their goal was to be anonymous, to facilitate others, and to "create an organization that is nonauthoritarian and nonhierarchical" (Bunn, 2003:62). Both the familiar journalistic dismissal of the public message capacity of these demonstrations, and Fithian's (possibly edited) notion of building distributed activist networks as an end in itself, seem to leave open the question of where ideas and coherent public messages come from.

Yet, ideas do seem to distill and diffuse, as endless meetings are reported and echoed through the dense information flows over thousands of electronic nodes in these networks (Polletta, 2002). Notice, for example, that the movement adopted a name—global social justice (GSJ), or simply global justice (GJ)—within a few years after the Seattle demonstrations. That name is now fairly well recognized among activists; a Google web search on "GSJ" produced over one million hits, including a broad mix of NGOs (e.g., Oxfam) and direct action networks (e.g., Indymedia) and various culture creators from Radiohead to Princeton University. A web search on "GJ" produced nearly two million hits, but the mix seemed less coherent than the first search. These movement names may also be filtering into mainstream journalism, as indicated in the *New York Times* passage above. Yet the linkages among groups and the convergence in their messages may not be crossing the media divide, as suggested in this activist news account:

> Anti-war groups such as United for Peace and Justice joined with the more de-centralized, affinity group-based wing of the global justice movement to organize direct action. Powerful labor groups like the AFL-CIO and the United Steelworkers made clear that despite tactical differences, there was solidarity among resistance movements. To emphasize this point, AFL-CIO president John Sweeney visited the mobilization convergence center where art-making, training, and planning was underway for un-permitted street actions. Yet this powerful display of successful solidarity is not what Americans saw on their television or read in their newspapers (Hogue and Reinsborough, 2003).

If the jury is still out on the public opinion-shaping capacity of these activist networks, what about their capacity to create effective power and influence relations with targets of their protest? Demonstrators often claim victories, from shutting down the 1999 WTO meetings in Seattle (which it seems they did), to helping small nations scuttle the 2003 Cancun meetings, which requires a bit more of a leap to comprehend.[7] As for the FTAA, the Miami talks fell far short of U.S. expectations, and, more importantly, solidified the formation of a group of southern nations that had blocked the WTO proposals earlier in Cancun. Now dubbed the G-20, the group held its first formal meeting in Brasilia shortly after the Miami FTAA. But what can we say in this case about accountability relationships between the protest movement and the FTAA results? The FTAA case illustrates the complex linkages involved in such relationships.

The short story here is that Brazil cohosted the Miami FTAA, represented by the newly elected regime of Luis Ignacio Lula da Silva, whose backing by labor and social movements at home put him in a delicate position between domestic forces aimed at killing the free trade initiative and the United States with its corporate, investment, World Bank, and IMF partners, who could punish Brazilian defection rather painfully. Brazil proposed a compromise agreement involving a national opt-out provision on key trade rules that so weakened the U.S. proposal that many in the G-20 bloc felt (and apparently hoped) it would be rejected by the United States. However, the United States provisionally endorsed it as a means of continuing the talks at a future date. Being party to this awkward result kept Brazil from further straining relations with the United States, but put the newly elected regime of Lula at odds with social movement supporters in Brazil and demonstrators in the streets.

Assessing the political capacity of the protest network in this case involves first establishing whether there are communication and brokerage relationships among the demonstrators, domestic Brazilian social movements, and Lula's government. One such linkage point is through the WSF network, which offers an ongoing transnational dialogue among government-linked social movements (e.g., labor, environment, land reform, women's rights), issue-advocacy NGOs, and direct action networks. Next, it is important to recognize that capacity runs in two directions: the upward capacity of protest networks to introduce social movement values and positions into the strategic thinking and choices of policymakers (e.g., the Brazilian delegation at the FTAA), and the downward capacity of such policymakers to induce more radical protest networks to accept pragmatic political compromises such as weakening and delaying the FTAA rather than killing it. This second flow is as crucial to building and sustaining political capacity as the first. This give-and-take essential to movement capacity could be affected by the move of some factions of the WSF network to hold a counter-forum at the 2004 Mumbai meeting, partly aimed at driving NGOs out of the protest network (Waterman, 2003). Such dynamics illustrate the tensions between earlier-generation NGO-centered transnational activism and newer, loosely structured direct activist networks that focus my more formal theoretical discussion below.

For now, here is how Tom Hayden's widely circulated *Alternet* report described some of these delicate linkages in this inside–outside political game (see Sikkink's chapter in this volume) involving social justice movement networks and policymakers:

> A huge but empty trade agreement—widely described as "FTAA Lite"—was all the US could achieve after being buffeted for weeks by rising fair trade winds. But the jolly ship of neo-liberalism was salvaged in Miami rather than torpedoed, receiving life support from its most formidable critic, Brazil, and causing confusing challenges for the global justice movement in its wake. . . .
>
> One unofficial Brazilian insider explained that, "We were counting on resistance from the US to the Brazilian proposal, but they decided to accept it. This puts our social movements in a difficult position, because Brazil will

accept the FTAA 'model' even if it does not include all the issues, and the FTAA official schedule also. So our campaign will have to make difficult decisions soon" (Hayden, 2003).

This story illustrates the complex linkages between the global justice movement and related domestic and transnational players. As a piece of journalism, the story also embodies the properties of the social justice networks through which it circulated. First, Hayden implicitly recognizes the *inclusive organizational model* of the transnational social justice movement, in the context of a larger political policy process with which the movement is engaged. Second, this piece of activist/journalism offered a useful model of the political relationships intersecting the movement, which helped it diffuse rapidly through social justice networks via the *communication technologies* of hyperlinking and blogging (creating online public dialogues that speed the diffusion of ideas and deliberation about them). A Google web search on *Hayden Miami FTAA* conducted on December 15, 2003, produced 427 hits, linking this report across a broad range of organizations and discussion networks. Third, Hayden's analysis highlights important concerns about the *political capacity* of the movement. The remainder of this discussion provides theoretical perspective on how direct activist networks fit with the NGO advocacy networks, which, until recently, defined transnational social movements.

THEORIZING ABOUT TWO GENERATIONS
OF TRANSNATIONAL ACTIVISM

How does this broad and diverse movement compare with the transnational activism described by Keck and Sikkink (1998) and Smith (1997), among others, as largely issue-specific (e.g., labor, environment, human rights), and constituted around NGOs and coalition campaigns aimed at national or international political institutions to achieve specific policy goals? The current era of social justice activism still includes NGO policy networks, of course, but they now operate in a more emergent movement environment of large-scale direct activism, multi-issue networks, and untidy "permanent" campaigns with less clear goals and political relationships with targets. Those targets range over combinations of trade organizations, G7 summits, European Union meetings, WEF gatherings, and major corporations and industrial sectors (apparel, forest products, food, and media, among others). The first step toward theory here is to clarify the intersection of emerging global social justice networks with more established NGO-centered issue networks of earlier transnational activism.

An Organizational Hybrid: Embedded Networks

Second-generation direct activism embeds established NGO-centered networks in sprawling, loosely interconnected network webs populated by organizations and individuals who are more resistant to conventional social movement practices of coalition-formation, brokerage, framing, and establishing straightforward institutional relationships to influence policy. The players identified in the FTAA Miami protests—from unions, to anarchists, to antiwar networks—illustrate this embedding process, along with the upside potential for scale shifts and the downside of disruptive tensions and outright disjuncture inherent in such networks. The intersections of conventional NGOs with growing networks of informal, voluntary associations and direct activists call for reformulating earlier accounts of transnational activism cast largely in terms of: a) NGO-centered, single issue policy networks, b) that run centrally organized campaigns, c) based on brokered coalitions, d) aimed mainly at extracting policy reforms from institutional targets (Keck and Sikkink, 1998).

The scale shift in the globalization protest era reveals many points of tension between first- and second-generation transnational activism. These include:

- less NGO dominance of campaign and policy networks;
- the evolution of multi-issue organizations (ATTAC in Europe, Global Exchange in the United States);
- more direct individual involvement aimed at setting the agenda from below;
- and the proliferation of permanent campaigns that are not centrally controlled by NGOs or coalitions of organizations (Bennett, 2003).

At the risk of oversimplifying Keck and Sikkink's (1998) now-standard account of the original transnational activist networks, table 9.1 offers a contrast between their account of what I term an NGO-led transnational activist order, and the more recent emergence of direct action social justice networks identified in the first half of this chapter.

Loose activist networks adopting self-organizing communication technologies (see below) and advocating multiple issues, multiple goals, and flexible identities not only challenge previous organizational forms of transnational activism. These networks also challenge social movement theories that focus on brokered coalitions, ideological framing, and collective movement identities fashioned around national politics. As noted in the chapters by della Porta and Sikkink in this volume, most social movement theory has emerged from national cases, with mobilization often keyed to national political opportunities, framed in terms of familiar cul-

TABLE 9.1
Defining Differences in Two Eras of Transnational Activism

	NGO Advocacy Order	Direct Activism
Scope	policy—issue—advocacy	diverse social justice agenda
Organization	NGO-centered issue networks	mass activism—multi-issue
Scale	limited by brokered coalitions	expanded by technology networks
Targets	government (all levels) some corporations	corporations, industrial sectors econ blocs (G7, WEF, IMF, WTO)
Tactics	strategic campaigns —limited political goals —turned on & off by lead orgs	permanent campaigns —diverse political goals —difficult to turn on & off
Goals	gov't (nat. & int'l) regulation establish information regimes maintain organizational identity	personal involvement in direct action establish communication networks hyper-orgs to empower individuals
Capacity	reform & crisis intervention	mass protest, value change

tural symbols, and aimed at national policy institutions. By contrast, as noted by Guidry, Kennedy, and Zald (2000a) and in the introductory chapter by della Porta and Tarrow in this volume, many contemporary transnational activists believe that national governments are part of the problem of global economic injustice—either because they have ideologically joined, or have been coerced by, the neoliberal economic trade and development regimes. This perception of the problem leaves many activists despairing of national-level policy solutions.

The recent era of transnational activism suggests an evolution to a different social movement organizational form in several respects: the diffusion of supranational targets and rallying symbols; the regular, cross-national occurrence of parallel demonstrations with similar targets and protest repertoires; and experiments, albeit fragile ones, with new kinds of political relationships involving nonnational mechanisms of political accountability and community, from standards monitoring and certification regimes, to demands for direct popular inclusion in supranational decision processes. Perhaps most important, as noted by della Porta in this volume, individuals in direct activist networks seem to move fairly easily across issues and targets of protest (recall the co-organization of

TABLE 9.2
Two Models of Transnational Social Movement Network Organization

Network	*NGO Advocacy Networks*	*Global Social Justice*
structure	centralized w/lead organizations	polycentric ~ distributed
formation	brokered strategic coalitions	affinity ties & permanent campaigns
stability	issue/goal framing & organization identity create fracture lines	organizational code of inclusive diversity—creates dense networks of weak ties
membership	sign up/pay up limited agenda control	opt-in/opt-out collective agenda-setting
mobilization	strategic campaigns, member alerts	technological infrastructure generates continuous protest calendar
bridging	high brokerage costs	low brokerage costs
diffusion	within homogeneous networks	across diverse networks

antiwar and global social justice actions from our earlier stories), without experiencing the kinds of ideological, membership, or identity stress that most social movement theories would suggest. Hence, transnational social movement organization differs from conventionally defined national social movement organization in various ways, with the scale of transnational protest accounted for by these organizational differences. Table 9.2 identifies points of comparison between traditional, issue-centered social movements, and global social justice activism.

The contrasting mix of first- and second-generation activism outlined in table 9.1, and the organizational differences between national and transnational social justice movements identified in table 9.2, enable us to think theoretically about both the potential and the problems of transnational activism. For example, these differences do not always permit the levels of convergence in protest repertoires indicated in the Miami FTAA story. Indeed, some of these tensions are serious enough that many prominent NGOs simply do not identify with the global social justice movement at all, and many direct activists see NGOs, at best, as plodding too narrowly to make a difference, and, at worst, as agents of imperialism helping to institutionalize the problems they are trying to solve. A Social Science Research Council report on technology and international civil society described this disjuncture as:

the chasm that exists between formalized institutional NGOs and less formally structured social movements. The "real" NGOs aim to stand for credible social change—gathering the resources and membership necessary to
pressure governments on a particular set of issues or policies. In contrast,
more informal movements and loose groups of activists tend to see themselves as the emerging vanguard, developing flexible, creative and responsive approaches to the fact that we are more often than not all but shut out
of formal political decision making. Both sides see the other as ineffective
at best and clueless at worst, with international NGOs being portrayed as
lumbering dinosaur elites, often based in the North and unaware of realities
on the ground, while activists are seen as an ineffective rabble that sometimes misrepresents the truth to make political gains (Surman and Reilly,
2003:7–8).

The authors of this report put the best face on this tension by arguing
that many synergies exist across the two types of networks, and that in
any event, different kinds of organizations are required for a healthy
world civil society to emerge. Yet, the potential exists for NGOs to continue to take their seats at elite decision-making sessions without opening
doors for the direct activists to come along. For example, a study of the
inside–outside game at the 2002 WEF meetings in New York indicated
increasing NGO representation over previous years, and a shift in the
organization's agenda toward addressing many of the issues raised by
critics at WSF meetings and elsewhere. However, the systematic exclusion
of demonstrators in the streets, both through the words of official WEF
spokespeople and in reports by the mainstream press, also served to
exclude those activists from legitimate ownership of their own ideas, not
to mention from seats at the panels and dinner tables where they were
being discussed (Bennett et al., 2004). On the other side, the move by more
radical (i.e., ideologically inclined) direct action factions to create a
counter-forum at the 2004 WSF seems intended to define NGOs as part
of the problem with globalization (Waterman, 2003). If this initiative gains
support, the organizational code of inclusive diversity that has enabled
the scale shift in protest may well be undermined.

Viewed in traditional social movement terms, these rifts may appear to
be classic examples of ideological divisions between moderate NGOs and
more radical factions. This is not entirely wrong, but it misses the theoretical mark if we are looking for what is new in transnational activism. If we
see these tensions less in terms of ideological frame struggles or collective
identity problems, we can focus instead on the organization-based ethos
of inclusiveness and diversity (i.e., on what della Porta, in her chapter,
calls "multiple belonging and flexible identities") employed by so many
direct activists. In that model, it seems to me, we see something that
might be termed "organization as ideology": a movement design code

that is attempting to confront the failures of past movement eras—the fragmentation of the Left, the slowness and fragility of coalition building, the frequent inability to bridge collective identities meaningfully, and the leadership disputes and failures that led to factionalism, co-optation, and limited goal achievement. The so-called *heterarchical* emphasis on poly-centric, leaderless, inclusive organization is aimed at avoiding these prob-lems, while sustaining large numbers of individual-level relationships that enable people to move relatively freely across different issue con-cerns and to see problems in their localities as related to those in more distant regions. As I understand it, this organizational code has emerged from at least three sources: reflection about past movement organization problems; resistance on the part of many younger generation activists to ideologies and collective identity requirements; and necessity born of the desire to form sustainable relationships with distant others. These origins of the organizational code of this movement help us understand the importance of the development and application of technologies.

Social Technology: It's Not the Internet, It's the Code

Are communication technologies in and of themselves organizing move-ments? No. Plenty of face-to-face coalition building goes into the produc-tion of large-scale protest (Levi and Murphy, 2002). But when direct action networks are added to the mix, the idea of coalition building needs to be augmented to accommodate the density of individual level techno-logically assisted interactions. Dense interpersonal networks flow around protest events, building new relationships while creating agendas for future action. Such personal relationships are at the core of most social movements (Polletta, 2002). However, the scale and diversity of transna-tional global justice networks are not likely to be maintained without the remarkable integration of on- and offline interaction facilitated by innova-tive information and communication technologies.

Thus, the most important theoretical move we can make in trying to understand the transnational social justice movement is to move beyond the distinction between on- and offline relationships. Technology is often aimed at getting people together offline, and one purpose of offline asso-ciations is often to clarify and motivate online relations.[8] As Surman and Reilly put it, "When we speak of 'online mobilization' we are talking pri-marily of online efforts to move people to action—to protest, intervene, advocate, support. Such efforts are much more about relationships and community than information" (2003:39).

The synergy between the organizational code of inclusive diversity and the technology codes that link and structure network interactions may account for the heightened levels of diffusion and emulation that Tarrow and McAdam associate with scale shift (this volume). Consider, for example, the broad diffusion of simultaneous demonstrations around the world during the time of the Seattle WTO protests in November 1999. A simple social technology sequence involved (1) e-mail that (2) directed people to websites that (3) offered protocols for coordinating simultaneous demonstrations based on inclusion rather than conventionally brokered differences:

> Under the code N30 (November 30) a series of actions were organized using the Internet. Organizing included both web sites and e-mail. The web site, "A Global Day of Action" (http://www.seattlewto.org/N30/) called for action in ten different languages and provided a directory of local contacts all over the world. It included slogans like: "Resistance, and Carnival against Global Capitalist System" or "May our resistance be as transnational as capital" (Baldi, 1999). The organizing was broad based, inclusive and heavily online. "It is evident that the whole appeal was based on an extensive use of IT. It is also interesting to note that the aim was to gather as many groups as possible in the protest. Even the wide range of local initiatives suggested is a clear sign of the wish to enlarge and diffuse the protest as much as possible" (Baldi, 1999) (Surman and Reilly, 2003:43).

It goes without saying that various technologies greatly magnify the capacity of organizers to reach people and to continue to reach them for future actions. But more than amplifying the mobilizing capacities of organizations, applications of social technologies are beginning to transform organizational forms. For example, the transnational protest network that produced and coordinated dozens of demonstrations around the world at the time of the Seattle WTO event was not an organization at all, in any conventional sense of the term. It was more a meta-organization, or, better, a *hyper-organization* that existed mainly in the form of the website, e-mail traffic, and linked sites noted above. Such hyper-organizations have now become familiar in transnational and other protest networks.

An early example of the hyper-organizational form was the Jubilee 2000 debt relief network. As described by Surman and Reilly, Jubilee was not the sort of network typically assembled by NGOs for campaigns (2003:21–22). It emerged remarkably quickly, with a remarkable absence of central organization. Its approximately three hundred members included an unprecedented North/South balance in terms of organizational inclusion and information flows. Jubilee even rejected the formation of an international secretariat at a crucial stage in its evolution, in favor of continued horizontal diffusion of e-mail lists that reached large numbers of Southern organizations with computers, who passed along issues and inputs to their offline constituencies through various local channels.

Critics argue that the technology was also something of a burden for the network in that Jubilee was dominated by the superior technology of Northern members, but my point here is more fundamental: for better or worse, the organization did not exist apart from the technology. In other words, Jubilee was not just an organization enhanced or magnified by the simple application of e-mail lists—it was constituted by that technology as well as by the offline meetings through which its members also interacted. Current technological innovations to correct the North/South imbalance in such organizations involve experiments with community information technology kiosks around the globe (Badash, Khan, and Garrido, 2003).

If e-mail remains the "killer application" that enabled Jubilee and thousands of other networks to grow, the development and layering of more sophisticated social technologies has produced phenomenal organizational capacities (if still limited to those with technological access). The mix of practitioners and programmers at work on these network design technologies is most impressive, and their visions for complex organizational forms constituted through technological code offer the potential of a virtual infrastructure for a global civil society (Jordan, Hauser, and Foster, 2003).

An ongoing project at the Center for Communication and Civic Engagement at the University of Washington is an inventory of social technology applications that have implications for democratic organization in these on/offline networks (Center for Communication and Civic Engagement, 2004).[9] We have catalogued technological code applications in the areas of democratic decision making; open publishing and automated editing; trust, social capital, and reputation; grassroots mobilizing; and self-organizing networks, among other areas relevant to understanding whether inclusiveness, diversity, and individual affinity can be sustainable network organizing principles.

Two things are now becoming clear from this project. First, the capacity to identify social codes and values inscribed in applications of technology is crucial for assessing the sustainability, coherence, and quality of democratic process in large-scale transnational protest organizations—a point made more generally by Feenberg (1995) about the social values inscribed in all technologies and their uses. Second, and more crucial to understanding the embedded, disjointed networks described above, the most innovative applications for organizing sustainable, low brokerage, large-scale movement networks are coming from the hyper-organizations and not from the NGO sector. This point is explored in some detail by Surman and Reilly (2003).

The general failure of traditional NGO networks to push applications of open source social network technology—even though they have the resources to do so—may signal their general commitment to centralized organization and selective coalition formation aimed at advancing organizational goals within a government-centered institutional order. The technology disjuncture thus mirrors the organizational codes of the different networks that are mutually embedded, but not always well connected within the transnational global justice order. Consider, for example, the remarkable network map created to show the links among various groups attending the Ruckus society summer camp of 2002. Some fifty organizations offered their URLs to Govcom.org (www.govcom .org), a technology development organization building communication among movement groups and between movements and governments. The resulting map revealed hundreds of direct action groups linked in dense patterns to form a complex network structure that contained few traditional NGOs either linking in or out of the network.[10]

Identifying the technological isolation of NGOs as an obstacle to better integrating the transnational social justice movement led to an impressive international gathering of open source social software developers and activists with connections to the NGO world. The 2003 Summer Source meeting in Croatia drew participants from over thirty countries, who shared the aim of better integrating nerds and activists to improve social software solutions and to help the diffusion of open source applications through NGO networks. The Govcom.org map of this Summer Source camp again reveals few links between direct action organizations and conventional NGOs, and something of a general network disjuncture between the developers and the activists (Surman and Reilly, 2003:26). The technological divide between the hyper-networks and the traditional NGO coalitions may ultimately limit the political capacity of the global social justice movement even more than the technology access issues confronting Southern activists.

Political Capacity: Be the Media, Create New Political Relationships

Until the disjuncture between NGO and direct activist networks can be addressed both socially and technologically, the voice of the movement that reaches general publics is likely to remain disproportionately the voice of established NGOs that have long cultivated relations with governments and journalists. The marginalization of radical voices in conventional news accounts is a familiar issue in social movements (Gitlin, 1980). In some ways, the global justice movement has failed to overcome this problem, generally attracting negative press, from being associated with soccer hooliganism in mainstream German papers, to images of lawlessness and violence in American news. Protest actions can attract news frames of violence and disruption even when demonstrations are generally peaceful, as occurred at the 2002 New York meetings of the WEF. As mentioned above, activists watched in frustration as the WEF successfully launched a publicity campaign claiming ownership of many of their issues, legitimized by inviting selected NGOs into the meetings and dismissing the crowds in the streets as bent on pointless disruption (Bennett et al., 2004). Kolb (in this volume) suggests that particular organizations such as ATTAC can cultivate better press relations, but this strategy may result in isolation from other wings of the movement in order to maintain press access.

State authorities have contributed their own divide-and-conquer tactics to undermine the political capacities of the social justice networks. It seems clear that the actions of police—from the Seattle WTO in 1999, to the Genoa G7 demonstrations in 2001, to the 2003 Miami FTAA conflict—reflect transnational governmental strategies of criminalizing direct action networks, both for purposes of disrupting them and for discrediting them in the eyes of publics. The Miami police even borrowed a page from the U.S. military book by embedding journalists inside police formations, creating an even stronger media definition of direct activists as the enemy. The War on Terror has provided police and other local authorities in the U.S. with added incentives to split the movement; nearly nine million dollars in police funding from the War on Terror budget was made available in Miami just by declaring particular groups as subversive (Klein, 2003).

Despite the many frustrations, the capacity to join in public discussion on their own terms remains a serious goal for many activists. Media strategies have generated considerable attention in protest networks, giving rise to a growing media reform movement (www.mediareform.org), a diffusion of culture jamming and hacktivism, and campaigns against corporations such as Monsanto, Nike, and Coca-Cola that have taken messages from desktops to newscasts around the world (Bennett, 2004). The activist-journalists who wrote one of the accounts of the FTAA demonstrations above identified themselves as cofounders of The smartMeme Project (www.smartmeme.com), "a strategy and training collective dedicated to combining grassroots movement-building with tools to inject new ideas into the culture." Their mission is to experiment with ways of sending messages through the mainstream media filters to reach publics on the other side. They called for an integrated media strategy when social justice networks descend on the 2004 Republican Party Convention:

> One power of mass mobilization is the creation of conflict and drama as any good story demands. Some mass mobilization organizations are calling for a

million people to descend on NY to protest the Republican agenda. This type of momentum is certain to attract a lot of sensational coverage. We need to use this opportunity to weave an alternative narrative to the Bush story of fear and dominance, in order to become more than just tabloid television coverage and background noise. We need to continue to use our alternative media outlets to document the real stories that compel change (Hogue and Reinsborough, 2003).

This reference to alternative media is an important factor that distinguishes this movement from others in its potential capacity to reach mass publics. As noted above, the very activists least likely to have voice in conventional media channels are those most responsible for innovative technologies with the potential for large-scale diffusion of information through the channels of micro (e-mail, lists, personal blogs, pagers, text messaging) and middle media (activist webzines, hyper-organization sites, community blogs). Whether or not their messages reach larger publics through mass media, the capacity to communicate and share rich information across social and temporal divides may in itself be counted as a political asset. Dozens of sites (Indymedia, Oneworld, Alternet, Znet, Infoshop) form an activist web sphere that is routinely harvested and archived on protest sites such as StoptheFTAA.org, which routinely posted links to high-quality reporting and commentary by such writers as Naomi Klein, Noam Chomsky, Derek Sheer, Jim Hightower, Bob McChesney, Tom Hayden, and thousands of activist journalists such as the authors of the FTAA story above.

The scale of this communication network may be unprecedented in the history of social protest movements. Most importantly, the network is broadly accessible to general publics, creating a public interface that may also be unparalleled in the history of radical politics. For all these reasons, this may be the first modern movement for which failure to communicate through mass media is not a fatal limit. Indeed, international polls on globalization and the protest movement reveal more favorable public attitudes toward the movement—particularly in the South—than one might suspect given the tone of press coverage (Pew Research Center, 2003). One implication here—and it is consistent with a great deal of research on publics and media audiences—is that mass publics are beginning to fragment in most modern societies, while media channels are proliferating, with the result that publics must be assembled through multimedia strategies. This is good news for activists who can now publish high-quality media content of their own. Activists can "Be the Media," as the well-traveled slogan of Indymedia puts it.

But what are the political aims of this movement, and how is it going about achieving them? Here again, we encounter the disjuncture between

NGOs who primarily seek relations with governmental entities, and direct action networks involved in all manner of political relationship building from simply trying to shut down trade meetings, to experimenting with stand-alone regulatory systems to monitor and discipline manufacturers and entire industrial sectors. It is impossible to evaluate all of these initiatives in this short space. I am tempted to adopt Coopman's generalization that these "dissentworks" primarily accomplish what he calls "resource burn"—distracting and wearing down larger opponents who have trouble fighting such nimble distributed networks (2003). His classic case is file swapping on the Internet, which seems to be changing the business model of the music industry.

If disrupting the business of the status quo can be included in assessing the capacity of a movement, the global justice protests have been fairly effective at several levels. For example, the trade protests have shut down meetings (Seattle WTO) and derailed agreements (Montreal Multilateral Agreement on Investments) with varying degrees of coordination between direct activist networks, hyper-organizations such as Jubilee, and traditional NGO coalitions (Surman and Reilly, 2003:43). Indeed, my preliminary impression of the success stories is that they typically involve overcoming network disjunctions—at least for purposes of short-term actions.

Another area in which the political capacity of this movement can be assessed involves the proliferation of corporate campaigns against multinationals from Monsanto to McDonald's. In many of these campaigns, activists have won compliance with demands for new industry practices and social responsibility standards.[11] Some of these campaigns are conventional NGO-style strategic coalitions that are turned on and off following the model of the now classic Nestlé infant formula boycott. A recent example involving a partnership between direct activists and an NGO was the culture jamming campaign of Greenpeace and Adbusters to force Coca-Cola to change its coolants.[12] However, many recent generation campaigns are what I call permanent campaigns, that have no center and little coordinated strategy—yet they also can drain resources and exact changes from their targets despite their hit and miss quality (Bennett, 2004).

CONCLUSION: THE VIRTUAL LIGHTNESS OF BEING NETWORKED

Large-scale transnational activism, framed loosely around social justice issues, has displayed remarkable organizational capabilities in recent years to wage sustained protests against corporations and transnational organizations at the core of global economic trade and development regimes. The Iraq War provided another view of transnational organizational capabilities, as peace and social justice activists joined in what may have been the largest simultaneous political demonstrations in the history of the world. And as noted above, peace and antiwar groups joined protests against the FTAA hemispheric trade regime. Both the scale and the organizational fluidity of this activism raise interesting questions for conceptions of transnational activism and for social movement theories.

The three core theoretical issues identified here involve: (1) how traditional NGO advocacy networks are embedded with, and relate to networks of direct activists; (2) how social technologies may create new organizational dynamics in coordinating and expanding protest; and (3) whether these mutually embedded networks can use their technological resources effectively to extend their political capacities to communicate with larger publics and develop accountability relations with corporations and transnational policy agencies. The picture in all three areas is not fully developed, because the patterns are still emerging as I write. For example, there have been enough examples of NGOs and direct activists acting together to suggest that bridging the divides between generational networks is possible; yet there are enough tensions (such as the specter of a counter-forum developing outside the WSF meetings) to suggest that clashing organizational forms have become obstacles in the present era similar to movement ideology and collective identity conflicts in the past. While the social technologies that facilitate dense online networking are clearly enabling the inclusive organization model to work among direct activists, the slow transfer of these technologies to NGOs indicates that conventional models of organizations and political relationships continue to define many NGOs, even as their potential next generation of supporters may be shifting allegiances toward direct action forms.

As for the political capacities of these networks of hyper-organizations, the problems of sustaining relationships and mobilizing action in diffuse "opt-in" networks seem to be addressed with some success by technologies that put individuals at the center of multiple networks, thus shifting the brokerage process in many cases from organizational leadership to dense interpersonal relationships. The importance of technologies that integrate on- and offline relationships in these networks is illustrated by a collaborative study of antiwar demonstrators in eight countries, in which I participated as leader of the U.S. research team. The overall results from the eight countries (Germany, United Kingdom [England and Scotland], Spain, Switzerland, Belgium, Italy, Netherlands, United States) showed that personal networks were overwhelmingly the main source through which participants learned about the February 15, 2003, antiwar demonstrations (Walgrave and Verhulst, 2003), followed by mass media, e-media (Internet and web), and flyers in different orders in different countries.

Some researchers in the February 15 study interpreted this as a sign that electronic communication channels are not as important as many of us think they are.[13] However, my own analysis of the U.S. data (705 cases from San Francisco, Seattle, and New York) shows that the participants who rely most on the Internet and other e-media (and least on mass media) for their general political information and communication were disproportionately more likely to have strong identifications with the global social justice movement. They were also more likely to have participated in the greatest number and thematic diversity of other protest activities, including globalization demonstrations. Conversely, those who were least e-media and more mass media- (TV, newspapers, radio) oriented were more likely to be single issue protesters (peace), to be first-timers to a demonstration, and to identify least with the global social justice movement, and least likely to have participated in a global justice demonstration. (Preliminary analysis suggests that these trends appear to hold for all of the other national data sets as well.) This issue-and-identity bridging facility of social technologies may explain the organizational capacity of what appears to be a movement with weak collective identity and a relatively weak core political agenda. At the same time, these defining features of the movement raise questions about other aspects of movement political capacity, from communicating clear messages to larger publics, to developing effective relationships with political targets.

As for the political change-producing capacity of this movement, my sense is that we should pay more careful attention to the proliferating experiments involving direct relationships with corporations, including labor standards monitoring in the apparel industry, forest certification regimes, and fair-trade campaigns in the coffee sector, among others.[14] Whether or not particular initiatives prove sustainable, they represent early ventures into citizen-driven transnational democratic institution building. Whether or not these direct action initiatives become better integrated with ongoing NGO efforts to pressure states and transnational agencies for particular reforms is perhaps the largest unanswered question of all. The eventual resolution of these linkage issues may hinge on the work done at social fora, at both world and regional levels, along with other world governance and civil society conferences.[15] These gatherings tend to attract the different players required to forge the linkages on which effective political capacity depends. Beyond their potential for changing how NGOs and direct activists mutually define and pursue goals, these gatherings of the social justice tribes also represent the first steps toward a global civil society populated not just by NGOs, but by citizens who seem to be making direct democratic claims beyond borders.

NOTES

1. See www.votenowar.org.

2. See www.internationalanswer.org/endorsers.html.

3. An inventory of these social technologies is located in the Democracy and Internet Technology section of the Center for Communication and Civic Engagement, www.engagedcitizen.org.

4. See www.stopwar.org.uk/.

5. See www.interwebnet.org/chasing_bush.

6. See www.infoshop.org/inews/ftaa_miami.html.

7. See www.nadir.org/nadir/initiativ/agp/free/cancun/.

8. This is precisely the model developed by the U.S. activism organization MoveOn. See www.moveon.org.

9. www.engagedcitizen.org.

10. www.govcom.org/publications/drafts/ruckus.html#1.

11. See the archives of campaigns and standards monitoring regimes at the Center for Communication and Civic Engagement (www.engagedcitizen.org) and the Global Citizen Project (www.globalcitizenproject.org).

12. See www.cokespotlight.org. Also, www.adbusters.org.

13. Dieter Rucht (in a personal communication) has noted the disproportionate reliance on interpersonal networks over Internet and web sources for learning about the demonstrations in the German survey. From WZB survey of German antiwar demonstrators.

14. See www.globalcitizenproject.org.

15. Consider the number of lists that went out in just one call to participate in the Global Governance Conference in Montreal, Oct. 13–16, 2002:

50 Years is Enough list on World Bank and IMF; Ad-Hoc List on the MAI; ATTAC's newsletter; BRIDGES Weekly Trade News Digest; Campaign for Labor Rights Action Alerts; Change-IMF, Bread for the World Debt and Development Project; Corporate Europe Observatory newsletter; Corpwatch action alerts; Corpwatch news; Drillbits and Tailings, on oil/gas/mining from Project Underground; Export Credit Agencies Watch; Eye on SAPs from Globalization Challenge Initiative; Focus on the Global South newsletter; Global economy network, Campaign for America's Future; Global environmental list with news updates; Global environmental news updates; Global Trade Watch list; Globalization Challenge Initiative list; International List on Challenges to the FTAA; Jubilee South updates and info; Jubilee USA Network news and information; List on WTO, MAI, and trade issues; News on the IMF, Essential Action; NGO forum on Asian Development Bank; Plan Puebla Panama Social Movements Organizing List; PRS-Watch (Eurodad), monitors World Bank PRSPS and civil society responses; Rights Action information list, commentary/analysis on globalization and Central America; Working group on International Finance Corporation; World Bank Bonds Boycott. Source: www.dasbistro.com/pipermail/nvgreen/2002-June/002437.html.

10

Conclusion: "Globalization," Complex Internationalism, and Transnational Contention

SIDNEY TARROW AND DONATELLA DELLA PORTA

On February 15, 2003, two and a half million people marched past the Coliseum against the impending American assault on Iraq. Those Romans were not alone: on the same day in Paris, 250,000 people demonstrated against the coming war. In Berlin, half a million marched past the Brandenburg gate; in Madrid, there were a million marchers; in Barcelona, 1.3 million, while, in London, 1.75 million people—the largest demonstration in the city's history—spread out across Hyde Park. Even in New York, in the face of rough post-9/11 treatment from the police, over 500,000 people managed to assemble on the East Side of Manhattan.

On that day in February, starting in New Zealand and Australia and following the sun around the world, an estimated sixteen million people marched, demonstrated, sang songs of peace, and occasionally small groupings—despite the strenuous efforts of organizers to restrain them—clashed with police. Even in the thin February sunshine of Ross Island in Antarctica, forty-six of the 250 residents of the McMurdo Sound station demonstrated against the American war on Iraq. This was probably the single largest international demonstration in history.

In some ways, the February 15 demonstration resembled the vast turnouts that swept across Western Europe against the Reagan arms program (Rochon, 1988). Those demonstrations, too, were mounted in a number of different capitals and attracted millions of people. But while the 1980s campaign was an isolated peak of protest during a period of movement quiescence, the antiwar movement of 2003 included activists from, and built on the momentum of, the concurrent movement against neoliberal globalization. It was a classical case of "social movement spillover" (Meyer and Whittier, 1994).

For some, the anti-Iraq war movement was no more than that. We think not: for its immediate target was not one of the great international financial institutions, or even American or global neoliberalism. Nor was it primarily composed of activists with a global vocation, though many of these also took up the antiwar cause. Most were what we will call "rooted cosmopolitans": ordinary citizens, more commonly involved in domestic politics or movements, who reached beyond their own home bases to join with millions of others around the world.

What was truly new in this movement? We will argue that it reflects not only globalization, but also the partial internationalization of the sphere of political authority in today's world. Second, it reflects not only the risks of global power, but also the political opportunities that internationalization offers a new generation of activists. Third, we will focus on the strategies and behaviors of the stratum of activists we call "rooted cosmopolitans." We also think the February 15 campaign reflected important changes in the sphere of contentious politics, ranging from challenges from emerging social movements, to the macro-developments that have been variously described under the heterogeneous label of "globalization."

WHAT'S OLD AND WHAT'S NEW?

When we speak of "emerging social movements," we do not wish to revive the by-now tired debate about their intrinsic newness or the search for a new class actor that, in the literature of the 1980s, was thought to be substituting for the central role of the working class. We think it more fruitful to single out some specific characteristics of contentious politics at the turn of the millennium. Even with this more modest aim in mind, we should be cautious about claiming too much, for some aspects of the antiwar movement of 2003 were familiar from the history of collective action:

- *Diffusion:* Much like the antislavery movement in the early nineteenth century and Gandhian nonviolence, it demonstrates how forms of contention can diffuse across space and over borders (Keck and Sikkink, 1998: ch. 2; Chabot and Duyvendak, 2002);
- *Mobilization from Organized Actors:* Much as May Day was transmitted to Europe from the U.S. eight-hour-day campaign by the Socialist International, it shows how mobilization can take place through transnational organizations;

- *Modularity:* Much as Chinese revolutionaries styled themselves as Jacobins and constructed China in the image of the French Old Regime, it shows how movements can be linked across boundaries through the modularity of the forms and the framing of contention (Anderson, 1991);
- *Externalization:* And it showed how transnational movements can be formed as people reach beyond their own borders to face external or internal opponents.

New Challenges

But if diffusion, mobilization from above, modularity, and externalization are familiar social processes, what then is new in the emerging dynamics and characteristics of the contemporary wave of transnational contention? And how have scholars and practitioners been approaching them? Since the mid-1990s, a number of changes in the "real world" have combined to expand and extend the reach of transnational contention:

- The neoliberal economic orthodoxy summarized in the term *Washington Consensus* began to bear bitter fruit in the collapse of the Asian "tigers" and in the increasingly evident inequalities between North and South.
- International institutions that enshrined neoliberalism—the International Monetary Fund, the World Bank, the World Trade Organization (WTO), and, with some countertendencies, the European Union (EU)—began to take on a more central role as the targets of resistance.
- These institutions and their actions have provided a focal point for the global framing of a variety of domestic and international conflicts.
- Transnational campaigns and transnational movement organizations (like Jubilee 2000 and ATTAC) have resulted from this dynamic.
- New electronic technologies, and broader access to them, have enhanced the capacity for movement campaigns to be organized rapidly and effectively in many venues at once.
- Counter-summits and boycotts of big corporations have emerged as new repertoires for protest addressing international targets.
- Within transnational contention, tendencies can be seen for a shift from the internal expression of claims against external targets (domestication), to greater externalization and, ultimately, to the formation of transnational campaigns and coalitions.
- Partial but highly visible successes of campaigns by nonstate actors (often in coalition with some governmental and international offi-

cials) such as the international support for the liberation movement in South Africa, the anti-landmine campaign, the international solidarity movement with the Zapatista rebellion, and the now-stalled Kyoto process.

Macro- and Micro-Approaches

In attempting to understand these new challenges, observers first turned to macro-level phenomena, like globalization, and to micro-level changes, such as the spreading use of the Internet by social movements. Neither factor is unimportant, but globalization "explains" so much and has been given so many meanings that it fails as an explanation for any single form of transnational contention (Tarrow, 2002). As for the Internet, while it has sped up and increased the range of intramovement communication, its reach is unequal and it poses problems as well as advantages for movement organizers (see Bennett's chapter for the concept of "social technology").

Moreover, neither globalization nor the Internet explains, per se, the passage from structure to action. Social movement studies confirmed long ago that grievances are not sufficient to produce mobilization; both macroeconomic and microtechnological change must be processed by actors in social networks who respond to concrete threats and avail themselves of opportunities and resources they can perceive and cope with. This is why scholars like Diani (1995 and in this volume), Tilly (2004), and the present authors have insisted on the importance of networks of trust and strategic seizure of opportunities in their work on contentious politics.

For example, while much of the earlier literature on globalization singled out its negative effects on the capacity for collective action, the thickening of cross-national social networks that it produced was largely ignored. As for the Internet, although it has indeed reduced the costs of communication (this was also the case for print, the telephone, radio, and television), it has to be mobilized by committed individuals and organizations in order to serve as an instrument of collective action.

Our Approach

Without denying the importance of either macro-level structural change or micro-level technological change, we point to a middle range interpretation. In particular, we look at how the changing structure of the international system—what we call "complex internationalism"—not only poses new threats and imposes new inequalities, but offers a new generation of activists the opportunities and resources to form transnational coalitions and movements. We derive this concept from Robert Keohane and Joseph Nye's (2001) concept of "complex interdependence" intending by our term not merely interdependence between states, but a triangular set of relationships among states, international institutions, and nonstate actors. We see this as the emerging structure in which multilevel opportunities appear for nonstate actors. And we see the latter both embedded in domestic political contexts, multiple memberships, and flexible identities. Rather than citizens in a not-yet-visible "global civil society," these "rooted cosmopolitans" are sustained by their domestic rooting, reaching out across borders to respond to threats using the opportunities of complex internationalism.

In order to accomplish this task, first, we want to sketch the tradition of social movement research out of which this book has come. Then we will survey available resources, both within and outside of that tradition. Third, we will put forward our own synthesis to help to answer the "what's new?" question. Fourth, we will examine new findings that emerge, both from this book and from recent work by other scholars. Finally, we will close with the knotty problems that social movement scholars face in confronting the new transnational contention, and with some new opportunities for research in this growing area of conflict and cooperation.

WHERE WE ARE COMING FROM

In 1995, a group of American and European social movement scholars met at Mont Pélerin, Switzerland, to discuss cross-national influences on social movements (della Porta, Kriesi, and Rucht, 1999:ix). In the book that came out of that conference, *Social Movements in a Globalizing World*, as two of the editors described it, "the underlying idea [was] that, in the contemporary world, social action in a given time and place is increasingly conditioned by social actions in very different places" (della Porta and Kriesi, 1999:3). In line with this idea, most of the contributors focused on "national mobilization within a globalizing world." A few of the contributors reached beyond the nation-state to examine transnational forms of collective action,[1] but even there, the focus was more on the interaction between the national and the transnational than on the autonomous dimensions of the latter (Rucht, 1999:206).

Moreover, much of the research reported in that volume was rooted in the countries of the North, where it was easiest for European and American scholars to observe the activities of transnational social movement organizations. In addition, much of it focused on the more routine forms of transnational contention mounted by nongovernmental organizations

(NGOs), instead of on the more contentious transnational activities that have exploded on the international scene since the book appeared. In fact, the book reflected the institutionalization, taming, and normalization of movement organizations that was a widespread trend in the 1980s and early 1990s (Smith, 1999; Rucht, 1999). And it paid little attention to parallel efforts going on in international relations and international political economy research. Our focus in that volume hardly prepared us for the wave of transnational political contention that would sweep over the planet beginning in the late 1990s.

Those limitations reflected less a narrow vision on the part of social movement scholars, than the "real world" of the early- to mid-1990s. In particular, that research depicted a period of NGO specialization on single issues, a widespread "retreat from politics," and the hope that "epistemic communities" of experts could work with international institutions to build a cooperative new world order. Still in the future lay the movement against the WTO in the "Battle of Seattle"; North/South coalitions like Jubilee 2000; the transnational arena for social movements represented by the World Social Forum; and the savage attacks of September 11 and the belligerent response to them that originated the February 15 movement.

Existing Traditions

Not that there were no attempts outside the social movement tradition to provide theoretical resources to understand the new transnationalism. Two important traditions were growing up largely independent of social movement scholarship: "transnational relations" and "global civil society." But much of this research was poorly specified precisely where specification was most needed: regarding the linkages between transnational and local contention.

In the international relations tradition, "transnational relations" were explored in a series of works begun by Keohane and Nye (1972; 2001), whose inspiration was taken up by research on international "regimes," "epistemic communities," and normative change. Where Keohane and Nye's work cried out for attention to nonstate actors in transnational space, in the course of the 1980s and early 1990s, work in the tradition they founded specialized on the study of international political economy, with an almost obsessive focus on the multinational corporation. Attention to NGOs largely closed down until the late 1990s, when European political scientists like Thomas Risse-Kappen (1995) and Americans like Kathryn Sikkink (1993) helped to reopen it, locating their work within a wave of "constructivist" research. They did international relations the service of "bringing norms back in" to its research agenda.[2]

A second stand of research came out of the "global civil society" and "transnational citizenship" traditions of the early to mid-1990s (Edwards and Hulme, 1996; Wapner, 1995; Soysal, 1994). Here, in a mixture of macro-analytical theorizing and organizational case studies, there was a direct move from the idea that globalization was advancing, to the hope that a brave new world of "global social movements" was just over the horizon. But this concept was never clearly conceptualized. It tended to enlarge into the vague category of "global civil society," and it focused on a relatively narrow range of institutionalized "good" movements—that is, environmentalism, human rights, and solidarity with the third world. It also left poorly specified the relationship of "global civil society" to states and international regimes and institutions (Tarrow, 2001b).

In his conclusions to *Social Movements in a Globalizing World*, Dieter Rucht was both more cautious and more empirical. In contrast to the international relations tradition, he focused on the domestic rooting of transnational phenomena; and in contrast to the utopian view of some proponents of a "global civil society," he pointed to the complex problems that transnational social movements face (1999:217–19).[3] But looking forward, Rucht also saw transnational SMOs becoming more significant, in part because the problems they address are increasingly international, and in part because of the opportunities for activism offered by international governmental bodies, which serve as both targets and frameworks for their activities (210–15).

AVAILABLE RESOURCES AND NEW APPROACHES

Since the Mont Pélerin conference, scholars from a variety of perspectives and disciplines have amply responded to Rucht's call for more research. Five areas of research and theorizing have been particularly creative:

- Students of social movements were quick to focus on the wave of international protest events that began to explode in 1999, the very year in which *Social Movements in a Globalizing World* was published.[4]
- At the same time, political economists and economic sociologists were offering broad interpretations of these events, emphasizing global capitalism, countermovements, and the shifting arenas of conflict between the forces of capital and labor.[5]
- "New" institutional sociologists were studying trends in global culture and using the growth of international institutions and organizations to draw a picture of a "world polity."[6]
- Focusing on microdynamics, anthropologists were tracking the rela-

tions between local actors and global trends, developing the concept of "cosmopolitanism" to describe transnational activists.[7]

- Students of international development, environmentalism, and human rights were focusing on the relations among NGOs, states, and international institutions in these important sectors of transnational activism.[8]

Social movement scholars began to reach out to scholars in international relations, comparative politics, law and development studies, and advocates and activists from the field.[9] Attention to specific transnational campaigns—such as those against the North American Free Trade Agreement (NAFTA), the Multilateral Agreement on Investments (MAI), or big dams financed by the World Bank—showed how networking occurred between very different types of associations, from environmental NGOs and indigenous people to unions from North and South (Ayres, 1998; Khagram, Riker, and Sikkink, 2002; Shoch, 2000). And a series of methodological innovations began to adapt to the new realities of transnational contention. Three important ones are the use of original movement Internet sources to trace the activities and the characteristics of participants in international protest; the administration of on-site or near-site surveys of participants in international demonstrations; and comparative research designs.[10]

COMPLEX INTERNATIONALISM, MULTILEVEL OPPORTUNITIES, AND TRANSNATIONAL ACTIVISM

Drawing on these different strands of research and on the contributions in this book, we propose to add a synthetic approach at a middle range of generalization, developed around the categories of complex internationalism, multilevel political opportunities, and transnational activism.

Complex Internationalism

Our concept of complex internationalism draws upon a group of international relations theorists whose work derives from the landmark study by Keohane and Nye, *Power and Interdependence* (2001). Keohane and Nye had separated themselves from the neorealism that dominated American international relations theory in the 1970s—which saw world politics hierarchically organized around state competition over security issues. They argued that this increasing international interdependence produces sustained interactions among states around many issues, leading to the creation of interstate and transgovernmental practices and institutions below and outside of the state level of international relations.

These authors made three cardinal assumptions: *first*, when multiple channels (and not only interstate relations) connect societies, then informal ties between governmental elites and transnational organizations develop below and beyond the state-to-state level; *second*, when there is no clear or consistent hierarchy of military and nonmilitary issues, a plurality of domestic actors are legitimized to participate in world politics; and, *third*, the multiplicity of ties in the international system lead to transnational and transgovernmental coalition building and political bargaining. These factors open an international space for transgovernmental relations and nonstate actors operating outside their own states (Keohane and Nye, 2001:35).

Keohane and Nye—like us—did not assume either the authority or the autonomy of international institutions (2001:240–41). Originally writing in the late 1970s (and well before the expansion in the authority of the EU), they saw these institutions more as fora for communication and coalition building than as supranational authorities. Also like us, they recognized the profound asymmetries of power between large and small states. But out of the communication and coalition-building role of international institutions, regimes, and practices, they saw a spillover effect that led to "the proliferation of international activities by apparently domestic agencies" (241).

We take Keohane and Nye's theory of "complex interdependence" a step further to deliberately include nonstate actors in the horizontal and vertical relations they posit among states and international institutions. By "complex internationalization," we mean *the expansion of international institutions, international regimes, and the transfer of the resources of local and national actors to the international stage, producing threats, opportunities and resources for international NGOs, transnational social movements and, indirectly, grassroots social movements.* Needless to say, these actors have widely varying levels of power and influence, with states the central actors, international institutions representing both state interests and their own bureaucratic claims, "insider" NGOs able to gain direct access to both states and institutions, and social movements attempting to operate from outside this structure to influence its policies. This takes us to the concept of "multilevel opportunity structure," and to the linkages between domestic and international levels of conflict and cooperation.

Multilevel Opportunity Structure

Many analyses of globalization tended initially toward a pessimistic forecast of the weakening of labor and other civil society groups as state protective legislation withers, leading to a presumed demise of classical social movements. For some observers, globalization was to blame for hindering the formation of collective subjects able to reverse or modify its course, and social movements were often seen as fragmented, single-issue and ephemeral (Castells, 1996:4). In the economic system, growing interdependence meant production being transferred to countries with lower wages, leading to a strengthening of multinational corporations and, especially, to the internationalization of financial markets. To prevent the hemorrhaging of capital, even left-wing governments would be obliged to swallow the bitter pill of "flexibilization" of the workforce and cuts in social spending. In the words of Susan Strange (1996), the "retreat of the state" and the "diffusion of power in the world economy" in the last quarter of the twentieth century, with the increasing role of private economic actors in global economic policies, has been the outcome of the political choices of an alliance of transnational corporations, financial international institutions, and the U.S. government.

However, alongside the costs of globalization, interdependence has had a dynamic effect on collective action. As the development of the EU, but also of the international financial institutions (WTO, World Bank, International Monetary Fund [IMF]) indicates, international institutions serve as a fulcrum for the formation of alliances of different state and nonstate actors. Such participation does not substitute for the power of states, but increases nonstate actors' visibility, their awareness of each other and, at times, even their power to influence events.

Access to supranational decision making by various collective actors is even more unequal than in national states with representative institutions. This is clearly the case for institutions such as the North Atlantic Treaty Organization (NATO) or the G8, which have no democratic pretensions and grant formal access only to state representatives. But even in institutions like those of the EU, with its elected Parliament and mixed intergovernmental and supranational structure, business and professional groups have found it much easier "to go European"—that is, to gain access to these institutions—than has labor. Civil society groups active at the EU level—such as the Platform of the European Social NGOs, the European Anti-Poverty Network, the Human Rights Contact Group, the European Migrant Forum, United (against racism), and the European Network of Women—are usually poorly staffed and lack the access of well-established business and professional groups (Rootes, 2002:382).

This distinction between "insiders" and "outsiders" should not be overdrawn. What we suggest is that if complex internationalism represents obstacles to political participation, it offers resources and opportunities for nonstate actors to challenge elites and—on occasion—to collaborate with insiders, just as domestic movements sometimes cooperate with political parties or interest groups. And as anticipated in *Social Movements in a Globalized World*, "supranational organizations increasingly provide *new arenas* for the articulation of claims and there is also a *new reference public* linked to them" (della Porta and Kriesi, 1999:16–17; della Porta, 2003b). In addition, some international institutions have been permeable to social movements that push for the establishment of general norms such as human rights or sustainable development. As the protests against the Iraq War showed, transnational movements can sometimes count on the support of sympathetic states.

The growth of international institutions, regimes, and practices provides multilevel targets—national, macroregional, international—for social movements. The protests at Seattle, Quebec, and Cancun showed that these international instances are perceived as co-responsible for increasing inequality and environmental disasters. If this does not increase the direct power of social movements, it increases their transnational visibility, their links to one another, and, on occasion, their ability to influence events.

A New Activist Stratum?

In our work (Tarrow, 2001b, 2003; della Porta, this volume), we have been struck by the growing importance of what we call "rooted cosmopolitans" with multiple belongings and flexible identities. These terms require some preliminary definition:

- By "rooted cosmopolitans," we mean *people and groups who are rooted in specific national contexts, but who engage in regular activities that require their involvement in transnational networks of contacts and conflicts;*
- By "multiple belongings," we refer to *the presence of activists with overlapping memberships linked within loosely structured, polycentric networks;*
- By "flexible identities," we mean *identities characterized by inclusiveness and a positive emphasis upon diversity and cross-fertilization, with limited identifications that develop especially around common campaigns on objects perceived as "concrete" and nurtured by search for dialogue.*

Let us walk briefly through these interlocking concepts and offer some examples to concretize them.

Rooted cosmopolitans. It was philosopher Anthony Appiah, writing of his Ghanaian father, who was the first to use the term *"rooted* cosmopolitan." "The favorite slander of the narrow nationalist against us cosmopolitans," he states, "is that we are rootless. What my father believed in, however, was a rooted cosmopolitanism, or, if you like, a cosmopolitan patriotism" (1996:22). Appiah's essay emphasizes both the normality of cosmopolitanism (e.g., the cosmopolitan is not *rootless*), and its broad sweep (that is, it does not depend on involvement in any particular movement or campaign, but underlies a number of different sectors of transnational activity).

As we use the concept, it includes: immigrant activists who are involved regularly in transnational political activities in their home countries or internationally (Portes, 2000:265); labor activists from the South who forge ties with northern unions and NGOs (Anner, 2001); members of transnational advocacy networks who link domestic activists to international institutions through international NGOs (Keck and Sikkink, 1998); and the organizers and even occasional participants in transnational protest campaigns (Andretta et al., 2002 and 2003; Fisher et al., 2003).

Our view is that the unusual character of the contemporary period of globalization is not its greater international economic integration—that was true even at the beginning of the world system—but the growth of a stratum of people who, in their lives and their cognitions, are able to combine the resources and opportunities of their own societies with what Margaret Keck and Kathryn Sikkink call "activism beyond borders" (1998).

Some of these activists become permanent transnational advocates, moving from primarily domestic involvements into international institutions, transnational NGOs, or social movement networks. But the vast majority are engaged in both domestic networks and international activities. As della Porta's chapter shows, participants in Italy, in Genoa and afterwards, had previous or current experience of participation in associations of various types, often overlapping: from NGOs to voluntary work, from trade unions to religious groups, from parties to social movements.

We still lack the necessary panel data to determine whether transnational involvements permanently "subtract" such activists from these domestic commitments. Anecdotal evidence, however, suggests the contrary: most of the activists from Seattle, Genoa, Quebec City, and Cancun returned to their domestic activism with the fruits of their international experiences. In fact, the long-term impact of the current wave of transnational campaigns may not be so much through externalization and transnational coalition formation, but through the implosion of international issues into domestic politics through the *multiple belongings* and *flexible identities* of these rooted cosmopolitans.

Multiple belongings. As for the next concept, overlapping membership and loose networks have long been considered typical of social movement activism (della Porta and Diani, 1999:119–27). Movement campaigns such as those against nuclear plants or the deployment of nuclear missiles have remobilized networks of activists from previous cycles of protest, who had disappeared from the public sphere (della Porta and Rucht, 2002). Movement coalitions, or even coalitions of movement organizations with other collective actors such as political parties, have frequently emerged on various issues, places, and moments in history. What is special about contemporary transnationalism is the persistence of mobilization involving a heterogeneous social basis, as well as a heterogeneous range of protest entrepreneurs.

From Seattle to the February 15 campaign against the Iraq War, marches have been filled with people of different generations (in Italy, the media often spoke of "protest carried out by fathers and sons, mothers and daughters"). Although demonstrators usually come from well-educated backgrounds, temporary workers and the unemployed in the North and industrial workers in the South have been going into the street to demonstrate against neoliberal policies. Peasants and indigenous peoples have also participated. The hundreds of organizations that signed calls for counter-summits and for international campaigns came from quite different traditions. For example, since Seattle, reporters often presented as "unlikely bedfellows" ecologists and unionists, feminists and religious groups, young squatters and middle-aged lobbyists for public interest groups, anarchists and consumers associations, communist parties and hackers.

What is more, research indicates that this convergence is far from sporadic or merely tactical: more and more, activists are simultaneously members of various and heterogeneous associations and groups. The "movement of movements"—as the Italian activists define themselves—is glued together by the multiple belongings of its members. We do not have, in fact, just the coming together of members of the ecological movement with unionists, but more and more activists who are members of both and constantly bridge ecological and labor approaches to world problems (see della Porta, 2003a for an analysis of trade union and ecological activists at the Florence European Social Forum). Long-lasting experiences of collaboration in local, national and cross-national campaigns (see Gabriel and Macdonald, 1994; Ayres, 2001; Rothman and Oliver, 2001) have created those dense ties that are a condition for the creation of sustained social movements.

Flexible identities. Heterogeneous networks of networks require special types of identity. Traditionally, movements have been considered as relevant examples of "identity politics," substituting symbolic resources for the material ones they lack. Especially in some moments in history, the closing of political opportunities as well as escalation processes have produced exclusive forms of militantism. More in general, in the development of protest cycles, loyalties tend to shift from the movement as a whole to single organizations, fueling processes of intramovement competition (della Porta, 1995). In the new transnational movements, the tensions among different individuals and organizations are reduced by the development of flexible identities. If past movements stressed equality—understood as "communities of equals"—activists in contemporary transnational mobilization stress diversity as a positive asset for collective actors. Concrete common campaigns are perceived not only as built upon a minimal common denominator, but as the basis for the development of a shared understanding of the external reality. Notwithstanding multiple belongings, activists stress the important role of "subjectivity" and individual involvement. Identification with global causes does not exclude other types of identifications.

To summarize: we think the combination of rooted cosmopolitans with multiple belongings and flexible identities, working within the structure of complex internationalization, offers new resources and opportunities for transnational social movements. Neoliberal globalization is one of the forces against which these movements mobilize, and the Internet is a tool they can use. But it is the nature and resources of the activists who link domestic and international institutions within the structure of the international system that provides both the challenges and opportunities for transnational contention.

OUR AUTHORS' CONTRIBUTIONS

We offer this approach as a middle-range synthetic framework for the analysis of the new transnational contention, but it is neither exclusive nor all-encompassing. We have brought together in this volume contributions from a variety of traditions to attempt to answer the questions we raised in our introduction. We turn to these different strands of research and to our contributors' work in the following sections. To this growing body of research, we think our colleagues have added both new and reinforcing elements.

In chapter 1, we asked five questions. Let us see to what extent our authors offer responses.

First, with respect to the *organizational forms* that have developed to connect loose networks of activists, the contributions to this volume reinforce our view that the modal unit of transnational contention is not the bureaucratic movement organization, but the loosely linked movement *campaigns*, social fora, or other types of weakly structured networks (Anheier and Themundo, 2002). Clearly, traditional forms of interpersonal network formation continue to be the main linkages in organizing such campaigns, but the Internet has proved to be a major innovation—possibly even a new form of movement organization, as Lance Bennett argues.

National movement organizations have not disappeared as new transnational forms have emerged. On the contrary, evidence from Christopher Rootes's chapter indicates that the center of gravity of national movement organizations is still the nation-state. Yet, within national settings, as Mario Diani's chapter reports, mobilizations on global issues constitute the focal point of specific alliances, based on specific identity bonds within British civil society. Not only do transnational NGOs build vital coalitions on issues such as environmental protection (see Johnson and McCarthy's chapter); but new transnational organizations emerge, with the explicit agenda of forming a supranational public sphere (see Kolb's chapter).

Second, we asked how the *repertoire of contention* has adapted to address international institutions with low democratic accountability and transparency. Earlier studies (for example, Marks and McAdam, 1999) suggested that, as social movements shift their activities from the national to the international level, they experience a shift from more contentious to more contained forms of collective action. Most of the activists who agitated around the EU in Imig and Tarrow's edited volume *Contentious Europeans* (2001) used institutionalized forms of influence.

Our studies indicate that if this was true in the 1990s, it is no longer the case today. In fact, protest against major international institutions—like the demonstrations studied by della Porta and her collaborators in Europe—are bringing together outsiders and insiders in complementary forms of collective action. The Internet itself offers new forms of protest, like "hacktivism," and mobile telephony allows protesters to rapidly deploy and redeploy their forces in response to new contingencies and police tactics (Tilly, 2004:ch. 5). Even the framing of new campaigns, like the "consumerist" repertoire of action analyzed by Diani in his chapter, suggests a redeployment of the traditional form of the boycott to target international firms and marketing practices, but also the growth of various initiatives of "fair trade."

Third, we asked whether *movement identities* are shifting as the result of transnational exposure and activism. Della Porta provides evidence for this shift with respect to the "flexible identities" of transnational activists. Similarly, Diani, in his chapter, shows how reference to global issues structures movement identities, even at a local level. And in his study of national environmental organizations, Rootes discovered that their members were much more cosmopolitan and interested in global issues than expected. We see this not as the "identity opportunism" of activists as they shift from one venue to another, but the result of what we have called "rooted cosmopolitanism"—the capacity of today's generation of activists to operate with equal ease on home ground and in the international arena.

The theme of global justice reflects this characteristic well: under that rubric, advocates of environmental justice, indigenous rights, North–South inequality, and labor rights find common cause. Whether this frame will give way to a new "master frame" in the form of a socialist alternative is a major open question.

Fourth, what are the major *movement resources* that movements mobilize in order to address political claims in a system of complex internationalism? Since we suggest, as Tarrow and McAdam argue in their chapter, that international activities *transpose* domestic movements, rather than transforming them, we believe that domestic networks and experiences continue to be important resources for transnational contention. But the converse is also true. As Tarrow and McAdam argued in their discussion of the American nuclear freeze movement, the need to tap into domestic resources and national movement traditions can also constrain movement organizations' capacity to form transnational coalitions.

Fifth, we asked how *national and local political opportunities* influence the strategies of social movements active on global issues. Because we do not believe in a distinct transnational sphere, we think these domestic factors are crucial determinants of the strategies of movements active transnationally. In work related to his chapter here, Rootes reports that although "a few mostly small and symbolic transnational demonstrations have been staged in Brussels or Strasbourg," "collective action occurs overwhelmingly *within* nation states in the form of mobilizations confined to the local or national level" (2002:383). Diani's chapter stresses the role of local opportunities in structuring mobilization on global issues. Della Porta's chapter suggests that, in spite of relevant similarities in the sociopolitical background of activists coming from different countries, national political opportunities still influence the configuration of the movement for global justice.

RESURGENT PROBLEMS AND
NEW OPPORTUNITIES

Those are solid and exciting achievements in an area of social movement research that barely existed a decade ago. But we should not claim too much: major new problems have emerged and a number of old problems continue to plague transnational movement research, just as they did at the rebirth of domestic research several decades ago.

Resurgent Problems

In 1986, when an international social movement group met in Amsterdam, they worried about an underlying lack of communication between North American and European social movement researchers (Klandermans and Tarrow, 1988). European researchers were animated by a "new social movement" framework, while their American colleagues were more wedded to resource mobilization and political process perspectives. In the following decade, a remarkable set of interactions and convergences cross-fertilized these two sets of perspectives. But the parallel discovery of transnational contention since the mid-1990s has led to somewhat different trajectories and research subjects on the two sides of the Atlantic. As American researchers were making major advances in organizational studies, on the Internet, and on international relations-related research, European researchers were carrying out original research on counter-summits, social networks, and EU-related research. These efforts are not contradictory, but if we are not careful, there is a risk of re-creating the trans-Atlantic segmentation of the field that shackled research progress until the mid-1980s.

The different evolution of the recent movements in the United States versus Europe, as well as the increase in large cross-national projects financed by the EU involving only European countries, can account, in part, for the reduced interaction between European and U.S. scholars. Research on social movements has in fact increased significantly in Europe, and has produced a large number of publications in Italian, French, Spanish, and German, many of which are invisible to American scholars absorbed in their country's unique situation. And, as in the 1980s, European scholars appear to share a deeper preoccupation with the structural origins of conflict than for its concrete processes, and for a dialogue with normative theorists of democracy whose work is less well known or appreciated across the Atlantic.

A second recurring problem—also typical of research on domestic social movements—is the persistent absence of the South in research on transnational social movements. This is in part due to the weakness of training in social movements in universities in that part of the world (with the notable exception of India, parts of Latin America, and South Africa), partly to the language limitations of Northern researchers, but in larger part to the greater ease of doing research in countries in which liberal democratic politics is well established. Important exceptions are research efforts on human rights (Risse, Ropp, and Sikkink, 1999), on World Bank-related projects (Clark, Fox, and Treakle, 2003), and coming out of the international norms tradition (Khagram, Riker, and Sikkink, 2002). Participatory budgeting in Porto Alegre and movements in the Muslim world

(Fung and Wright, 2001; Souza, 2000; Baiocchi, 2001; Sintomer and Gret, 2002; Bannani-Chraibi and Fillieule, 2003) have increased attention to contentious politics in the South in recent years. Southern-based research centers are making their own contributions, until recently poorly appreciated by North American and Western European social movement researchers.

Finally, there is yet little systematic collection of information about the quantitative evolution of transnational contentious politics over time. In our introduction, we suggested a number of processes of transnationalization that we think will help to specify the overall process of internationalization. Some of our authors have posited other theoretical trends. Fine empirical studies, like those carried out by Boli and Thomas (1999); Smith, Chatfield, and Pagnucco (1997); and, more recently, Smith (forthcoming), trace the growth of transnational movement organizations. But few studies allow us to say definitively that a certain kind of transnational social movement campaign is increasing, declining, or stable, or that activists formed in domestic arenas are moving permanently into transnational forms of activism.

New Opportunities

Is transnational contention increasing? And, if so, around what issues, in which regions of the world, and in what form? Are the newer forms of transnational contention, like counter-summits or corporate campaigns, replacing older ones like transnational NGOs, or are new hybrid forms such as ATTAC developing out of the encounter between domestic movements and transnational mobilization? How do "pragmatic" and "radical" identities combine or interact? To what extent is anti-neoliberalism merely a replay of traditional socialist thought—or does it signal a new departure in this intellectual tradition?

There are more specific questions on the agenda as well. Is there a growing interaction among the different sectors of transnational activism—human rights, labor, global justice, and the environment—or will they be weakened by separate agendas and competition for funds, public attention, or support? Does the appearance on the agenda of a burning new issue, like the war in Iraq, displace movement activity from these by now traditional sectors, or will anti-imperialism merge with the already broad frame of "global justice?" How do transnational social movements solve the "transaction costs" of coalition formation over great distances and in the face of shifting global issues? Finally, how deeply will current transnational movements affect domestic politics and intersect with political parties and other institutionalized groups?

To these questions, we and our collaborators have offered some tentative, promising but partial answers. We hope the next generation of scholars of transnational contention now in the field will take the discussion further.

NOTES

The authors thank Jackie Smith for her helpful comments on a draft of this chapter.

1. Gary Marks and Doug McAdam focused on collective action in the EU (chapter 6); Florence Passy examined supranational opportunities to defend the rights of indigenous peoples of the South (chapter 9); Jackie Smith analyzed the transnational campaign against trade in toxic wastes (chapter 10); and Christian Lahusen described the structure and practice of international campaigns (chapter 11).

2. Particularly important was the inspiration of international relations theorist Peter Katzenstein (1996) and a group of his students, particularly Klotz, 1996; Price, 1997; and Thomas, 2001. For a summary of the constructivist tradition, see Finnemore and Sikkink, 1998.

3. Other authors in the volume shared his caution. For example, Doug Imig and Sidney Tarrow pointed out in their chapter that much of what passes for "transnational" activity in the EU is actually aimed at national governments (chapter 7; also see Koopmans and Statham, 2000).

4. On international protest events, see della Porta and Mosca, 2003; Levi and Murphy, 2002; Lichbach and Almeida, 2001; and Smith, 2004. On transnational social movements, see Guidry, Kennedy, and Zald, 2000b; and Smith and Johnston, 2002.

5. For different political economy perspectives, see Arrighi and Silver, 1999; McMichael, 1996; and Silver, 2003.

6. The work of new institutional sociologists is best reflected in the work by Boli and Thomas, 1999 and Soysal, 1994.

7. For anthropological perspectives, see Edelman, 1999; Hannerz, 1996; and Kearney, 1995.

8. For good examples of institutionally rooted studies of transnational activism in these sectors, see Fox and Brown, 1998; Risse, Ropp, and Sikkink, 1999; Clark, Fox, and Treakle, 2003; and O'Brien et al., 2000.

9. Here we can only mention a few landmark studies: Margaret Keck and Kathryn Sikkink's study of transnational advocacy networks in the areas of human rights, the environment and women's rights (1998), and the follow-up study for human rights networks (Risse, Ropp, and Sikkink, 1999); O'Brien and his colleagues' (2000) detailed studies of the interactions of transnational NGOs with the World Bank, the IMF and the WTO within an overall social movement perspective.

10. The use of Internet-based sources can be seen in Almeida and Lichbach, 2003 and Bennett, 2003. On-site surveys have been used by Andretta et al., 2002

and 2003; della Porta, 2003a (see also www.unifi.it/grace); della Porta and Diani, 2004a; Bandler and Sommier, 2003; van Aelst and Walgrave, 2001; Bédoyan, Van Aelst, and Walgrave, 2003; Walgrave and Verlust, 2003; and Fisher et al., 2003. Surveys have been combined with focus group techniques (for instance, della Porta, 2003b). Comparative designs have been used in research financed by the European Commission such as the TEA project on environmental activism (Rootes, 2003c); the UNEMPOL project on the contentious politics of unemployment (www.leeds.ac.uk/ics/euro/unempol); and the EUROPUB project on the Europeanization of the public sphere (www.europub.wz-berlin.de).

Appendix A

Organizational Consolidation

Differences in organizational consolidation were measured in reference to four indicators: amounts of budget; dependence on public funds, that is, public agencies being an organization's two most important income sources; level of formalization, corresponding to the sum of nine dummy variables measuring the presence of formal organizational properties such as a statute, chief executive, formal board, etc.; and years in existence. Given the strong correlations between these variables, a single factor summarizing them was generated through maximum likelihood analysis. The resulting factor scores have been used in the regression analysis, to prevent risks of multicollinearity.

	Factor
Formalization (0–9 scale)	.887
Budget Levels	.755
Public Funds as Major Source of Income	.656
Years in Existence	−.426
Explained Variance	62%

Appendix B

Repertoires of Action

Organizations were given a list of eighteen forms of action and asked whether they had used, or would consider using, any of them. Maximum likelihood analysis generated four rotated (Varimax solution) factors with eigenvalue above 1. They can be associated to a *protest repertoire*, a *pressure repertoire*, an *electoral repertoire*, and a *consumerist repertoire*. For the purpose of data analysis, 1–100 scales were constructed for each factor by calculating the percentage of the form of action, strongly correlated ($r > .5$) to one factor, which one group included in its possible repertoire, and multiplying the resulting scores by 100. The same logic was applied to data measuring orientations to issues (see table 3.1 in the text).

	Have Done/ Would Do	Pressure	Protest	Electoral	Consumerist
Contact a National Politician	79%	.766			
Contact a Local Politician	89%	.762			
Contact a Public Official	79%	.702			
Contact the Local Media	88%	.659			
Contact the National (UK) Media	65%	.555			
Promote/Support a Petition	70%	.534			
Contact a Solicitor or Judicial Body	60%	.497			
Promote/Support Occupations of Building Sites	19%		.884		
Promote/Support Blockades/Sit-ins	23%		.853		
Promote/Support Attacks on Property/Land	15%		.682		
Promote/Support a Strike	22%		.519		
Promote/Support Illegal Billboarding/Graffiti	13%		.562		
Promote/Support a Public Demonstration	55%	.402	.472		
Support Candidates in National Elections	10%			.968	
Support Candidates in Local/Regional Elections	11%			.857	
Promote/Support Ethical Trade/Investment	45%				.758
Promote/Support a Boycott of Certain Products	38%				.730
Promote/Support Cultural Performances	58%				
Explained Variance		18%	17%	10%	9%

References

Acostavalle, Melanie, Devashree Gupta, Doug Hillebrandt, and Dana Perls. 2003. "Transnational Politics: A Bibliographic Guide to Recent Research on Transnational Movements and Advocacy Groups." Working Paper 2003–05, Workshop on Transnational Contention, Cornell University, Ithaca, N.Y.

Aguiton, Christophe. 2001. *Il mondo ci appartiene*. Milan: Feltrinelli.

———. 2002. *Was bewegt die Kritiker der Globalisierung? Von Attac zu Via Campesina*. Cologne, Germany: Neuer ISP-Verlag.

Aldrich, Howard. 1999. *Organizations Evolving*. Thousand Oaks, Calif.: Sage.

Almeida, Paul D., and Mark Irving Lichbach. 2003. "To the Internet, from the Internet: Comparative Media Coverage of Transnational Protests." *Mobilization* 8:249–72.

Ancelovici, Marcos. 2002. "Organizing against Globalization: The Case of ATTAC in France." *Politics & Society* 30:427–63.

Anderson, Benedict. 1991. *Imagined Communities: Reflections on the Origin and Spread of Nationalism*. Rev. ed. London: Verso.

———. 1998. *The Spectre of Comparisons: Nationalism, Southeast Asia and the World*. London: Verso.

Andretta, Massimiliano, Donatella della Porta, Lorenzo Mosca, and Herbert Reiter. 2002. *Global, Noglobal, New Global, La protesta contro il G8 a Genova*. Rome: Laterza.

———. 2003. *NO GLOBAL—NEW GLOBAL: Identität und Strategien der Antiglobalisierungsbewegung*. Frankfurt: Campus.

Anheier, Helmut, and Nuno Themundo. 2002. "Organizational Forms of Global Civil Society: Implications of Going Global." In *Global Civil Society 2002*, ed. Marlies Glasius, Mary Kaldor, and Helmut Anheier. Oxford: Oxford University Press, pp. 191–216.

Anner, Mark. 2001. "The International Trade Union Campaign for Core Labor Standards in the WTO." *Working USA: The Journal of Labor and Society* 4.

Appiah, Anthony Kwame. 1996. "Cosmopolitan Patriots." In *For Love of Country: Debating the Limits of Patriotism*, ed. Joshua Cohen and Martha Nussbaum. Boston, Mass.: Beacon, pp. 21–29.

Arrighi, Giovanni, and Beverly Silver. 1999. *Chaos and Governance in the Modern World System*. Minneapolis: University of Minnesota Press.

Auyero, Javier. 2003. "The Gray Zone: The Practice and Memory of Collective Violence in Argentina." Unpublished paper presented to the Columbia Workshop on Contentious Politics, September.

Ayres, Jeffrey M. 1998. *Defying Conventional Wisdom: Political Movements and Popular Contention against North American Free Trade*. Toronto: University of Toronto Press.

———. 2001. "Transnational Political Processes and Contention against the Global Economy." *Mobilization* 6(1):55–68.

Badshah, Akhtar, Sarbuland Khan, and Maria Garrido, eds. 2003. *Connected for Development: Information Kiosks and Sustainability*. United Nations Information and Communication Technology Task Force Report. www.unicttf.org/wsis/publications/Connected%20for%20Development.pdf.

Baglioni, Simone. 2003. "Bridging Local and Global: Experiences from the Organizations of the Unemployed Movement in Italy." Paper presented at the conference on Transnational Process and Social Movements, Bellagio, Italy, July 22–26.

Baiocchi, Gianpaolo. 2001. "Participation, Activism, and Politics: The Porto Alegre Experiment and Deliberative Democratic Theory." *Politics and Society* 29(1):43–72.

Baldi, Stefano. 1999. *The Internet for International Political and Social Protest: The Case of Seattle*. hostings.diplomacy.edu/baldi/articles/protest.htm.

Ball, Patrick. 2000. "State Terror, Constitutional Traditions, and National Human Rights Movements." In *Globalizations and Social Movements: Culture, Power and the Transnational Public Sphere*. Ann Arbor: University of Michigan Press, pp. 54–75.

Balme, Richard, and Didier Chabanet. 2002. "Introduction: Action collective et gouvernance de l'Union Européenne." In *L'action collective en Europe*, ed. Richard Balme, Didier Chabanet, and Vincent Wright. Paris: Presses de Sciences Po, pp. 21–120.

Bandler, Marko, and Isabelle Sommier. 2003. "Le contre sommet G8 d'Évian. Éléments pour une sociographie des militants altermondialistes." Paper presented at the conference on Anti/Alterglobalisation, Paris, Fondation Nationale des Sciences Politiques, December 5–7.

Bandy, Joe, and Jackie Smith. 2004. "What Have We Learned? Factors Affecting Conflict and Cooperation in Transnational Movement Networks." In *Coalitions across Borders: Transnational Protest and the Neoliberal Order*, ed. J. Bandy and J. Smith. Boulder, Colo.: Rowman & Littlefield.

Bannani-Chraibi, and Olivier Fillieule. 2003. *Résistances et protestations dans les sociétés musulmanes*. Paris: Presses de Sciences Po.

Baum, Joel A. C., and Christine Oliver. 1996. "Toward an Institutional Ecology of Organizational Founding." *The Academy of Management Journal* 39(5):1378–427.

Baumgartner, Frank R., and Bryan D. Jones. 1993. *Agendas and Instability in American Politics*. Chicago: University of Chicago Press.

BBC. 2003a. "Millions Join Global Anti-War Protests." February 17. news.bbc.co.uk.

———. 2003b. "Thousands protest against Bush." November 21. BBC News, World Edition, news.bbc.co.uk/2/hi/uk_news/politics/3223780.stm.

Bédoyan, Isabelle, Peter Van Aelst, and Stefaan Walgrave. 2003. *Limitations and Possibilities of Transnational Mobilization: The Case of the EU Summit Protesters in Brussels, 2001.* Paper presented at the conference on Anti/Alterglobalisation, Paris, Fondation Nationale des Sciences Politiques, December 5–7.

Bennett, W. Lance. 2003. "Communicating Global Activism: Strengths and Vulnerabilities of Networked Politics." *Information, Communication & Society.* 6(2):143–68.

———. 2004. "Branded Political Communication: Lifestyle Politics, Logo Campaigns, and the Rise of Global Citizenship." In *Politics, Products, and Markets: Exploring Political Consumerism Past and Present,* ed. Michele Micheletti, Andreas Follesdal, and Deitlind Stolle. New Brunswick, N.J.: Transaction.

Bennett, W. Lance, Victor P. Pickard, David P. Iozzi, Carl L. Schroeder, Taso Lagos, and Courtney Evans-Caswell. 2004. "Managing the Public Sphere: Journalistic Construction of the Great Globalization Debate." Unpublished manuscript.

Béroud, Sophie, René Mouriaux, and Michel Vakaloulis. 1998. *Le movement social en France: Essai de sociologie politique.* Paris: La Dispute.

Beyeler, Michelle, and Hanspeter Kriesi. 2003. "The Impact of the Anti-Globalization Movement in the Public Sphere." Paper presented at the conference "Transnational Processes and Social Movements" at the Villa Serbelloni, Bellagio, Italy, July 22–26.

Bob, Clifford. 2001. "Marketing Rebellion: Insurgent Groups, International Media, and NGO Support." *International Politics* 38:311–34.

Boli, John, and George M. Thomas, eds. 1999. *Constructing World Culture: International Nongovernmental Organizations Since 1875.* Stanford, Calif.: Stanford University Press.

Brand, Urlich, and Markus Wissen. 2002. "Ambivalenzen praktischer Globalisierungskritik: Das Beispiel ATTAC." *Kurswechsel* 17.

Brooks, Thomas R. 1974. *Walls Came Tumbling Down: A History of the Civil Rights Movement, 1940–1970.* Englewood Cliffs, N.J.: Prentice Hall.

Brysk, Alison, ed. 2002. *Globalization and Human Rights.* Berkeley: University of California Press.

Bullert, B. J. 2000. "Strategic Public Relations, Sweatshops, and the Making of a Global Movement." In Joan Shorenstein Center on the Press, Politics and Public Policy, Working Paper Series 2000–14, Harvard University.

Bunn, Austin. 2003. "Them against the World, Part 2." *New York Times Magazine,* November 16:58–62.

Burbach, R. 2001. *Globalization and Postmodern Politics: From Zapatistas to High-Tech Robber Barons.* London: Pluto Press.

Bush, Evelyn, and Pete Simi. 2001. "European Farmers and Their Protests." In *Contentious Europeans: Protest and Politics in an Emerging Polity,* ed. Doug Imig and Sidney Tarrow. Lanham, Md.: Rowman & Littlefield, pp. 97–121.

Buttel, Frederick H. 2000. "World Society, the Nation-State, and Environmental Protection: Comment on Frank, Hironaka, and Schofer." *American Sociological Review* 65:117–121.

Caniglia, Beth Schaefer. 2001. "Informal Alliances vs. Institutional Ties: The Effects of Elite Alliances on Environmental TSMOs Networks." *Mobilization* 6:37–54.

———. 2002. "Elite Alliances and Transnational Environmental Movement Organizations." In *Globalization and Resistance: Transnational Dimensions of Social Movements*, ed. Jackie Smith and Hank Johnston. Lanham, Md.: Rowman & Littlefield, pp. 153–72.

Carmin, JoAnn, and Barbara Hicks. 2002. "International Triggering Events, Transnational Networks and the Development of Czech and Polish Environmental Movements." *Mobilization* 7:305–24.

Carroll, Glenn R. 1984. "Organizational Ecology." *Annual Review of Sociology* 10:71–93.

Cassen, Bernard. 2003. "On the Attack." *New Left Review* 19:41–60.

Castells, Manuel. 1996. *The Rise of the Network Society*. Oxford: Blackwell.

Center for Communication and Civic Engagement. 2004. "Democracy and Internet Technology." depts.washington.edu/ccce/digitalMedia/demonet.html.

Chabanet, Didier. 2002. "Les marches européennes contre le chomage, la précarité et les exclusions." In *L'action collective en Europe*, ed. Richard Balme, Didier Chabanet, and Vincent Wright. Paris: Presses de Sciences Po, pp. 461–94.

Chabot, Sean, and Jan Willem Duyvendak. 2002. "Globalization and Transnational Diffusion between Movements: Reconceptualizing the Dissemination of the Ghandian Repertoire and the 'Coming Out' Routine." *Theory and Society* 31:697–740.

Charlesworth, Andrew. 1978. "Social Protest in a Rural Society: The Spatial Diffusion of the Captain Swing Disturbances of 1830–1831." Historical Geography Research Series, Working Paper no. 1, Department of Geography, University of Liverpool, Liverpool.

Chatfield, Charles. 1997. "Intergovernmental and Nongovernmental Associations to 1945." In *Transnational Social Movements and Global Politics*, ed. J. Smith, C. Chatfield, and R. Pagnucco. Syracuse, N.Y.: Syracuse University Press.

Clark, Dana, Jonathan Fox, and Kay Treakle, eds. 2003. *Demanding Accountability: Civil Society Claims and the World Bank Inspection Panel*. Lanham, Md.: Rowman & Littlefield.

Clayton, Edward, ed. 1964. *The SCLC Story*. Atlanta, Ga.: The Southern Christian Leadership Conference.

Cockburn, Alexander, Jeffrey St. Clair, and Allan Sekula. 2000. *Five Days That Shook the World: Seattle and Beyond*. London: Verso.

Coopman, T. M. 2003. "Dissentworks: Identity and Emergent Dissent as Network Structures." Paper presented at the Association of Internet Researchers Conference, Toronto, Canada.

Cortright, David, and Ron Pagnucco. 1997. "Transnational Activism in the Nuclear Weapons Freeze Campaign." In *Coalitions and Political Movements: The Lessons of the Nuclear Freeze*, ed. Thomas R. Rochon and David S. Meyer. Boulder, Colo.: Rienner, pp. 81–96.

Costain, Anne N. 1994. *Inviting Women's Rebellion: A Political Process Interpretation of the Women's Movement*. Baltimore: Johns Hopkins University Press.

Cunningham, Hilary. 2001. "Transnational Politics at the Edges of Sovereignty: Social Movements, Crossings and the State at the US–Mexico Border." *Global Networks* 1:369–87.

Dalton, Russell J. 1994. *The Green Rainbow: Environmental Groups in Western Europe.* New Haven, Conn.: Yale University Press.

———. 1996. *Citizen Politics in Western Democracies.* Chatham, N.J.: Chatham House.

Dehousse, Renaud. 1998. *The European Court of Justice.* New York: Macmillan.

della Porta, Donatella. 1995. *Social Movements, Political Violence and the State.* New York: Cambridge University Press.

———. 1996. "Social Movements and the State: Thought on the Policing of Protest." In *Comparative Perspectives on Social Movements,* ed. Doug McAdam, John D. McCarthy, and Mayer N. Zald. Cambridge: Cambridge University Press.

———. 2001. *I partiti politici.* Bologna, Italy: Il Mulino.

———. 2003a. "Ambientalismo e movimenti sociali globali." Paper presented at conference "I conflitti ambientali nella globalizzazione," Florence, Forum per i problemi della pace e della guerra, May 9–10.

———. 2003b. "Democracy in Movement: Organizational Dilemma and Globalization from Below." Paper presented at the conference on Anti/Alterglobalisation, Paris, Fondation Nationale des Sciences Politiques, December 5–7.

———. 2003c. *I new global.* Bologna, Italy: Il Mulino.

———. 2003d. "Social Movements and Democracy at the Turn of the Millennium." In *Social Movements and Democracy,* ed. Pedro Ibarra. New York: Palgrave Macmillan, pp. 105–36.

———. 2003e. "Social Movements and Europeanisation: A Typology and Some Empirical Evidence." Paper presented at the symposium on Europeanization and social movement, ECPR Conference, Marburg, September 18–21.

———. 2004. "Deliberation in Movement: Why and How to Study Deliberative Democracy and Social Movements." Paper presented at the conference on Empirical Approaches to Deliberative Politics, Florence, May 22–23.

della Porta, Donatella, Massimiliano Andretta, and Lorenzo Mosca. 2003. "Movimenti sociali e sfide globali: politica, antipolitica e nuova politica dopo l'11 settembre." In *Rassegna Italiana di Sociologia,* pp. 43–76.

della Porta, Donatella, and Mario Diani. 1999. *Social Movements: An Introduction.* Oxford: Blackwell.

———. 2004a. " 'Contro la guerra senza se né ma': The Protests against the Iraqi War." In *Italian Politics Yearbook 2003,* ed. V. della Sala and S. Fabbrini. Providence, R.I.: Berghan Books.

———. 2004b. *Movimenti senza protesta? L'ambientalismo in Italia.* Bologna, Italy: Il Mulino.

della Porta, Donatella, and Hanspeter Kriesi. 1999. "Social Movements in a Globalizing World: An Introduction." In *Social Movements in a Globalizing World,* ed. Donatella della Porta, Hanspeter Kriesi, and Dieter Rucht. New York: Macmillan, pp. 3–23.

della Porta, Donatella, Hanspeter Kriesi, and Dieter Rucht, eds. 1999. *Social Movements in a Globalizing World.* New York: Macmillan.

della Porta, Donatella, and Lorenzo Mosca, eds. 2003. *Globalizzazione e movimenti sociali*. Roma: Manifestolibri.

della Porta, Donatella, and Herbert Reiter, eds. 1998. *Policing Protest: The Control of Mass Demonstrations in Western Democracies*. Minneapolis: University of Minnesota Press.

della Porta, Donatella, and Dieter Rucht. 1995. "Left-Libertarian Movements in Context: A Comparison of Italy and West Germany, 1965–1990." In *The Politics of Social Protest: Comparative Perspectives on States and Social Movements*, ed. J. Craig Jenkins and Bert Klandermans. Minneapolis: University of Minnesota Press, pp. 229–72.

———. 2002. "The Dynamics of Environmental Campaigns." In *Comparative Environmental Campaigns* (special issue of *Mobilization*, no. 7), pp. 1–14.

della Porta, Donatella, and Sidney Tarrow. 2001. "After Genoa and New York: The Antiglobal Movement, the Police and Terrorism." *Items & Issues* 2:9–11.

Denton, Peter. 1993. *World Wide Fund for Nature*. Watford, UK: Exley.

Desai, Meghnad, and Yahia Said. 2001. "The New Anti-Capitalist Movement: Money and Global Civil Society." In *Global Civil Society 2001*, ed. Helmut K. Anheier, Marlies Glasius, and Mary Kaldor. Oxford: Oxford University Press, pp. 51–78.

Diani, Mario. 1992. "The Concept of Social Movement." *Sociological Review* 40:1–25.

———. 1995. *Green Networks: A Structural Analysis of the Italian Environmental Movement*. Edinburgh: Edinburgh University Press.

———. 2002. "Network Analysis." In *Methods of Social Movement Research*, ed. B. Klandermans and S. Staggenborg. Minneapolis: University of Minnesota Press, pp. 173–200.

———. 2003. "Networks and Social Movements: A Research Program." In *Social Movements and Networks: Relational Approaches to Collective Action*, ed. M. Diani and D. McAdam. Oxford: Oxford University Press, pp. 299–319.

Diani, Mario, and Ivano Bison. 2004. "Organizations, Coalitions, and Movements." *Theory and Society* 33.

Diani, Mario, and Doug McAdam, eds. 2003. *Social Movements and Networks: Relational Approaches to Collective Action*. Oxford: Oxford University Press.

Dines, N. 1999. "Centri sociali: Occupazioni autogestite a Napoli negli anni novanta." *Quaderni di sociologia* 21:90–111.

Doherty, Brian, Alex Plows, and Derek Wall. 2001. "Comparing Radical Environmental Activism in Manchester, Oxford and North West Wales." Paper for the Workshop on Local Environmental Activism, ECPR Joint Sessions, Grenoble, April 6–11.

Donnelly, Elizabeth. 2002. "Proclaiming Jubilee: The Debt and Structural Adjustment Network." In *Restructuring World Politics: Transnational Social Movements, Networks, and Norms*, ed. Sanjeev Khagram, James Riker, and Kathryn Sikkink. Minneapolis: University of Minnesota Press.

Drescher, Seymour. 1987. *Capitalism and Antislavery: British Mobilization in Comparative Perspective*. New York: Oxford University Press.

Edelman, Marc. 1999. *Peasants against Globalization: Rural Social Movements in Costa Rica*. Stanford, Calif.: Stanford University Press.

Eder, Klaus. 2000. "Zur Transformation nationalstaatlicher Oeffentlichkeit in Europa." *Berliner Journal fuer Soziologie* 2:167–84.

Edwards, Bob, and Kenneth T. Andrews. 2002. "Methodological Strategies for Examining Populations of Social Movement Organizations." Paper presented at the Annual meetings of the American Sociological Association, Chicago, August.

Edwards, Michael, and David Hulme, eds. 1996. *Beyond the Magic Bullet: NGO Performance and Accountability in the Post–Cold War World.* West Hartford, Conn.: Kumarian.

Epstein, B. 2000. "Not Your Parents' Protest." *Dissent* (Spring): 8–11.

Eskola, Kaisa, and Felix Kolb. 2002a. "Attac: Entstehung und Profil einer globalisierungskritischen Bewegungsorganisation." In *Globaler Widerstand: Internationale Netzwerke auf der Suche nach Alternativen im globalen Kapitalismus,* ed. Heike Walk and Nele Boehme. Münster, Germany: Westfälisches Dampfboot, pp. 157–68.

———. 2002b. "Attac—Globalisierung ist kein Schicksal." In *Zivilgesellschaft international: Alte und neue NGOs,* ed. Christiane Frantz and Annette Zimmer. Opladen, Germany: Leske + Budric, pp. 199–212.

Evans, Peter, Harold K. Jacobson, and Robert Putnam, eds. 1993. *Double-Edged Diplomacy: Bargaining and Domestic Politics.* Berkeley: University of California Press.

Evans, Sara M. 1980. *Personal Politics: The Roots of Women's Liberation in the Civil Rights Movement and the New Left.* New York: Vintage.

Everett, Kevin Djo. 1992. "Professionalization and Protest: Changes in the Social Movement Sector, 1961–1983." *Social Forces* 70:957–75.

EZLN. 1994. *Zapatistas! Documents of the New Mexican Revolution; December 31, 1993–December 12, 1994.* Brooklyn, N.Y.: Autonomedia.

Fagan, Adam. 2004. *Environment and Democracy in the Czech Republic: The Environmental Movement in the Transition Process.* Cheltenham, England: Edward Elgar.

Fagan, Adam, and Petr Jehlicka. 2003. "Contours of the Czech Environmental Movement: A Comparative Analysis of Hnuti Duha (Rainbow Movement) and Jihoceske matky (South Bohemian Mothers)." *Environmental Politics* 12(2):49–70.

Feenberg, Andrew. 1995. *Alternative Modernity: The Technical Turn in Philosophy and Social Theory.* Berkeley: University of California Press.

Fillieule, Olivier. 2003. "France." In *Environmental Protest in Western Europe,* ed. Christopher Rootes. Oxford: Oxford University Press, pp. 59–79.

Finnemore, Martha. 1993. "International Organizations as Teachers of Norms." *International Organization* 47(4):565–628.

———. 1996. *National Interests in International Society.* Ithaca, N.Y.: Cornell University Press.

Finnemore, Martha, and Kathryn Sikkink. 1998. "International Norm Dynamics and Political Change." *International Organization* 52:887–917.

Fisher, Dana, David Berman, Gina Neff, and Kevin Stanley. 2003. "Do Organizations Matter? Mobilization and Support for Participants at Five Globalization Protests." American Sociological Association, August.

Forsberg, Randall. 1982. "A Bilateral Nuclear Weapons Freeze." *Scientific American* 247(5):52–61.

Fox, Jonathan, and L. David Brown, eds. 1998. *The Struggle for Accountability: The World Bank, NGOs and Grassroots Movements*. Cambridge, Mass.: MIT Press.

Frank, David John. 1997. "Science, Nature, and the Globalization of the Environment, 1870–1990." *Social Forces* 76(2):409–37.

Frank, David J., Ann Hironaka, John W. Meyer, Evan Schofer, and Nancy Brandon Tuma. 1999. "The Rationalization and Organization of Nature in World Culture." In *Constructing World Culture: International Nongovernmental Organizations since 1875*, ed. John Boli and George M. Thomas. Stanford, Calif.: Stanford University Press, pp. 81–99.

Frank, David J., Ann Hironaka, and Evan Schofer. 2000. "The Nation-State and the Natural Environment over the Twentieth Century." *American Sociological Review* 65(1):96–116.

Fung, Archon, and Erik Olin Wright. 2001. "Deepening Democracy: Innovations in Empowered Participatory Governance." *Politics and Society* 29(1):5–41.

Gabriel, Christina, and Laura Macdonald. 1994. "NAFTA, Women and Organising in Canada and Mexico: Forging a 'Feminist Internationality.'" *Millennium* 23:535–62.

Gamson, William A. 1975. *The Strategy of Social Protest*. Homewood, Ill.: Dorsey Press.

———. 2001. "Promoting Political Engagement." In *Mediated Politics: Communication in the Future of Democracy*, ed. W. Lance Bennett and Robert M. Entman. Cambridge: Cambridge University Press, pp. 56–74.

Gamson, William A., and David S. Meyer. 1996. "Framing Political Opportunity." In *Comparative Perspectives on Social Movements: Political Opportunities, Mobilizing Structures, and Cultural Framings*, ed. Doug McAdam, John D. McCarthy, and Mayer N. Zald. Cambridge: Cambridge University Press.

Gamson, William A., and Gadi Wolfsfeld. 1993. "Movements and Media as Interacting Systems." *ANNALS* :114–25.

Gardner, Sarah Sturges. 1995. "Major Themes in the Study of Grassroots Environmentalism in Developing Countries." *Journal of Third World Studies* XII(2):200–44.

George, Susan. 2002. "Was ist Attac—und was nicht?" *Blätter für deutsche und internationale Politik* 47:419–30.

Gerhards, Jürgen, and Dieter Rucht. 1992. "Mesomobilization: Organizing and Framing in Two Protest Campaigns in West Germany." *American Journal of Sociology* 98:555–95.

Gill, Stephen. 2000. "Toward a Postmodern Prince? The Battle of Seattle as a Moment in the New Politics of Globalisation." *Millennium* 29(1):131–40.

Gitlin, Todd. 1980. *The Whole World Is Watching: Mass Media in the Making and Unmaking of the New Left*. Berkeley: University of California Press.

Giugni, Marco, and Florence Passy. 2002. "Le champ politique de l'immigration en Europe: Opportunités, mobilisations et héritage de l'Etat national." In *L'action collective en Europe*, ed. Richard Balme, Didier Chabanet, and Vincent Wright. Paris: Presses de Sciences Po, pp. 433–60.

Goldberg, Michelle. 2003. "Dazed and Confused about Iraq." Salon.com. October 25.

Goldenberg, Edie N. 1975. *Making the Papers: The Access of Resource-Poor Groups to the Metropolitan Press.* Lexington, Mass.: Lexington Books.

Goldstein, Judith, and Robert Keohane, eds. 1993. *Ideas and Foreign Policy: Beliefs, Institutions, and Political Change.* Ithaca, N.Y.: Cornell University Press.

Gottlieb, Robert. 1993. *Forcing the Spring: The Transformation of the American Environmental Movement.* Washington, D.C.: Island Press.

Gourevitch, Peter. 2002. "Domestic Politics and International Relations." In *The Handbook of International Relations*, ed. Walter Carlsnaes, Thomas Risse, and Beth Simmons. Newbury Park, Calif.: Sage.

Grefe, Christiane, Mathias Greffrath, and Harald Schumann. 2002. *Attac: Was wollen die Globalisierungskritiker?* Berlin: Rowohlt.

Guarnizo, Luis E., Alejandro Portes, and Patricia Landolt. 2003. "Assimilation and Transnationalism: Determinants of Transnational Political Action among Contemporary Migrants." *American Journal of Sociology* 108:1211–48.

Guidry, John A., Michael D. Kennedy, and Mayer N. Zald. 2000a. "Globalizations and Social Movements." In *Globalizations and Social Movements: Culture, Power, and the Transnational Public Sphere*, ed. J. Guidry, M. Kennedy, and M. Zald. Ann Arbor: University of Michigan Press, pp. 1–32.

———, eds. 2000b. *Globalizations and Social Movements: Culture, Power, and the Transnational Public Sphere.* Ann Arbor: University of Michigan Press.

Habermann, Friederike. 2002. "Peoples Global Action: Für viele Welten! In pink, silber und bunt." In *Globaler Widerstand: Internationale Netzwerke auf der Suche nach Alternativen im globalen Kapitalismus*, ed. Heike Walk and Nele Boehme. Münster, Germany: Westfälisches Dampfboot, pp. 143–56.

Hannan, Michael T., and Glenn R. Carroll. 1992. *The Dynamics of Organizational Populations: Density, Legitimation and Competition.* New York: Oxford University Press.

Hannan, Michael T., and John Freeman. 1987. "The Ecology of Organizational Foundings: American Labor Unions, 1936–1985." *American Journal of Sociology* 92:910–43.

———. 1989. *Organizational Ecology.* Cambridge: Harvard University Press.

Hannerz, Ulf. 1996. *Transnational Connections: Culture, People, Places.* London: Routledge.

Harvey, Neil. 1998. *The Chiapas Rebellion: The Struggle for Land and Democracy.* Durham, N.C.: Duke University Press.

Haveman, Heather A. 2000. "The Future of Organizational Sociology: Forging Ties among Paradigms." *Contemporary Sociology* 29:476–86.

Hayden, Tom. 2003. "FTAA Ship Runs Aground, but Party Goes On." Alternet, December 1. www.alternet.org/story.html?StoryID=17284.

Heirich, Max. 1968. *The Beginning, Berkeley 1964.* New York: Columbia University Press.

Helfferich, Barbara, and Felix Kolb. 2001. "Multilevel Action Coordination in European Contentious Politics: The Case of the European Women's Lobby." In *Contentious Europeans: Protest and Politics in an Emerging Polity*, ed. Douglas R. Imig and Sidney G. Tarrow. Lanham, Md.: Rowman & Littlefield, pp. 143–61.

Hellman, Judith Adler. 1999. "Real and Virtual Chiapas: Realism and the Left." In *Socialist Register 2001*, ed. Leo Panitch and Colin Leys. London: Merlin Press, pp. 161–86.

Hey, Christian, and Uwe Brendle. 1994. *Umweltverbände und EG: Strategien, politische Kulturen und Organisationsformen*. Opladen, Germany: Westdeutscher Verlag.

Higgins, Nicholas. 2000. "Zapatista Uprising and the Poetics of Cultural Resistance." *Alternatives: Social Transformation and Humane Governance* 25(3).

Hilgartner, Stephen, and Charles L. Bosk. 1988. "The Rise and Fall of Social Problems: A Public Arenas Model." *American Journal of Sociology* 94:53–78.

Hocke, Peter. 2001. *Massenmedien und lokaler Protest: Eine empirische Fallstudie zur Medienselektivität in einer westdeutschen Bewegungshochburg*. Opladen, Germany: Westdeutscher Verlag.

Hofrichter, Jürgen, and Karlheinz Reif. 1990. "Evolution of Environmental Attitudes in the European Community." *Scandinavian Political Studies* 13(2):119–46.

Hogue, Ilyse, and Patrick Reinsborough. 2003. "Information Warfare in Miami." Alternet, December 1. www.alternet.org/story.html?StoryID=17293.

Hooghe, Liesbet. 2002. "The Mobilization of Territorial Interests and Multilevel Governance." In *L'action collective en Europe*, ed. Richard Balme, Didier Chabanet, and Vincent Wright. Paris: Presses de Sciences Po, pp. 347–74.

Imig, Doug, and Sidney Tarrow. 1999. "The Europeanization of Movements? Contentious Politics and the European Union. October 1983–March 1995." In *Social Movements in a Globalizing World*, ed. Donatella della Porta, Hanspeter Kriesi, and Dieter Rucht. New York: Macmillan, pp. 112–33.

———. 2001. "Mapping the Europeanization of Contention." In *Contentious Europeans: Protest and Politics in an Emerging Polity*, ed. D. Imig and S. Tarrow. Lanham, Md.: Rowman & Littlefield, pp. 27–49.

———. 2002. "La contestation politique dans l'Europe en formation." In *L'action collective en Europe*, ed. Richard Balme, Didier Chabanet, and Vincent Wright. Paris: Presses de Sciences Po, pp. 195–223.

———, eds. 2001. *Contentious Europeans: Protest and Politics in an Emerging Polity*. Lanham, Md.: Rowman & Littlefield.

Infoshop. 2003. www.infoshop.org/ftaa_miami.html.

Jackson, Maurice, Eleanora Peterson, James Bull, Sverre Monsen, and Patricia Richmond. 1960. "The Failure of an Incipient Social Movement." *Pacific Sociological Review* 3:35–40.

Johnson, Erik. 2000. "Policy Issue Diffusion among Major Environmental Social Movement Organizations." Thesis (MS), Pennsylvania State University.

Jordan, Ken, Jan Houser, and Steven Foster. 2003. "The Augmented Social Network: Building Identity and Trust into the Next Generation Internet." White Paper for the Planetwork Linktank. collaboratory.planetwork.net/linktank _whitepaper/.

Katzenstein, Peter J., ed. 1996. *The Culture of National Security: Norms and Identities in World Politics*. New York: Columbia University Press.

Kearney, Michael. 1995. "The Local and the Global: The Anthropology of Globalization and Transnationalism." *Annual Review of Anthropology* 24:547–65.

Keck, Margaret, and Kathryn Sikkink. 1998. *Activists beyond Borders: Advocacy Networks in International Politics.* Ithaca, N.Y.: Cornell University Press.

Keeler, John T. S. 1993. "Opening the Window for Reform: Mandates, Crises, and Extraordinary Policy-Making." *Comparative Political Studies* 25:433–86.

Kempton, Willett, Dorothy C. Holland, Katherine Bunting-Howarth, Erin Hannan, and Christopher Payne. 2001. "Local Environmental Groups: A Systematic Enumeration in Two Geographical Areas." *Rural Sociology* 66:557–78.

Keohane, Robert O. 1984. *After Hegemony: Cooperation and Discord in the World Political Economy.* Princeton, N.J.: Princeton University Press.

———. 2002. *Power and Governance in a Partially Globalized World.* New York: Routledge.

Keohane, Robert O., and Joseph S. Nye, eds. 1972. *Transnational Relations and World Politics.* Cambridge, Mass.: Harvard University Press.

———. 2001. *Power and Interdependence: World Politics in Transition.* 3rd ed. New York: Addison Wesley.

Khagram, Sanjeev, James V. Riker, and Kathryn Sikkink, eds. 2002. *Restructuring World Politics: Transnational Social Movements, Networks, and Norms.* Minneapolis: University of Minnesota Press.

Khagram, Sanjeev, and Kathryn Sikkink. 2002. "From Santiago to Seattle: Transnational Advocacy Groups Restructuring World Politics." In *Restructuring World Politics: Transnational Social Movements, Networks, and Norms,* ed. Sanjeev Khagram, James Riker, and Kathryn Sikkink. Minneapolis: University of Minnesota Press, pp. 3–23.

Kim, Jae-On, and Charles Mueller. 1978. *Introduction to Factor Analysis.* London: Sage.

Klandermans, Bert. 1988. "The Formation and Mobilization of Consensus." In *From Structure to Action: Comparing Social Movement Research across Cultures: International Social Movement Research I,* ed. Bert Klandermans, Hanspeter Kriesi, and Sidney Tarrow. Greenwich, Conn.: JAI Press, pp. 173–97.

———. 1992. "The Social Construction of Protest and Multiorganizational Fields." In *Frontiers in Social Movement Theory,* ed. Aldon Morris and Carol McClurg Mueller. New Haven, Conn.: Yale University Press, pp. 77–103.

———. 1997. *The Social Psychology of Protest.* Oxford: Blackwell Publishers.

Klandermans, Bert, and Sidney Tarrow. 1988. "Mobilization into Social Movements: Synthesizing European and American Approaches." In *From Structure to Action: Comparing Social Movement Research across Cultures: International Social Movement Research I,* ed. Bert Klandermans, Hanspeter Kriesi, and Sidney Tarrow. Greenwich, Conn.: JAI Press, pp. 1–38.

Klandermans, Bert, Hanspeter Kriesi, and Sidney Tarrow, eds. 1988. *From Structure to Action: International Social Movement Research Vol. 1,* Greenwich, Conn.: JAI Press.

Kleffner, Heike, Katharina Koufen, and Stephanie Von Oppen. 2001. "Globaler Protest im Rampenlicht." P. 3 in *taz, die tageszeitung.* Berlin.

Klein, Naomi. 2003. "The War on Dissent." *The Globe and Mail* November 25:A21. www.globeandmail.com/servlet/ArticleNews/TPStory/LAC/20031125/CONAOMI25/Column ists/Idx.

Kliment, Tibor. 1996. "Kollektive Gewalt und Massenmedien. Anmerkungen zur Forschungslage." *Forschungsjournal Neue Soziale Bewegungen* 9:46–58.

Klotz, Audie. 1996. *Norms in International Relations: The Struggle against Apartheid.* Ithaca, N.Y.: Cornell University Press.

Knopf, Jeffrey. 1998. *Domestic Society and International Cooperation: The Impact of Protest on U.S. Arms Control Policy.* Cambridge: Cambridge University Press.

Kolb, Felix. 2001. "Eine andere Welt ist möglich. Alternativen der Globalisierung." *Politische Ökologie* 59–60.

———. 2002. "Das Weltsozialforum und die globalisierungskritische Bewegung." *Forschungsjournal Neue Soziale Bewegungen* 15:80–82.

Koopmans, Ruud, and Paul Statham. 2000. *Challenging Immigration and Ethnic Relations Politics: Comparative European Perspectives.* Oxford: Oxford University Press.

Koufen, Katharina. 2002. "Ich stehe in der Zeitung, also bin ich." P. 17 in *taz, die tageszeitung.* Berlin.

Koufen, Katharina, and Hannes Koch. 2001. "Grüne werben um Attac." P. 1 in *taz, die tageszeitung.* Berlin.

Kriesi, Hanspeter. 1996. "The Organizational Structure of New Social Movements in a Political Context." In *Comparative Perspectives on Social Movements: Political Opportunities, Mobilizing Structures, and Cultural Framings,* ed. Doug McAdam, John D. McCarthy, and Mayer N. Zald. Cambridge: Cambridge University Press.

Lahausen, Christian. 1999. "International Campaigns in Context: Collective Action between the Local and the Global." In *Social Movements in a Globalizing World,* ed. Donatella della Porta, Hanspeter Kriesi, and Dieter Rucht. London: Macmillan, pp. 189–205.

Lamb, Robert. 1996. *Promising the Earth.* London: Routledge.

Laumann, Edward O., and David Knoke. 1987. *The Organizational State: Social Choice in National Policy Domains.* Madison: University of Wisconsin Press.

Lefébure, Pierre, and Eric Lagneau. 2002. "Le moment Vilvorde: Action protestataire et espace publique européen." In *L'action collective en Europe,* ed. Richard Balme, Didier Chabanet, and Vincent Wright. Paris: Presses de Sciences Po, pp. 495–529.

Leggewie, Claus. 2003. *Die Globalisierung und ihre Gegner.* München, Germany: Beck.

Le Grignou, Brigitte. 2002. "The Expert Always Knows Best? ATTAC Uses of the Internet." Unpublished paper.

Levi, Margaret, and Gillian Murphy. 2002. "Coalitions of Contention: The Case of the WTO Protests in Seattle." Presented at the International Sociological Association Meetings, Brisbane, Australia.

Levi, Margaret, and David Olson. 2000. "The Battles in Seattle." *Politics & Society* 28(3):309–29.

Lewis, Tammy L. 2002. "Conservation TSMOs: Shaping the Protected Area Systems of Less Developed Countries." In *Globalization and Resistance: Transnational Dimensions of Social Movements,* ed. Jackie Smith and Hank Johnston. Lanham, Md.: Rowman & Littlefield, pp. 75–96.

Lichbach, Mark I., and Paul Almeida. 2001. "Global Order and Local Resistance: The Neoliberal Institutional Trilemma and the Battle of Seattle." Riverside, Calif., unpublished manuscript.

Lindsay, Isobel, and Satnam Virdee. 2002. "Ethnic Minority/Left Coalition Building in Glasgow." Paper for the Annual Democracy and Participation Conference, University of Essex, January.

Lipschutz, Ronnie. 1992. "Reconstructing World Politics: The Emergence of Global Civil Society." *Millennium* 21(3):389–420.

Lofland, John. 1989. "Consensus Movements: City Twinnings and Derailed Dissent in the American Eighties." *Research in Social Movements, Conflict and Change* 11:163–96.

Long, Tony. 1998. "The Environmental Lobby." In *British Environmental Policy and Europe: Politics and Policy in Transition*, ed. P. Lowe and S. Ward. London: Routledge, pp. 105–18.

Lowe, Phillip, and Jane Goyder. 1983. *Environmental Groups in British Politics*. London: Allen and Unwin.

Lowe, Phillip, Jonathon Murdoch, and Andrew Norton. 2001. *Professionals and Volunteers in the Environmental Process*. Newcastle-upon-Tyne, England: Centre for Rural Economy.

Lumsdaine, David H. 1993. *Moral Vision in International Politics: The Foreign Aid Regime, 1949–1989*. Princeton, N.J.: Princeton University Press.

Lutz, Ellen, and Kathryn Sikkink. 2001. "The Justice Cascade: The Evolution and Impact of Foreign Human Rights Trials." *Chicago Journal of International Law* 2(1):1–33.

Marks, Gary, and Doug McAdam. 1996. "Social Movements and the Changing Structure of Political Opportunity in the European Union." *West European Politics* 19(2)(April):249–78.

———. 1999. "On the Relationship of Political Opportunities to the Form of Collective Action: The Case of the European Union." In *Social Movements in a Globalizing World*, ed. Donatella della Porta, Hanspeter Kriesi, and Dieter Rucht. London: Macmillan, pp. 97–111.

Martin, Andrew, and George Ross. 2001. "Trade Union Organizing at the European Level: The Dilemma of Borrowed Resources." In *Contentious Europeans: Protest and Politics in an Emerging Polity*, ed. Doug Imig and Sidney Tarrow. Lanham, Md.: Rowman & Littlefield.

Martin, Lisa, and Kathryn Sikkink. 1993. "U.S. Policy and Human Rights in Argentina and Guatemala, 1973–1980." In *Double-Edged Diplomacy: International Bargaining and Domestic Politics*, ed. P. Evans, H. Jacobson, and R. Putnam. Berkeley: University of California Press.

Marullo, Sam. 1991. "U.S. Grass-Roots Opposition to the Euromissile Deployment." In *Peace Movements in Western Europe and the United States*, ed. Bert Klandermans. Greenwich, Conn.: JAI Press, pp. 283–310.

Mazey, Sonia. 2002. "L'Union Européenne et les droits des femmes: De l'européanisation des agendas nationaux à la nationalisation d'un agenda européen?" In *L'action collective en Europe*, ed. Richard Balme, Didier Chabanet, and Vincent Wright. Paris: Presses de Sciences Po, pp. 405–32.

Mazey, Sonia, and Jeremy Richardson. 1997. "The Commission and the Lobbying." In *The European Commission*, ed. G. Edwards and G. Spence. London: Cartermill.

McAdam, Doug. 1982. *Political Process and the Development of Black Insurgency, 1930–1970*. Chicago: University of Chicago Press.

———. 1988. *Freedom Summer*. Chicago: University of Chicago Press.

———. 1996. "Conceptual Origins, Current Problems, Future Direction." In *Comparative Perspectives on Social Movements: Political Opportunities, Mobilizing Structures, and Cultural Framings*, ed. Doug McAdam, John D. McCarthy, and Mayer N. Zald. Cambridge: Cambridge University Press, pp. 23–40.

———. 1998. "On the International Origins of Domestic Political Opportunities." In *Social Movements and American Political Institutions*, ed. Anne N. Costain and Andrew S. McFarland. Lanham, Md.: Rowman & Littlefield, pp. 251–67.

———. 1999. *Political Process and the Development of Black Insurgency, 1930–1970*. Chicago: University of Chicago Press.

———. 2003. "Beyond Structural Analysis: Toward a More Dynamic Understanding of Social Movements." In *Social Movements and Networks: Relational Approaches to Collective Action*, ed. Mario Diani and Doug McAdam. Oxford: Oxford University Press, pp. 281–98.

McAdam, Doug, John D. McCarthy, and Mayer N. Zald, eds. 1996. *Comparative Perspectives on Social Movements: Political Opportunities, Mobilizing Structures, and Cultural Framings*. Cambridge: Cambridge University Press.

McAdam, Doug, and Dieter Rucht. 1993. "The Cross-national Diffusion of Movement Ideas." *Annals of the American Academy of Political and Social Science* 528:56–74.

McAdam, Doug, and Young Su. 2001. "The War at Home: Anti-War Protests, Public Opinion, and Congressional Voting, 1965–1973." Unpublished paper, Stanford University, Stanford, Calif.

McAdam, Doug, Sidney Tarrow, and Charles Tilly. 2001. *Dynamics of Contention*. New York: Cambridge University Press.

McCarthy, John D. 1996. "Constraints and Opportunities in Adoption, Adaption and Inventing." In *Comparative Perspectives on Social Movements: Political Opportunities, Mobilizing Structures, and Cultural Framings*, ed. Doug McAdam, John D. McCarthy, and Mayer N. Zald. Cambridge: Cambridge University Press.

———. 1997. "The Globalization of Social Movement Theory." In *Transnational Social Movements and Global Politics: Solidarity beyond the State*, ed. Jackie Smith, Charles Chatfield, and Ron Pagnucco. Syracuse, N.Y.: Syracuse University Press, pp. 243–59.

———. Forthcoming. "Franchising Social Change: Logics of the Variable Structures of National Social Movement Organizations with Local Chapters." In *Social Movements and Organizational Theory*, ed. Gerry Davis and Mayer N. Zald. Ann Arbor: University of Michigan Press.

McCarthy, John D., Clark McPhail, and Jackie Smith. 1996. "Images of Protest: Dimensions of Selection Bias in Media Coverage of Washington Demonstrations, 1982 and 1991." *American Sociological Review* 61:478–99.

McCarthy, John D., and Mark Wolfson. 1992. "Consensus Movements, Conflict

Movements, and the Cooptation of Civic and State Infrastructures." In *Frontiers in Social Movement Theory*, ed. A. Morris and C. McClurg Mueller. New Haven, Conn.: Yale University Press, pp. 273–98.

McCarthy, John D., and Mayer N. Zald. 1977. "Resource Mobilization and Social Movements: A Partial Theory." *American Journal of Sociology* 82(6):1212–41.

McMichael, Philip. 1996. *Development and Social Change: A Global Perspective*. Thousand Oaks, Calif.: Pine Forge Press.

Melucci, Alberto. 1989. *Nomads of the Present*. London: Hutchinson Radius.

———. 1996. *Challenging Codes*. Cambridge: Cambridge University Press.

Mendelson, Sarah E., and John K. Glenn. 2002. *The Power and Limits of NGOs*. New York: Columbia University Press.

Meyer, David S. 1990. *A Winter of Discontent: The Nuclear Freeze and American Politics*. New York: Praeger.

———. 1993. "Protest Cycles and Political Process: American Peace Movements in the Nuclear Age." *Political Research Quarterly* 47:451–79.

———. 2003. "Political Opportunities and Nested Opportunities." *Social Movement Studies* 2:17–35.

Meyer, David S., and Rob Kleidman. 1991. "The Nuclear Freeze Movement in the United States." In *Peace Movements in Western Europe and the United States*, ed. Bert Klandermans. Greenwich, Conn.: JAI Press, pp. 231–62.

Meyer, David S., and Sidney Tarrow. 1998. *The Social Movement Society: Contentious Politics for a New Century*. Lanham, Md.: Rowman & Littlefield.

Meyer, David S., and Nancy Whittier. 1994. "Social Movement Spillover." *Social Problems* 41(2):277–98.

Meyer, John W., John Boli, George M. Thomas, and Francisco O. Ramirez. 1997. "World Society and the Nation State." *American Journal of Sociology* 103:144–82.

Meyer, John W., David John Frank, Ann Hironaka, Evan Schofer, and Nancy Brandon Tuma. 1997. "The Structuring of a World Environmental Regime, 1870–1990." *International Organization* 51:623–51.

Minkoff, Debra C. 1995. *Organizing for Equality: The Evolution of Women's and Racial–Ethnic Organizations in America, 1955–1985*. New Brunswick, N.J.: Rutgers University Press.

———. 1997. "The Sequencing of Social Movements." *American Sociological Review* 62:779–99.

———. 1999. "Bending with the Wind: Strategic Change and Adaptation by Women's and Racial Minority Organizations." *American Journal of Sociology* 104(6):1666–703.

Mokhiber, Russell, and Robert Weissman. 2003. "Nike Gets a Pass." September 23. lists.essential.org/pipermail/corp-focus/2003/000161.html.

Moldenhauer, Oliver. 2003. E-mail exchange with the author.

Molotch, Harvey. 1979. "Media and Movements." In *The Dynamics of Social Movements: Resource Mobilization, Social Control, and Tactics*, ed. Mayer N. Zald and John D. McCarthy. Cambridge, Mass.: Winthrop Publishers, pp. 71–93.

Myers, Daniel J. 2000. "Media, Communication Technology, and Protest Waves." Paper prepared for the conference Social Movement Analysis: The Network Perspective, Ross Priory, Loch Lomond, Scotland, June 23.

Nadelmann, Ethan. 1990. "Global Prohibition Regimes: The Evolution of Norms in International Society." *International Organization* 44:479–526.

Nelson, Paul. 2002. "Agendas, Accountability, and Legitimacy among Transnational Networks Lobbying the World Bank." In *Restructuring World Politics: Transnational Social Movements, Networks, and Norms*, ed. Sanjeev Khagram, James V. Riker, and Kathryn Sikkink. Minneapolis, University of Minnesota Press, pp. 131–54.

Nicholson, Max. 1987. *The New Environmental Age*. New York: Cambridge University Press.

Oberschall, Anthony. 1996. "Opportunities and Framing in the Eastern European Revolts of 1989." In *Comparative Perspectives on Social Movements: Political Opportunities, Mobilizing Structures, and Cultural Framings*, ed. Doug McAdam, John D. McCarthy, and Mayer N. Zald. Cambridge: Cambridge University Press, pp. 93–121.

O'Brien, Robert, Anne Marie Goetz, Jan Aart Scholte, and Marc Williams, eds. 2000. *Contesting Global Governance: Multilateral Institutions and Global Social Movements*. Cambridge: Cambridge University Press.

O'Connor, Jim. 2000. "Die Konferenz von Seattle und die Anti-WTO-Bewegung." *PROKLA* 30:157–70.

Olesen, Thomas. 2002. "Long Distance Zapatismo: Globalization and the Construction of Solidarity." Doctoral Dissertation, Department of Political Science, University of Aarhus, Denmark.

———. 2003. *International Zapatismo: The Construction of Solidarity in the Age of Globalization*. London: ZED Books.

Olien, Clarice N., Phillip J. Tichenor, and George A. Donohue. 1989. "Media Coverage and Social Movements." In *Information Campaigns: Balancing Social Values and Social Change*, ed. Charles T. Salmon. Newbury Park, Calif.: Sage, pp. 139–63.

Oliver, Pamela E., and Gregory M. Maney. 2000. "Political Processes and Local Newspaper Coverage of Protest Events: From Selection Bias to Triadic Interactions." *American Journal of Sociology* 106:463–505.

Oliver, Pamela E., and Daniel J. Myers. 1999. "How Events Enter the Public Sphere: Conflict, Location, and Sponsorship in Local Newspaper Coverage of Public Events." *American Journal of Sociology* 105:38–87.

Oppenheimer, Martin. 1963. "The Genesis of the Southern Negro Student Movement (Sit-in Movement): A Study in Contemporary Negro Protest." Doctoral Dissertation, University of Pennsylvania.

Orum, Anthony. 1972. *Black Students in Protest: A Study of the Origins of the Black Student Movement*. Washington, D.C.: American Sociological Association.

Passy, Florence. 1999. "Supranational Political Opportunities as a Channel of Globalization of Political Conflicts: The Case of the Rights of Indigenous People." In *Social Movements in a Globalizing World*, ed. Donatella della Porta, Hanspeter Kriesi, and Dieter Rucht. New York: Macmillan, pp. 148–69.

Paulson, Justin. 2000. "Peasant Struggles and International Solidarity: The Case of Chiapas." In *Socialist Register 2001*, ed. Leo Panitch and Colin Leys. London: Merlin Press, pp. 275–88.

Peterson, M. J. 1992. "Transnational Activity, International Society and World Politics." *Millennium* 21(3):375–76.

Petrocik, John. 1996. "Issue Ownership in Presidential Elections with a 1980 Case Study." *American Journal of Political Science* 40:825–50.

Pew Research Center. 2003. "Views of a Changing World." June 3. www.people press.org.

Pianta, Mario. 2001. *La globalizzazione dal basso*. Rome: Manifestolibri.

Pianta, Mario, and Federico Silva. 2003. *Globalizers from Below: A Survey on Global Civil Society Organizations*. Globi Research Report.

Pinard, Maurice. 1971. *The Rise of a Third Party: A Study in Crisis Politics*. Englewood Cliffs, N.J.: Prentice Hall.

Pizzorno, A. 1996. "Mutamenti nelle istituzioni rappresentative e sviluppo dei partiti politici." In *Storia d'Europa*, vol. 5. Turin, Italy: Einaudi, pp. 961–1031.

———. 2001. "Natura della disuguaglianza, potere politico e potere privato nella società in via di globalizzazione." *Stato e Mercato* 2:201–36.

Polletta, Francesca. 2002. *Freedom Is an Endless Meeting: Democracy in American Social Movements*. Chicago: University of Chicago Press.

Portes, Alejandro. 2000. "Globalization from Below: The Rise of Transnational Communities." In *The Ends of Globalization: Bringing Society Back In*, ed. Don Kalb et al. Lanham, Md.: Rowman & Littlefield, pp. 253–70.

Price, Richard. 1997. *The Chemical Weapons Taboo*. Ithaca, N.Y.: Cornell University Press.

———. 1998. "Reversing the Gunsights: Transnational Civil Society Targets Land Mines." *International Organization* 52:613–44.

Purdue, Derrick, and Mario Diani. 2003. "Voice and Leadership in Civic Networks in Bristol (and Glasgow)." Voice, Leadership and Accountability Conference, Centre for Local Democracy, University of the West of England, September 8–10.

Putnam, Robert. 1988. "Diplomacy and Domestic Politics: The Logic of Two-Level Games." *International Organization* 42(3):427–60.

Rawcliffe, Peter. 1998. *Environmental Pressure Groups in Transition*. Manchester, England: Manchester University Press.

Reising, Uwe. 1999. "United in Opposition? A Cross-National Time-Series of European Protest in Three Selected Countries, 1980–1995." *Journal of Conflict Resolution* 43:317–42.

Rheingold, Howard. 2002. *Smart Mobs: The Next Social Revolution*. Cambridge, Mass.: Perseus.

Risse, Thomas. 2002. "Transnational Actors and World Politics." In *Handbook of International Relations*, ed. Walter Carlsnaes, Thomas Risse, and Beth Simmons. London: Sage.

Risse, Thomas, Stephen Ropp, and Kathryn Sikkink, eds. 1999. *The Power of Human Rights: International Norms and Domestic Change*. New York: Cambridge University Press.

Risse, Thomas, and Kathryn Sikkink. 1999. "The Socialization of International Human Rights Norms into Domestic Practices." In *The Power of Human Rights: International Norms and Domestic Politics*, ed. T. Risse, S. Ropp, and K. Sikkink. Cambridge: Cambridge University Press.

Risse-Kappen, Thomas. 1995. "Bringing Transnational Relations Back In: An Introduction." In *Bringing Transnational Relations Back In: Non-State Actors, Domestic Structure and International Institutions*, ed. T. Risse-Kappen. Cambridge: Cambridge University Press.

———, ed. 1995. *Bringing Transnational Relations Back In: Non-State Actors, Domestic Structure and International Institutions*. Cambridge: Cambridge University Press.

Rochon, Thomas R. 1988. *Mobilizing for Peace: The Antinuclear Movements in Western Europe*. Princeton, N.J.: Princeton University Press.

Rogers, Everett M. 1983. *Diffusion of Innovations*. New York: Free Press.

Rohrschneider, Robert, and Russell Dalton. 2002. "Global Network? Transnational Cooperation among Environmental Groups." *Journal of Politics* 64:510–33.

Roht-Arriaza, Naomi. 2004. *The Pinochet Effect*. Philadelphia: University of Pennsylvania Press.

Roose, Jochen. 2003a. *Die Europäisierung von Umweltorganisationen: Die Umweltbewegung auf dem langen Weg nach Brüssel*. Wiesbaden, Germany: Westdeutscher Verlag.

———. 2003b. "Multi-level Governance as Strategic Opportunity: The Case of National Environmental Organisations." Paper presented at the SVPW workshop, Berne, November 15.

Rootes, Christopher. 1997. "Environmental Movements and Green Parties in Western and Eastern Europe." In *International Handbook of Environmental Sociology*, ed. M. Redclift and G. Woodgate. Cheltenham, England: Edward Elgar, pp. 319–48.

———. 2000. "Environmental Protest in Britain 1988–1997." In *Direct Action in British Environmentalism*, ed. B. Seel, M. Paterson, and B. Doherty. London: Routledge, pp. 26–61.

———. 2002. "The Europeanization of Environmentalism." In *L'action collective en Europe*, ed. Richard Balme, Didier Chabanet, and Vincent Wright. Paris: Presses de Sciences Po, pp. 377–404.

———. 2003a. "Britain." In *Environmental Protest in Western Europe*, ed. C. Rootes. Oxford: Oxford University Press, pp. 20–58.

———. 2003b. "Conclusion: Environmental Protest Transformed?" in *Environmental Protest in Western Europe*, ed. C. Rootes. Oxford: Oxford University Press, pp. 234–57.

———. 2003c. "The Transformation of Environmental Activism: An Introduction." In *Environmental Protest in Western Europe*, ed. C. Rootes. Oxford: Oxford University Press, pp. 1–19.

———. 2004. "Is There a European Environmental Movement?" In *Europe, Globalisation and the Challenge of Sustainability*, ed. Brian Baxter, John Barry, and Richard Dunphy. London: Routledge.

———, ed. 2003. *Environmental Protest in Western Europe*. Oxford: Oxford University Press.

Rootes, Christopher, and Alexander Miller. 2000. "The British Environmental Movement: Organisational Field and Network of Organisations." Paper presented at ECPR Joint Sessions, Copenhagen, April 14–19. www.essex.ac.uk/ecpr/jointsessions/Copenhagen/papers/ws5/rootes_miller.pdf.

Rothman, Franklin Daniel, and Pamela E. Oliver. 2001. "From Local to Global: The Anti-Dam Movement in Southern Brasil, 1979–1992." In *Contentious Europeans: Protest and Politics in an Emerging Polity*, ed. Doug Imig and Sidney Tarrow. Lanham, Md.: Rowman & Littlefield, pp. 115–32.

Rothschild, Mary Aiken. 1979. "White Women Volunteers in the Freedom Summers: Their Life and Work in a Movement for Social Change." *Feminist Studies* 5:466–95.

———. 1982. *A Case of Black and White: Northern Volunteers and the Southern Freedom Summers, 1964–65*. Westport, Conn.: Greenwood.

Rucht, Dieter. 1989. "Environmental Movement Organizations in West Germany and France: Structure and Interorganizational Relations." *International Social Movements Research* 2:61–94.

———. 1993. "'Think Globally, Act Locally'? Needs, Forms and Problems of Cross-National Cooperation among Environmental Groups." In *European Integration and Environmental Policy*, ed. J. D. Liefferink, P. D. Lowe, and A. P. J. Mol. London: Belhaven Press, pp. 75–95.

———. 1994. "Öffentlichkeit als Mobilisierungsfaktor für soziale Bewegungen." In *Öffentlichkeit, öffentliche Meinung, soziale Bewegungen*, ed. Friedhelm Neidhardt. Opladen: Westdeutscher Verlag, pp. 337–58.

———. 1999. "The Transnationalization of Social Movements." In *Social Movements in a Globalizing World*, ed. Donatella della Porta, Hanspeter Kriesi, and Dieter Rucht. London: Macmillan, pp. 206–22.

———. 2001. "Transnationaler politischer Protest im historischen Längsschnitt." In *Politische Partizipation im Zeitalter der Globalisierung*, ed. A. Klein, R. Koopmans, and H. Geiling. Opladen, Germany: Leske + Budrich, pp. 77–96.

———. 2002a. "The EU as a Target of Political Mobilization: Is There a Europeanization of Conflict." In *L'action collective en Europe*, ed. Richard Balme, Didier Chabanet, and Vincent Wright. Paris: Presses de Sciences Po, pp. 163–94.

———. 2002b. "Rückblicke und Ausblicke auf die globalisierungskritische Bewegungen." In *Globaler Widerstand: Internationale Netzwerke auf der Suche nach Alternativen im globalen Kapitalismus*, ed. Heike Walk and Nele Boehme. Münster, Germany: Westfälisches Dampfboot, pp. 57–82.

———. 2003a. "Media Strategies and Media Resonance in Transnational Protest Campaigns." Paper presented at the conference "Transnational Processes and Social Movements" at the Villa Serbelloni, Bellagio, Italy, July 22–26.

———. 2003b. "Social Movements Challenging Neo-liberal Globalization." In *Social Movements and Democracy*, ed. Pedro Ibarra. New York: Palgrave Macmillan, pp. 211–28.

———. forthcoming. "The Quadruple 'A': Media Strategies of Protest Movements since the 1960s." In *Cyberprotest: New Media, Citizens and Social Movements*, ed. Wim van den Donk, Brian D. Loader, Paul G. Nixon, and Dieter Rucht. London: Routledge.

Rucht, Dieter, and Jochen Roose. 2001. "Neither Decline nor Sclerosis: The Organizational Structure of the German Environmental Movements." *West European Politics* 24:55–81.

Rudé, George. 1964. "The French Rural Riot of the Eighteenth Century." In *The*

Crowd in History: A Study of Popular Disturbances in France and England, 1730–1848, ed. G. Rudé. London: Lawrence and Wishart, pp. 19–32.

Ruggiero, Vincenzo. 2002. "'Attac': A Global Social Movement?" *Social Justice* 29:48–60.

Ryan, Charlotte. 1991. *Prime Time Activism: Media Strategies for Grassroots Organizing*. Boston, Mass.: South End Press.

Scott, W. Richard. 2001. *Institutions and Organizations*. 2nd ed. Thousand Oaks, Calif.: Sage.

———. 2002. *Organizations: Rational, Natural and Open Systems*. 5th ed. New Jersey: Prentice Hall.

Seidman, Gay W. 2002. "Adjusting the Lens: What Do Globalizations, Transnationalism and the Anti-Apartheid Movement Mean for Social Movement Theory?" In *Globalizations and Social Movements: Culture, Power and the Transnational Public Sphere*. Ann Arbor: University of Michigan Press, pp. 339–58.

Shoch, J. 2000. "Contesting Globalization: Organized Labor, NAFTA, and the 1997 and 1998 Fast-Track Fights." *Politics & Society* 28(1):119–50.

Sikkink, Kathryn. 1993. "Human Rights, Principles, Issue-Networks, and Sovereignty in Latin America." *International Organization* 47:411–41.

Sikkink, Kathryn, and Jackie Smith. 2002. "Infrastructures for Change: Transnational Organizations, 1953–1993." In *Restructuring World Politics: Transnational Social Movements, Networks, and Norms*, ed. S. Khagram, J. Riker, and K. Sikkink. Minneapolis: University of Minnesota Press, pp. 24–44.

Silver, Beverly J. 2003. *Forces of Labor: Workers' Movements and Globalization since 1870*. New York: Cambridge University Press.

Singh, Jitendra V., and Charles J. Lumsden. 1990. "Theory and Research in Organizational Ecology." *Annual Review of Sociology* 16:161–95.

Sintomer, Yves, and Marion Gret. 2002. *Porto Alegre: L'éspoir d'un autre démocratie*. Paris: La découverte.

Skjelsbaek, Kjell. 1972. "The Growth of International Nongovernmental Organizations in the Twentieth Century." In *Transnational Relations and World Politics*, ed. R. Keohane and J. Nye. Cambridge, Mass.: Harvard University Press, 70–92.

Sklair, Leslie. 1995. "Social Movements and Global Capitalism." *Sociology* 29(3):495–512.

———. 1997. "Social Movements for Global Capitalisms: The Transnational Capitalist Class in Action." *Review of International Political Economy* 4:514–38.

Smith, Jackie. 1997. "Characteristics of the Modern Transnational Social Movement Sector." In *Transnational Social Movements and Global Politics*, ed. J. Smith, C. Chatfield, and R. Pagnucco. Syracuse, N.Y.: Syracuse University Press.

———. 1999. "Global Politics and Transnational Campaign against International Trade in Toxic Waste." In *Social Movements in a Globalizing World*, ed. Donatella della Porta, Hanspeter Kriesi, and Dieter Rucht. New York: Macmillan, pp. 170–88.

———. 2001. "Globalizing Resistance: The Battle of Seattle and the Future of Social Movements." *Mobilization* 6:1–20.

———. 2002a. "Bridging Global Divides? Strategic Framing and Solidarity in Transnational Social Movement Organizations." *International Sociology* 1:505–28.

———. 2002b. "Globalization and Transnational Social Movement Organizations." Paper presented at the Michigan Conference on Social Movements and Organizations. Ann Arbor: University of Michigan.

———. 2004. "Exploring Connections between Global Integration and Political Mobilization." *Journal of World Systems Research* 10(1):255–85.

———. Forthcoming. "Persistence and Change among Federated Social Movement Organizations." In *Social Movements and Organizational Theory*, ed. G. Davis, D. McAdam, W. R. Scott, and M. Zald. New York: Cambridge University Press.

Smith, Jackie, Charles Chatfield, and Ron Pagnucco, eds. 1997. *Transnational Social Movements and Global Politics: Solidarity beyond the State.* Syracuse, N.Y.: Syracuse University Press.

Smith, Jackie, and Hank Johnston, eds. 2002. *Globalization and Resistance: Transnational Dimensions of Social Movements.* Lanham, Md.: Rowman & Littlefield.

Smith, Jackie, Ron Pagnucco, and Winnie Romeril. 1994. "Transnational Social Movement Organisations in the Global Political Arena." *Voluntas* 5:121–54.

Snow, David A., and Robert D. Benford. 1988. "Ideology, Frame Resonance, and Participant Mobilization." In *From Structure to Action: Social Movement Participation across Cultures*, ed. Bert Klandermans, Hanspeter Kriesi, and Sidney Tarrow. Greenwich, Conn.: JAI Press, pp. 197–217.

———. 1992. "Master Frames and Cycles of Protest." In *Frontiers in Social Movement Theory*, ed. Aldon Morris and Carol McClurg Mueller. New Haven, Conn.: Yale University Press, pp. 133–55.

———. 1999. "Alternative Types of Cross-National Diffusion in the Social Movement Arena." In *Social Movements in a Globalizing World*, ed. Donatella della Porta, Hanspeter Kriesi, and Dieter Rucht. New York: Macmillan, pp. 23–39.

Social Trends 33. 2003. Carol Summerfield and Penny Babb, eds. London: The Stationery Office (HMSO) for the Office for National Statistics.

Soule, Sarah A. 1997."The Student Divestment Movement in the United States and Tactical Diffusion." *Social Forces* 75:855–82.

———. 1999. "The Diffusion of an Unsuccessful Tactic: The Case of the Shantytown Protest Tactic." *The Annals of the American Academy of Political and Social Science* 566 (November):120–31.

Souza, Celina. 2000. "Participatory Budgeting in Brazilian Cities: Limits and Possibilities in Building Democratic Institutions." *Environment and Urbanization* 13(1):159–84.

Soysal, Yasemine. 1994. *Limits of Citizenship: Migrants and Postnational Membership in Europe.* Chicago: Chicago University Press.

Stock, Christian. 2001. "Tränengas im Rückenwind: Die Proteste von Genua werden von der Politik instrumentalisiert." P. 7 in *iz3w.*

Stokke, Olav Schram, and Øystein B. Thommessen. 2002. "Friends of the Earth International" and "Greenpeace International." In *Yearbook of International Cooperation on Environment and Development 2002/2003*, ed. O. Stokke and Ø. Thommessen. London: Earthscan, pp. 196–98.

Strang, David, and John W. Meyer. 1993. "Institutional Conditions for Diffusion." *Theory and Society* 22:487–511.

Strange, Susan. 1996. *The Retreat of the State: The Diffusion of Power in World Economy.* Cambridge: Cambridge University Press.

Surman, Mark, and Katherine Reilly. 2003. "Appropriating the Internet for Social Change: Towards the Strategic Use of Networked Technologies by Transnational Civil Society Organizations." Version 1.0. New York: Social Science Research Council. www.ssrc.org/programs/itic.

Szasz, Andrew. 1994. *EcoPopulism: Toxic Waste and the Movement for Environmental Justice.* Minneapolis: University of Minnesota Press.

Szczepanski, Maxime. 2002. "Du militantisme à la militance. Une étude microsociologique des modalités de participation des militants 'antimondialisation', à travers l'exemple d'un comité local de l'Association pour la taxation des transactions financières pour l'aide aux citoyens (A.T.T.A.C.)." *Regards sociologiques* 24.

Tarrow, Sidney. 1989. *Democracy and Disorder: Protest and Politics in Italy 1965–1975.* Oxford: Clarendon Press.

———. 1994. *Power in Movement: Social Movements, Collective Action, and Politics.* New York: Cambridge University Press.

———. 1995. "Europeanisation of Conflict: Reflections from a Social Movement Perspective." *West European Politics* 18(2)(April):223–51.

———. 1996. "States and Opportunities: The Political Structuring of Social Movements." In *Comparative Perspectives on Social Movements*, ed. Doug McAdam, John D. McCarthy, and Mayer N. Zald. Cambridge: Cambridge University Press.

———. 2001a. "Contentious Politics in a Composite Polity." In *Contentious Europeans: Protest and Politics in an Emerging Polity*, ed. D. Imig and S. Tarrow. Lanham, Md.: Rowman & Littlefield, pp. 233–52.

———. 2001b. "Transnational Politics: Contention and Institutions in International Politics." *Annual Review of Political Science* 4:1–20.

———. 2002. "From Lumping to Splitting: Specifying Globalization and Resistance." In *Globalization and Resistance: Transnational Dimensions of Social Movements*, ed. Jackie Smith and Hank Johnston. Lanham, Md.: Rowman & Littlefield, pp. 229–49.

———. 2003. "The New Transnational Contention: Social Movements and Institutions in Complex Internationalism." Revision of a paper presented at the 2002 Annual Meeting of the American Political Science Association.

Thomas, Daniel. 2001. *The Helsinki Effect: International Norms, Human Rights, and the Demise of Communism.* Princeton, N.J.: Princeton University Press.

Thomas, Janet. 2000. *The Battle in Seattle: The Story behind and beyond the WTO Demonstrations.* Golden, Colo.: Fulcrum.

Tilly, Charles. 1978. *From Mobilization to Revolution.* Reading, Mass.: Addison Wesley.

———. 2001. "Mechanisms in Political Processes." *Annual Review of Political Science* 4:21–41.

———. 2003. *The Politics of Collective Violence.* New York: Cambridge University Press.

———. 2003–2004. "Rhetoric, Social History, and Contentious Politics." *International Review of Social History.* Forthcoming.

———. 2004. *Social Movements, 1768–2004.* Boulder, Colo.: Paradigm.

————. Forthcoming. "WUNC." In *Crowds*, ed. Jeffrey T. Schnapp and Matthew Tiews. Stanford, Calif.: Stanford University Press.

————. In preparation. *Trust and Rule*. Unpublished ms.

Touraine, A. 1981. *The Voice and the Eye: An Analysis of Social Movements*. Cambridge: Cambridge University Press.

Ullrich, Peter. 2003. *Gegner der Globalisierung? Protest-Mobilisierung zum G8-Gipfel in Genua*. Sachsen/Berlin: GNN Verlag.

Van Aelst, Peter, and Stefaan Walgrave. 2001. "Who Is the (Wo)man in the Street? From the Normalisation of Protest to the Normalisation of Protester." *European Journal of Political Research* 39:461–86.

Vanderford, Audrey. 2003. "Ya Basta!—A Mountain of Bodies That Advances, Seeking the Least Harm Possible to Itself." In *Media, Civil Disobedience and the Global Justice Movement*, ed. Andy Opel and Donnalyn Pompper. Westport, Conn.: Greenwood.

van der Heijden, Hein-Anton. 2002. "Dutch Environmentalism at the Turn of the Century." *Environmental Politics* 11(4):120–30.

Van Dyke, Nella. 1998. "Hotbeds of Activism: Locations of Student Protest." *Social Problems* 45(2):205–20.

von Lucke, Albrecht. 2002. "Made by Attac: Eine Marke und ihr Marketing." In *Globaler Widerstand: Internationale Netzwerke auf der Suche nach Alternativen im globalen Kapitalismus*, ed. Heike Walk and Nele Boehme. Münster, Germany: Westfälisches Dampfboot, pp. 169–74.

Wahl, Peter. 2002. "Globalisierungskritik im Aufwind: Zu den Bedingungen des Erfolgs der globalisierungskritischen Bewegung." In *Globaler Widerstand: Internationale Netzwerke auf der Suche nach Alternativen im globalen Kapitalismus*, ed. Heike Walk and Nele Boehme. Münster, Germany: Westfälisches Dampfboot, pp. 175–81.

Walgrave, Stefaan, and Jan Manssens. 2000. "The Making of the White March: The Mass Media as a Mobilizing Alternative to Movement Organizations." *Mobilization* 5:217–39.

Walgrave, Stefaan, and Joris Verhulst. 2003. "Worldwide Anti-war-in-Iraq Protest: A Preliminary Test of the Transnational Movement Thesis." Working paper, Center for Media, Movements, and Politics. University of Antwerp, Belgium.

Walker, Jack L., Jr. 1983. "The Origins and Maintenance of Interest Groups in America." *American Political Science Review* 77:390–406.

————. 1991. *Mobilizing Interest Groups in America: Patrons, Professions, and Social Movements*. Ann Arbor: University of Michigan Press.

Waller, Doug. 1987. *Congress and the Nuclear Freeze: An Inside Look at the Politics of a Mass Movement*. Amherst: University of Massachusetts Press.

Walton, John. 2001. "Debt, Protest and the State in Latin America." In *Power and Popular Protest: Latin American Social Movements*, ed. Susan Eckstein. Berkeley: University of California Press, chap. 10.

Wapner, Paul. 1995. "Politics beyond the State: Environmental Activism and World Civic Politics." *World Politics* 47(3):311–40.

————. 1996. *Environmental Activism and World Civic Politics*. Albany: State University of New York Press.

Ward, Stephen, and Phillip Lowe. 1998. "National Environmental Groups and Europeanisation." *Environmental Politics* 7(4):155–65.

Wasserman, Stan, and Katherine Faust. 1994. *Social Network Analysis.* Cambridge: Cambridge University Press.

Waterman, Peter. 2003. "Archaic Left Challenges the World Social Forum." *open-Democracy.* November 12. www.opendemocracy.net/debates/article-6–91–1576.jsp#.

Watters, Pat. 1971. *Down to Now: Reflections on the Southern Civil Rights Movements.* New York: Pantheon.

Westby, David L. 2002. "Theorizing the Emergence of Transnational Movements: The Swedish Anti-Bomb Movement." *Journal of Political and Military Sociology* 30:1–35.

Willetts, Peter. 2000. "From 'Consultative Arrangements' to 'Partnership': The Changing Status of NGOs in Diplomacy at the UN." *Global Governance* 6(2):191–213.

Wissen, Markus. 2002. "Stern oder Sternschnuppe? Über die Notwendigkeit einer Radikalisierung von Attac." Unpublished manuscript.

Wolff, Reinhard. 2001. "Gewalt um der Gewalt willen." P. 6 in *taz, die tageszeitung.* Berlin.

Wood, Lesley J. 2002. "Bridging the Chasms: The Case of People's Global Action." Unpublished paper.

Wright, Will. 1992. *Wild Knowledge: Science, Language and Social Life in a Fragile Environment.* Minneapolis: University of Minnesota Press.

Yashar, Deborah J. 2002. "Globalization and Collective Action." *Comparative Politics* 34(3).

———. 2005. *Contesting Citizenship: Indigenous Movements, the State, and the Postliberal Challenge in Latin America.* New York: Cambridge University Press.

Yearley, Steven. 1992. "Green Ambivalence about Science: Legal-Rational Authority and the Scientific Legitimation of a Social Movement." *British Journal of Sociology* 43(4):511–32.

Index

About the Contributors

W. Lance Bennett is professor of political science and Ruddick C. Lawrence Professor of Communication at the University of Washington. He has published widely on media and politics, with an emphasis on press–government relations, citizen engagement and opinion formation, and the political impact of global media systems from commercial conglomerates to personal digital networks. Current interests include how social technologies can engage citizens in conventional and contentious politics at local and transnational levels. He is director of the Center for Communication and Civic Engagement (www.engagedcitizen.org), where many of these projects can be found.

Donatella della Porta is professor of sociology at the European University Institute, Florence. Among her publications in the field of contentious politics are: *Social Movements, Political Violence and the State* (1995); *Policing Protest* (1998, edited with Herbert Reiter); *Social Movements in a Globalizing World* (1999, edited with Hanspeter Kriesi and Dieter Rucht); *Social Movements: An Introduction* (1999, with Mario Diani); and *Global, Noglobal, New Global* (University of Minnesota Press, forthcoming, with Massimiliano Andretta, Lorenzo Mosca, and Herbert Reiter).

Mario Diani is professor of sociology at the University of Trento and honorary research professor at the University of Strathclyde in Glasgow. Recent books include *Social Movements and Networks* (with Doug McAdam, 2003) and *Social Movements* (with Donatella della Porta, 1999). Current research interests include the network structure of civil society in British cities and the structure of overlapping memberships in recent antiwar protests.

Erik Johnson is a doctoral student in sociology at The Pennsylvania State University. His research areas include social movements, organizations,

285

and environmental sociology. These interests are reflected in a dissertation project that traces the evolution of the modern environmental movement in the United States, focusing on time-series analyses of national environmental movement organization foundings and disbandings.

Felix Kolb is a PhD candidate at the Free University of Berlin working on his dissertation on the policy outcomes of social movements. He is the recipient of a scholarship from the German National Academic Foundation. He is also an experienced activist and campaigner and one of the founding members of ATTAC Germany.

Doug McAdam is professor of sociology at Stanford University and director of the Center for Advanced Study in the Behavioral Sciences. He is the author or coauthor of eight books and more than fifty articles in the area of political sociology, with a special emphasis on the study of social movements and revolutions. Among his best-known works are *Political Process and the Development of Black Insurgency, 1930–1970*, a new edition of which was published in 1999; *Freedom Summer* (1988), which was awarded the 1990 C. Wright Mills Award as well as being a finalist for the American Sociological Association's best book prize for 1991; and *Dynamics of Contention* (2001), with Sidney Tarrow and Charles Tilly. He was elected to membership in the American Academy of Arts and Sciences in 2003.

John D. McCarthy is professor of sociology and director of the Graduate Program at The Pennsylvania State University. His research interests continue to include social movements and collective behavior, the sociology of protest, the policing of protest, and the sociology of organizations. Currently he is collaborating with Andrew Martin and Clark McPhail on a study of campus community public order disturbances, and with Frank Baumgartner on a study of the expansion of U.S. interest organizations during the last four decades.

Christopher Rootes is reader in political sociology and environmental politics at the University of Kent at Canterbury. He is joint editor of the journal *Environmental Politics*, and convenor of the Green Politics Standing Group of the European Consortium for Political Research. Publications include *The Green Challenge* (with Dick Richardson, 1995); *Environmental Movements: Local, National and Global* (1999); *Environmental Protest in Western Europe* (2003); and "Environmental Movements" in Snow, Kriesi, and Soule (eds.), *Blackwell Companion to Social Movements* (2003).

Kathryn Sikkink is the Arleen C. Carlson Professor of Political Science at the University of Minnesota. She has an MA and PhD in political science from Columbia University. Her publications include *Ideas and Institutions: Developmentalism in Brazil and Argentina; Activists beyond Borders: Advocacy Networks in International Politics* (coauthored with Margaret Keck); *The Power of Human Rights: International Norms and Domestic Change* (coedited with Thomas Risse and Stephen Ropp); and *Restructuring World Politics: Transnational Social Movements, Networks, and Norms* (coedited with Sanjeev Khagram and James Riker).

Sidney Tarrow is the Maxwell M. Upson Professor of Government and professor of sociology at Cornell University. His first book was *Peasant Communism in Southern Italy* (1967). He continued working on contentious politics with *Democracy and Disorder* (1989). His most recent books are *Power in Movement*, with Doug McAdam and Charles Tilly (1994, 1998); *Dynamics of Contention* (2001), with McAdam and Tilly; and *Contentious Europeans*, with Doug Imig (2001).